THE BIG BOOK OF BOY STUFF

CAN'T GET ENOUGH BOY STUFF?
READ MORE IN *THE BIG BOOK OF GROSS STUFF*!

COLLECT ALL BART KING'S BOOKS,
INCLUDING THE POCKET GUIDES.

Now available at bookstores or
directly from Gibbs Smith

1.800.835.4993

www.gibbs-smith.com

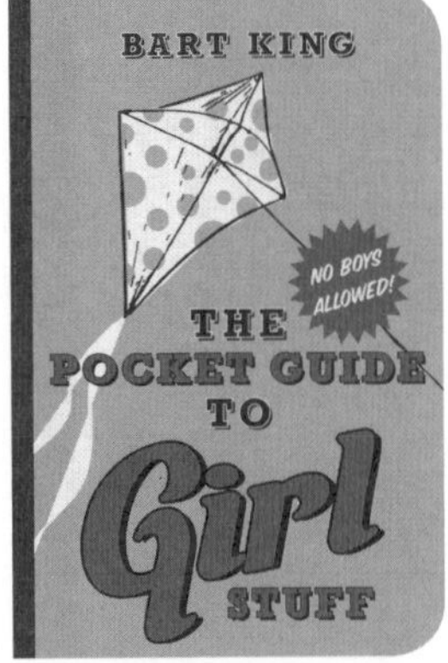

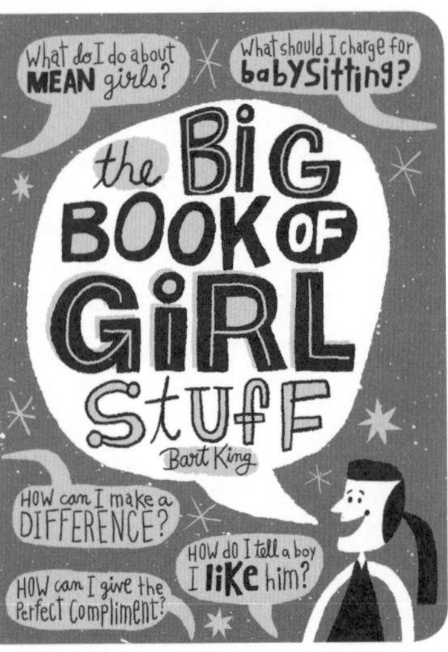

the BIG BOOK OF BOY STUFF

Bart King

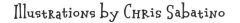

Illustrations by Chris Sabatino

GIBBS SMITH
TO ENRICH AND INSPIRE HUMANKIND

Manufactured in Dongguan, China, in November 2014 by Crash Paper Co.

Revised Edition
18 17 16 15 14 7 6 5 4 3

This book makes mention of some activities that carry an element of risk or danger. Readers of the book are urged to make wise decisions and to consult prudent adults before engaging in some of these activities and projects. The author and publisher disclaim all responsibility for injury resulting from the performance of any activities described in this book. Readers assume all legal responsibility for their actions.

I have relied on my own experience as well as many different sources for this book, and I have done my best to check facts and to give credit where it is due. In the event that any material is incorrect or has been used without proper permission, please contact me in care of the publisher so that the oversight can be rectified.

Published by
Gibbs Smith
P.O. Box 667
Layton, Utah 84041

1.800.835.4993 orders
www.gibbs-smith.com

Cover designed by Nate Williams
Interior designed by Renee Bond
Gibbs Smith books are printed on either recycled, 100% post-consumer waste, FSC-certified papers or on paper produced from sustainable PEFC-certified forest/controlled wood source. Learn more at www.pefc.org.

Library of Congress Cataloging-in-Publication Data
King, Bart.
The big book of boy stuff / Bart King ; illustrations by Chris Sabatino.—1st ed.
p. cm.
ISBN 13: 978-1-58685-333-4 (first edition)
ISBN 13: 978-1-4236-3761-5 (Revised edition)
1. Teenage boys—Life skills guides—Juvenile literature. 2. Teenage boys—Conduct of life—Juvenile literature. 3. Teenage boys—Anecdotes. I. Title.
HQ775 .K565 2004
646.7'0084'2—dc22
2003024951

DEDICATION

This book is dedicated to Suzanne Taylor . . . after all, it was HER idea!

CONTENTS

ADULT INTRODUCTION

If you think a boy can turn to any page in this book and find something to do, laugh at, or think about, you're right.

I began work on this project by consulting writers from ages past. Starting with the perspective of an older time, I found a variety of suggested activities for boys that today's safety-conscious culture can't stomach—bottle-rocket wars at midnight, survival hikes, rifle practice with live ammunition, skydiving without a helmet, that sort of thing. Yet while I researched these works with wide eyes, I couldn't help wondering whether (with the proper precautions) some of these dangerous activities were *more* preferable for a boy than, say, video games.

A book by Boy Scouts founder and World War I veteran Sir Robert Baden-Powell described three indispensable elements of a boy's world: *"Fun, feeding, and fighting."* Although this sounds simplistic and rambunctious, my mind kept returning to that phrase: Fun, feeding, and fighting.

As a longtime middle school teacher, I believe there is some truth to Sir Baden-Powell's statement. (To his list, I would add a few more elements, like sports, noise, and a fascination with bodily functions.) If you give a boy a doll (oops, I mean "action figure"!), the odds are good that he'll eventually use it as a sword or try to blow it up. So my hope is that the specters of social nicety and fear of litigation have been held at bay just long enough to infuse these pages with the spirit of *true* boyish fun. (But don't worry; there are no references to bare-knuckle boxing or live ammo in here!)

I hope the result *is* a book in which a boy may turn to any page and find something to do, laugh at, or think about.

Just like you thought!

BOY INTRODUCTION

Maybe someone gave you this book as a gift. Maybe you don't want to read it. Maybe you think this book stinks.

Think again.

Read this book. You're going to like it.

TRUST ME!

ACTIVITIES!

So, you're looking for something to do, huh? Well, you've come to the right place. The best kind of fun is the fun you make on your own. Remember when you were a little ankle-biter and you'd make a fort by throwing a blanket or some old sheets over the couch? Or the time that you tied a garbage bag around yourself and slid down the snow-covered hill? And remember how you made your own jet plane and flew to Timbuktu?

Before reading on, you must promise to use the following outstanding activities for good, not evil. Do you promise? Are your fingers crossed? Are your eyes crossed? Okay, then take a look below! I have listed the activities from the easiest to the most challenging.

The Most Dangerous Dance in the World! Be careful when you learn the traditional Polish dance called the *zbojnicke* (djeh-BOHJ-nick-ee). That's the one where the man swings an axe in circles above the ground and the woman has to jump over it, duck under it, and basically look out. Then *she* takes the axe!

I AM AN IDIOT

This is probably the stupidest activity of all time. Because of this, it always cracks me up.

You Need: to have the alphabet memorized

Try to say the alphabet without moving your lips or your tongue at all. No cheating! Whenever I do this, every letter sounds exactly the same; try it for yourself. (Hey, I said I would start with the easy stuff. If you find this activity too challenging, you may want to put this book down and go eat a Popsicle.)

TREASURE HUNT IN THE COUCH

For those on the lookout for spare change and cracker crumbs!

You Need: a couch or sofa

If you are tough enough to brave the sight of lint, small toys, dirt, and crumbs, you might make enough money to buy a candy bar by playing this game.

Here's what you do: Put on coveralls and plastic gloves. (Protective eyewear is optional.) Drag a garbage can over to the sofa. Now lift up one of the sofa cushions. Careful! You never know what kind of filthy varmint might be hiding down there! There could be cockroaches, or even that annoying kid from down the block.

Anyway, keep pulling up the cushions. As you find disgusting pieces of rancid and dried-out food, throw them out. If you find any clothes you've been missing, put them in the laundry. If that annoying neighbor kid is down there, send him home pronto! And finally, the treasure: nickels, dimes, quarters, maybe even dollars! Heck, maybe there's a credit card down there! I just did this, and I made $1.35, so try this amazing game every few months or so and see what you come up with.

COUNTERCLOCK WISDOM!

You Need: a friend
a couch or chair

Since you're by the couch, have a friend take a seat. Then give him the following directions:

1. Tell your friend to cross his legs, with the right leg on top.

2. Then have him move the end of his right foot in a *clockwise* direction.

3. Finally, ask him to draw a "6" in the air with his right hand while he keeps rotating his foot clockwise.

Now watch—as soon as he draws the "6," his foot will reverse direction! Act surprised, then say, "I must just be naturally coordinated!"

Now take your friend's place on the couch and follow the same steps. But as you draw the "6" in the air, draw it from the bottom *up*. This lets you do the trick without your foot changing direction. (It also will show your friend how superior you are!)

MIXED MARTIAL AIR ARTS

You Need: a long-sleeved shirt
a spastic attitude
a friend who's wearing a long-sleeved shirt

If you and a friend are just sitting around killing time AND if you both have long sleeves on, try this.

Pull your arms in from their sleeves and hold them behind your back.

Then start twisting your body at the hip (sort of like playing with a hula hoop) so that your arm sleeves swing out and around. Once you and your friend get your arms swinging, it will look like the craziest fake fight of all time!

Be sure to do this out in public where you can blow people's minds. (And you'll get Extra Credit Points if either of you gets knocked out by an empty sleeve!)

TALK THE COP TALK, WALK THE COP WALK

Looking for official police officer activities? Use the following information.

For Activity 1, you Need: this book!

For Activity 2, you Need: Krazy Glue
any box with a lid

ACTIVITY 1

You've probably noticed that police officers have lots of codes and lingo that they use. Codes are not only practical, but they sound cool too. For example, if an officer is radioing in a suspicious license plate, he doesn't say, "Run a check on license *174 DBP.*" The problem is that some letters sound like other things; in this license, D sounds like B and P, which could mess things up. (*"One-Adam-12, did someone pee on your license plate?"*)

Instead, the officer might say, "Run a check on *174 Delta Bravo Papa.*" This is cool cop talk that keeps things sensible! Here is the cop talk alphabet:

Alpha, Bravo, Charlie, Delta, Echo, Foxtrot, Golf, Hotel, India, Juliet, Kilo, Lima, Mike, November, Oscar, Papa, Quebec, Romeo, Sierra, Tango, Uniform, Victor, Whiskey, X-ray, Yankee, Zulu

Use these words to spell things out ("Please be advised that I would like some *Golf-Uniform-Mike* now") as well as for general silliness. ("Dad, take cover! We have a *Zulu alert*! Repeat, a *Zulu alert*!")

ACTIVITY 2

Detecting fingerprints is one of the most important police tools there is. If you have ever wanted to do this yourself, here's what you do.

Get a small box with a lid (a shoebox works great). Pour a small puddle of Krazy Glue on a piece of foil or waxed paper (or anything). Put that at one end of the box. Put the item you want to check for fingerprints at the other end of the box. This method will work best on hard, smooth items: anything glass, metal, or hard plastic will work, like a mirror or a knife blade. Make sure the lid is on tight. Leave the box in the sun for four to five hours. Come back and check for prints! (The molecules from the glue will get stuck to the greasy fingerprints!)

If you want to compare the prints to a suspect's, have your suspect push their finger on an inkpad and roll their finger one time on a sheet of white paper.

KUNG FU EGG

It's time to use lightning-quick reflexes on an egg!

You Need: an egg
a piece of aluminum foil
a glass
a playing card

Don't use a hard-boiled egg for this trick; it's more exciting if you don't! The setup for this activity only takes a moment. You just need to make a foil-ring platform to hold up the egg. Cut or tear a rectangular piece of foil and make a ring with it that will support the egg with its fat end down.

Now fill the glass about two-thirds of the way with water. Put the playing card over the glass. Finally, set the foil ring and egg in the center of the card.

Practice a few good kung fu yells and moves! Scream, chop, and kick! Finally, approach the egg. With a show of great concentration, reach out your hand and quickly and sharply flick the card hard, so that it shoots off the glass. The egg will sink into the water, and it won't even break!

Don't try this activity with an ostrich egg! Ostriches lay the biggest eggs of any bird. One of their eggs could support your weight if you stood on it, and its contents are equal to 24 chicken eggs.

RING FINGER!

Your volunteer is going to be making some pretty funny faces.

You Need: a dollar bill
a volunteer

It's impossible for most people to lift their ring finger from this position.

So here's what you do! First, spread your hand out flat on a table, with your palm facing the table. Ask another person to do the same thing. Have the person imitate you as you raise and then lower each of your fingers individually, as shown at right.

Now take out a dollar bill. Raise your hand and turn it, palm out, toward the other person. Bend down your middle finger. Have the other person do the same thing, then press your hands together, as shown at left.

Slip the dollar bill between your two ring fingers. Tell your subject he can have the dollar if he can lift his ring finger away from yours so that the dollar falls down to the table. (No cheating by just pulling the whole arm back or moving the finger to the side.)

The weird faces your volunteer will make are going to be priceless!

MONSTER TEETH

This is the perfect thing to do if you are babysitting some young kids and want to scare them!

You Need: an orange
a knife (careful!)
some kitchen scissors

Cut an orange from top to bottom into halves. (Be careful; if you cut your finger off, this isn't as much fun.) Then cut the halves in half from top to bottom so that you have four quarters of an orange.

Peel one of the sections. Then take the orange peel and cut it lengthwise down the middle. *Not all the way!* Leave about ½ inch at each end.

Now you need to make the teeth. About every ¼ inch on both sides of your first cut, make a ¼-inch cut with your scissors. (These little cuts should be toward the edge of the orange peel.)

You're ready! Turn the orange peel inside out, put it under your lips, and go look in the mirror. *Most excellent!*

SHOOTING THE AIR BALL

The coolest thing that you've never done!

You Need: 2 heavy nonflammable objects
a blow-dryer
a Ping-Pong ball

Take the blow-dryer and place it between your two heavy objects. (Don't block the blow-dryer's intake vent with either of these.) Point the blow-dryer straight up. Then plug it in and turn it on to its highest setting. Now take your Ping-Pong ball and place it in the airstream about a foot over the dryer. Amazing! It should stay suspended in the air. If it doesn't, try placing it farther up or down in the airstream. As gravity pulls down, the air pushes up, and the ball stays in the middle!

Now if you want to shoot your air ball, just go get the peashooter that you can design in the "Weapons!" chapter, page 277, and have at it!

THE PRIMITIVE PHONE

Yeah, you could use a real phone, but why?

You Need: a couple of cans
some string or a long garden hose
2 funnels
some duct tape

I'm assuming you've probably already made a phone line by tying a piece of string between two cans. That is a really primitive phone, where the sound waves of your voices follow the string to the cans.

So let's take it a step further. If you have an old garden hose (the longer, the better) lying around that your parents don't want anymore, have your parents cut off the metal ends with a hacksaw. Stick one funnel in each end and tape them in place.

If you put one funnel up to your mouth and the other up to your ear, you can say something and then hear it a second or two afterward. Now give one end to your friend and have him go out of sight. Have secret conversations! Use the hose as the way to communicate with your hideout!

AREN'T YOU GLAD YOU USE SUNDIALS?

Some people can tell the time by just looking at the sun, but even when I wear sunglasses, I can never see its numbers!

You Need: a pencil
clay or Play-Doh
a flowerpot
a wooden stick (like a chopstick)

You know not to look at the sun, but there are ways to tell the time from the sun *without* looking at it! After all, people have used sundials for thousands of years to tell time. One way to make a sundial is to take a blob of clay and stick it in the bottom of your flowerpot. Then put your stick into the clay so that it stands straight up. It should stick up about 3 inches over the rim of the flowerpot; if it doesn't, get a longer stick or a smaller pot!

To "set" your sundial, you need to put it in a place where the pot will be in the sun all day. Find a good area for it; once you set it, don't move it again. Now, at the top of every hour, make a mark on the edge of the pot where the stick's shadow is. Write down what time it is on the edge at that spot!

It may take a couple of days to get all the hours marked, but once you have, your sundial will be a pretty reliable clock that you made yourself!

If you ever make a sundial in the classic shape, make sure that the piece that casts a shadow is pointing due north. Use a compass or just point it at the North Star.

MESSIN' WITH THE HOMEYS ON THE THREE-WAY

This works best if one of your friends calls you. You can have a three-way conversation with just one person! This is a great way to kill some time and have some laughs. Although it sounds simple, it works like a charm, and once you start doing it, you can't stop!

You Need: a phone
some acting ability

Your friend Ty calls you up and you're talking with him. Suddenly, your friend hears *somebody else* in the room with you. This new person doesn't seem to like Ty very much. From his end of the phone, Ty can hear the person who is with you say, *"Is that Ty? I need to talk to that jerk! He owes me money!"*

Naturally Ty wants to know who is there, but you just apologize for the interruption and keep talking. You might even tell the person in the room with you, "Look, it's not even Ty, okay? Just take it easy."

Of course, *you* are that other person in the room. To make it seem like someone else is there, all you have to do is turn the phone receiver away from your mouth and extend your arm all the way away from you. Now turn your head in the opposite direction of the phone and yell out your comments. Don't try to disguise your voice very much; just yell.

This works best if you do your yelling while Ty is saying something on the other line. Then quickly pull the phone back in and speak in a conversational tone.

If you think this is too simple to work very well, *try it*. It works like a charm!

LAND OF TATTOOS

Tattoos are fun, but the problem is that you eventually get tired of them. This is why many adults who get tattoos either have the tattoo removed or keep getting more and more of them. Temporary tattoos are the way to go, but sticker tattoos are for wussies. Here are a couple of ways to get tattoos that will be your own design.

SUN TATTOOS

Here comes the sun . . . and it's going to tattoo you!

You Need: the sun
a permanent marker
some sunscreen (optional)

Method A

Use a permanent marker to draw your design on your belly, arms, legs, or back. After the ink dries, put on sunscreen and go have fun in the sun!

When you are done in the sun, soak some cotton balls in rubbing alcohol and clean off the marker ink. *Voilà!* There is a light tattoo of your design! If you don't like it, just go out in the sun some more and tan over it! If you do like it, *keep* using marker on the design before going outside.

Method B

Create your design, and then draw it on your body with a sunscreen that has a high SPF number (30 and higher should work.) This method is easier to clean up after, although it is harder to draw the tattoo with.

PAINTED TATTOOS

Just paint yourself and then hang out with some bikers!

You Need: tempera paints (dry or wet)
small bowls
lotion
cotton swabs or paintbrushes

If your tempera paints are wet, just put the different colors into different bowls. If they are dry, put some lotion in the bowls first, then mix the tempera paint color into it until it looks right.

Once the colors are ready, start painting yourself! You can use cotton swabs, paintbrushes, or your fingers to make designs. Cover your face completely with designs! Go native! Take pictures!

FREAK FACE

If you want to get absolutely wacky and you don't mind a little discomfort, try this!

You Need: school-supply-style rubber cement
a crazy attitude
a willingness to have a red face for an hour or so after the activity

(**WARNING:** *Do NOT use Krazy Glue, model glue, or Elmer's Glue for this activity. Use rubber cement ONLY.*)

This should be done in front of a mirror. Take the rubber cement. Apply a 1- to 2-inch band of it around your mouth, starting about 1/4 inch from your lips. Let it dry a little. Now turn your lips inside out and stick them to the rubber cement. You will be amazed at the effect!

The rubber cement will stick to itself, your lips will be flipped, and you will look completely insane! Try not to talk while you wander around scaring people, or your lips will come undone. When you're done, gently pry your lips off your face and wash with soap and warm water.

If you don't want to do your whole mouth the first time you try this, just do your upper or lower lip to get a feel for it.

SECRET MESSAGE MAN

If you don't know how to write in invisible ink yet, here's how to do it!

You Need: white paper
a mirror

Method A (easy)

Get out a pad of paper and stand in front of a mirror. Practice writing while looking at the message in the mirror. It will seem weird at first because you will be writing backwards; the mirror reverses everything!

If you find this too hard, just sit down to write. Write your message in regular writing first. Then carefully write it on a separate sheet in reverse! Remember that *everything* must be reversed; the last word of the sentence becomes the first. The word is spelled backwards and written backwards. A "d" should look like a "b." Once you're done writing your secret message, nobody will be able to read it . . . except for someone who holds it up to a mirror (or who is dyslexic!).

If this gives you trouble, take a piece of paper and rub a layer of dark crayon or pencil lead on it. Then take another sheet of paper, set it on the colored sheet, and write with a ballpoint pen or sharpened pencil. The message's reverse imprint will show up on the back.

Method B (Not Hard)

You Need: a raw potato

Take the potato and cut it in half. Using the cut end, write a message on the bathroom mirror. (I've always liked messages like *"Prepare to die!"*) The message is invisible. BUT when someone takes a shower next, the message will show up on the mirror because of the steam! Whoohoo!

Method C (not much Harder)

You Need: lemon juice (or milk)
a small glass or jar
a cotton swab
white paper

First, pour the liquid into your glass. *Mmmm, lemony!* Now just dip the cotton swab into the liquid and then use the swab to write your message on the white paper. Dip the swab into the liquid again if it dries out.

Let your writing dry out; it should become invisible. When you are ready to read the message, hold it up to a strong light or fire; the words will magically appear! Another way to get the message to appear is to have an adult use an iron at low temperature to "iron" the piece of paper. Because lemon juice and milk darken when heated, the message shows up.

If you ever want to read *someone else's message* in a sealed envelope, spray the envelope with hair spray. It works pretty well!

THE SNORER

Re-create the adventure of snoring while still awake!

You Need: a pocketknife
1 piece of wood about 8 inches long, 2 inches wide, and 1/4 inch thick
some string

If you have ever wanted to imitate the sound a snoring person makes, this is your lucky day! Take your pocketknife out and cut notches into the side edges of the wood. Then whittle the end to a point and bore or cut a hole there that you can run some string through. Tie the string off and leave about 3 feet to use as a handle. Then take it outside and spin it around your head in a circle. It should sound like a lumberjack in a coma!

For a person to snore, gravity must pull down parts of the mouth and throat, which makes them vibrate. Astronauts report that in outer space, nobody snores.

INTRUDER ALERT

How to make your own burglar alarm.

You Need: wood glue

Alarm A 4 small blocks of wood
2 small cans
some marbles

Alarm B a screw eye or an L-shaped metal bracket
a bell
some string
a staple gun
a piece of stiff wire

Here are two different ways to warn yourself that an intruder is coming in your room. Whether it's little Timmy from down the street or a mean guy with a big knife, it's nice to have advance warning!

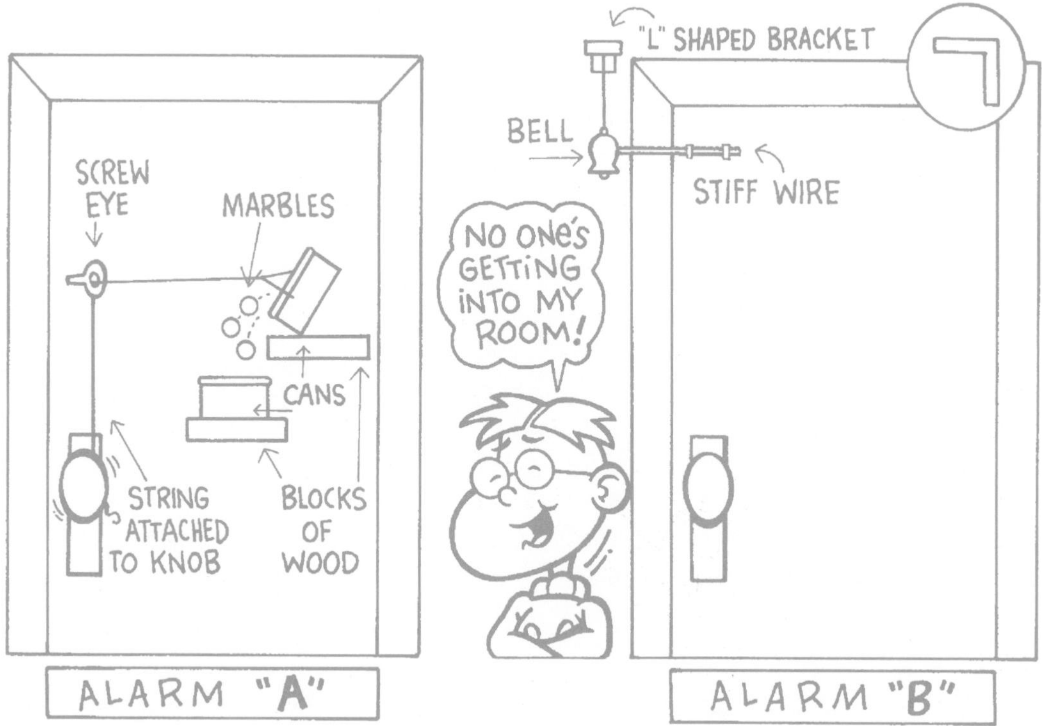

Method A

For the first method, glue or screw the blocks of wood onto the door as the illustration shows. Make sure that 1) they are wide enough to hold the cans, and 2) one can is high and close enough to tilt its marbles into the other one. Make sure you get this right!

Once your mounts are set, screw in the screw eye. Run a tightly wound string around the doorknob, through the screw eye, and into the upper can (which has marbles in it). You may want to put additional blocking around the upper can so that it doesn't simply fall off its mount when pulled by the string.

Method B

The second method is even easier. Screw your L-shaped metal bracket into the wall near the door. Hang your bell from it with the string. Staple a piece of stiff wire (like from a coat hanger) so that it lines up with the bell. *Voilà!* When the door opens, the bell is rung and you can be out the window before your mom can set down the milk and cookies!

FORT BUILDING

You've made forts out of the usual pillows and cardboard boxes. Now it is time for the ultimate fort!

You Need: newspaper

Godzilla grocery bags
tape

Igloo 100 or more empty, clean milk jugs
duct tape

GODZILLA-STYLE FORT

Take about a dozen sheets of newspaper and crumple them into paper balls. (Don't squish them too tightly.) Now fill a paper bag about three-quarters of the way up with the paper balls. Make sure to fill it evenly, but don't wad them down into the bag.

Now neatly fold the top of the paper bag over and tape it shut. You should now have a large, light block. Make about 10 more of these and start building. These are perfect for making large structures that you want to walk through and destroy, like King Kong or Godzilla!

IGLOO-STYLE FORT

To do this, you'll need a lot of plastic jugs . . . like, 100 or more. If your neighborhood recycles (like they should!), it will be easy to get some jugs from your neighbors. Make sure to wash them out so your igloo doesn't stink.

Take 20 of the milk jugs and make a circle with them. The tops should face inward, the ends should face outward. Then remove four or five of the jugs from one spot. (This will be the bottom of your door.) Tape the jugs that are left in the semicircle together with duct tape. If you want a huge igloo, make the circle bigger. If you want a smaller igloo, start with 15 jugs.

Now, put another row of jugs on top of the first row. But bring it in a little bit, so that this row comes inward toward the inside of the circle. Tape them together and leave room for the door. Keep going for five or so rows. Each row should come inward and use less jugs than the one before it.

When you get to the sixth or seventh row, close over the top of the door. When you get to the very top, just tape that last jug in place, and be cool in your igloo. *Ice, ice, baby!*

 If you decide to tear the igloo down later, just untape and recycle it!

FOLLOW-UP ACTIVITY

Are you kidding me? You want a follow-up activity for a chapter called "Activities"? That would be "Hyper-Activity"!

DOGS AND OTHERS!

Animals are the best! This chapter will focus on *domesticated* animals. These are the animals that make great pets. There are turtles, fish, mice, guinea pigs, cats, saltwater crocodiles, and many others. (Actually, I am just kidding about the cats.) I only have space to write about a few of these animals, so this chapter will focus on the one species of animal on the planet that has more varieties than any other.

I am talking, of course, about *dogs*.

Boys love dogs! Dogs are loyal, brave, friendly, and a pain in the butt, just like you! But before you get a dog of your own, there is something you have to do.

Don't get a dog.

That's right, *don't* get a dog. Dogs live a long time, sometimes 15 years or more. If you can't commit to taking care of a dog for that long, *DON'T GET A DOG*. If your family is not going to help you take care of it, DON'T GET A DOG. If you can't commit to giving the dog love, food, and exercise every day of its life, DON'T GET A DOG! If you're going to be one of those jerks who ties his dog up all day, or ignores the dog as it barks at anything that moves because it's bored out of its mind, then *DON'T GET A DOG!!*

Okay, I've calmed down. If you are *responsible* and your family can keep a dog happy, then *think* about getting a dog. But should you get a male or female dog? Some people think that females are more obedient and easier to handle. Some people are wrong. Just think about your sister (or any girl) and you'll see what I mean. And what about the dog's age? Remember that if you get a puppy, that means you have to clean up the puppy's dookie. You have to train the puppy and keep your temper when he drools on your cell phone. *D'oh!*

YOU'VE GOTTA GET ME OUTTA HERE, KID!

Save a dog's life. There are lots of adult dogs at your local animal shelter that already need a home. The beauty of it is, most of these dogs are already housebroken! You can see their personality, plus the dog will be incredibly grateful to you. That's because about 60 percent of the dogs at your local animal shelter eventually end up being "put to sleep." Like I said, you *really* can save a life by getting a dog at the animal shelter.

Dogs come in so many sizes and personalities, you really need to do some homework to pick the right type for you. But the animal shelter has ALL kinds. Go take a look. If you get a puppy, make sure it's more than eight weeks old.

Think about the size of your home and your yard when getting your dog, and be sure to ask the breeder or animal shelter worker a lot of questions before bringing home a dog. They should have questions for you, too.

Okay, so now you have a dog. Time to name it, right? Well, hold on a second! If you are going to name a dog (or even a cat), be *original*! Here is a list of the most popular names for dogs and cats in the United States. DON'T USE ANY OF THESE! Millions of pets already have these names: *Max, Sam, Lady, Bear, Smokey, Shadow, Kitty, Molly, Buddy, Brandy, Ginger, Baby, Misty, Missy, Pepper, Jack, Bandit, Tiger* (or *Tigger*), *Samantha, Lucky, Muffin* (or *Muffy*), *Princess, Maggie, Charlie, Sheba, Rocky, Patches, Rusty, Buster, Casey, Sadie, Riley*, and *Midnight*. Believe it or not, *Fido* and *Rover* don't get used much. Hey, here's an idea: if you get a dog that has bad breath a lot, just call it a "Germy shepherd"! (Sorry about that.)

Okay, now your dog has a name. What else? Well, maybe we should just ask the dog!

A VERY SPECIAL MESSAGE FROM YOUR DOG TO YOU

Hey, it's me. Why are you surprised? Heck, you taught me to *speak*, so why is it so amazing that I can write? Anyway, the nice man who wrote this book asked me to pass along a few things to *you*, so why don't you try listening to *me* for once, huh, punk? (This is fun! *Ruff!*)

First of all, *thank you* for not tying me up in the backyard all day and night, like the people who live down the street do with *their* dog. That only makes a dog feel isolated and depressed . . . kind of how *you* would feel if you were tied up and all alone!

I do have a few bones to pick with you, though. You know how you sometimes yell at me for barking at cats and the mail carrier? I just wanted to remind you that I'M A DOG! It's what I do!

Back to the "*thank yous.*" I really appreciate the fact that you trained me well. It sure saved my life the time I saw a cat (*GRRR!*) on the other side of that busy street. I would have been a goner if you hadn't yelled, "*Stay!*" and I knew what to do. Thanks again!

Now for a question: You know how you say "*Shake*" and I shake your hand? Well, here's a news flash: WE'VE MET ALREADY! Would you go up to your human friends every time you see them and say "Shake"? They would think you were a nutcake!

Thanks for letting me smell exciting things like pee and dirt when we go for walks. I see lots of dogs getting dragged along by their owners and not getting to stop for the best part of the walk: smelling dookie!

Well, that's about it. Oh yeah, you know how there is *something* you blame on me when guests are around? Stop doing that. Everyone knows it's you.

Thanks again!
Your Dog

SPECIAL FEATURE: DOG SAFETY TIPS

Every year, over four million people in the United States are bitten by dogs. So beware, and please read the following very *important information!*

LESSON 1: TRAIN YOUR DOG!

Train your dog not to go berserk when a mail carrier comes to the door. Also, don't allow your dog to bite the mail as it comes through the mail slot; this will only teach your dog to attack innocent envelopes.

LESSON 2: A STRANGE DOG APPROACHES YOU!

Stand still with your hands at your sides. Pretend you are a tree until the dog leaves. Perhaps your "bark" will scare it away! (For obvious reasons, do not imitate a fire hydrant unless you want wet pants.) Practice this technique with a stuffed toy dog. If the stuffed dog attacks you anyway, take it to an animal doctor or a psychiatrist. If that does not solve the problem, take yourself to an animal doctor or a psychiatrist.

Once the dog loses interest in you, slowly back away until it is out of sight. Then run like the wind! If the dog begins to chase you, stop immediately, especially if it is driving a car.

LESSON 3: THE STRANGE DOG IS AGGRESSIVE!

If a dog tries to bite you, try to "feed" him your jacket, homework, bicycle, cat, or anything else that can serve as a barrier between you and the dog.

LESSON 4: THAT STUPID DOG BIT YOU!

Immediately wash the wound thoroughly with soap, then report the bite to your local animal control agency. Tell the animal official everything you know about the dog. If the dog is a stray, tell the official what the dog looked like and in which direction it left. If the dog was driving, try to get its license plate number.

 Watch Your Step! New York City once had 75 tons of dog poop piled up on the sidewalks every DAY. (That's how the city got nicknamed the "Big Crapple"!)

OTHER ANIMALS

Okay, so you don't really want a dog, but you are considering getting a pet. Maybe you live in an apartment, so you're worried about room. Think about how much interaction with the pet you want. For example, with an aquarium of fish, you won't have much interaction. You can't take the fish out and play with them (at least not if you're smart). But that's not a bad thing! I had an aquarium for years, and I loved watching the different species of fish swimming around, having conversations, and building cities.

For boys who don't want a *big* animal, maybe a "stinky aquarium-mammal" will work. These are "pocket pets" such as rats, gerbils, hamsters, mice, etc., that live in aquariums filled with cedar shavings in boys' bedrooms. If you get one of these, remember to let it out of its habitat to play, but don't let it be eaten by larger pets, or make a dramatic, mysterious escape!

POLECATS

For people who like a *lot* of interaction with an indoor pet, a good choice is a cat. Not a kitty-cat, but a *polecat.* Also called *ferrets,* these fun-loving animals will amuse you to no end. But keep in mind that ferrets need a good couple of hours of play *every* day. They need lots of interaction. If you buy two ferrets at once, you can save yourself a little time because they can play with each other. (Oh, by the way, ferrets aren't allowed in Hawaii or California. Sorry about that.)

Ferrets are a kick in the pants, but be aware that they are full of mischief. They like to poke their nose into anything they can get it into. When your ferrets are out of their cage (it should be a big cage with lots of toys), you need to make sure your house has been ferret-proofed. This means put all food away, clear breakable items off of shelves and counters, and don't leave any credit cards out!

If you want a ferret, start with your local animal shelter or, if you have one, ferret shelter. Adult ferrets are usually already housebroken and aren't quite as full of pep as youngsters.

 Other names for ferrets: polecats, carpet sharks, ferts, fuzzballs

 Interesting Information!

Ferrets can be trained to use litter boxes for their dookie!

Ferrets can be taken outside on leashes!

Cats can tolerate ferrets, but always keep an eye on any dog near a polecat!

A higher number of humans than ferrets get rabies!

FERRETS IN HISTORY

Genghis Khan (1167–1227) conquered the largest land empire in the history of the world. He loved ferrets. (Of course, he also shot his brother full of arrows for stealing a fish that he himself had caught, but never mind that.) And one of England's greatest monarchs, Queen Elizabeth I, loved her ferrets so much that she had a picture of herself painted with her pets. Ferrets were often kept aboard sailing ships to keep the rat population down and were especially useful to the U.S. Navy. We even named one of our ships after them!

CATS

Even though some people say that cats are just walking meatloaf, maybe there are a few of you who think a cat is a good pet. Well, you're right. Cats can take care of themselves better than most other pets. They're pretty quiet and lovable, and they don't need a lot of interaction either.

So what's the problem? I'll tell you the problem: cats are like girls. They're disobedient and you never know what they're thinking. You never know why they do the things that they do. Heck, even *they* don't know why they do the things they do! Some people call this "mysterious." Puh-leeze. There's nothing mysterious about hair balls!

Cats aren't very loyal, either. If a bad guy broke into your house and threatened you with a wet noodle, you know that your dog would bark like crazy at the intruder, and maybe even attack the wet noodle just to make sure you were safe! But a cat would lick itself, yawn, and wander into another room. And here's a good one: try putting a leash on a cat sometime. Forget it! It's no wonder that dogs were used as pets a good 6,000 years before cats were!

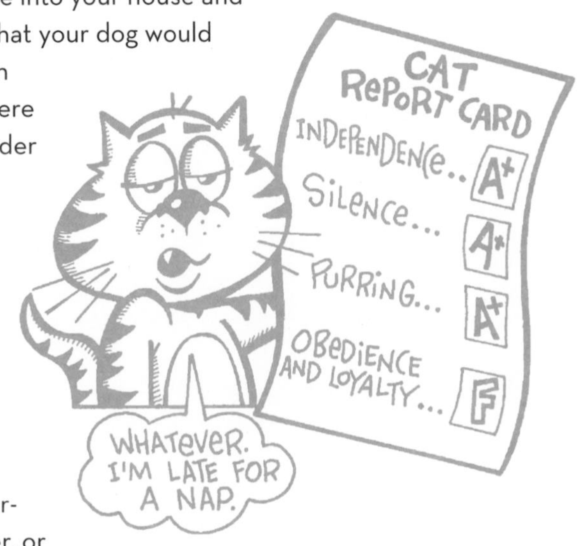

CAT REPORT CARD
INDEPENDENCE... A+
SILENCE... A+
PURRING... A+
OBEDIENCE AND LOYALTY... F
WHATEVER. I'M LATE FOR A NAP.

But cats are good at being by themselves, and they are good for living in apartments or small homes. In addition, watching a cat play with catnip is pretty cool. So if you don't mind being called a "cat dandy," feel free to get yourself a kitty. Get one at your local animal shelter, or try to tame one of the wild ones in your neighborhood. And just remember that I warned you!

SPECIAL FEATURE: CAT'S EYES

The eyes of a cat are something special. When you look at them, you will see that the "iris" of the eye is a vertical slit or line, unlike the round iris of a human. The long vertical opening of their eye lets them see very well right in front of them. This is called an "elliptical pupil." (Try saying *that* 10 times fast!) Cats are predators, so they look for movement *right* in front of them. If a cat is watching something that goes above or below its vision, it loses interest. Watch a cat sneak up on a bird; it will get closer and closer, but if the bird flies away, the cat often doesn't even look up. To the cat, the bird just vanished into thin air!

 Presidential Animal Lovers: President Dwight D. Eisenhower (1890–1969) was usually a nice guy, but he *hated* cats. He hated cats so much, he gave orders that any cat found on the White House grounds was to be shot. (He wasn't kidding around either.)

AMAZING ANIMAL FACTS

- In Pennsylvania in 1924, a black Labrador named Pep was sentenced to life in prison. Pep had made the mistake of killing the cat of Governor Gifford Pinchot of Pennsylvania. The governor was the judge in the case, and there was no jury. Pep was sent to prison and even given an inmate number: C2559.

  The good news is that, like most dogs, Pep loved attention. Pep was allowed to wander about the prison, and he was loved by hundreds of inmates. *Good dog!* Pep lived in the penitentiary from 1924 until his natural death in 1930.

- Elephants are the only mammal that can't jump. This is because the elephant is the only mammal with four knees.

- Kangaroo Tales! The famous English explorer Captain James Cook (1728–1779) traveled to Australia. In 1770, his men saw a strange animal bounce past them. According to legend, they asked a native Aborigine hunter what the animal was called. The man replied, "Kan-na-gu-ru."

  "So the beast is called a *kangaroo*!" the Englishmen exclaimed. They wrote this down, and the name stuck. But what the English didn't know was that *Kan-na-gu-ru* means "I do not understand you" in the language of the Aborigines!

- In South Africa, termites are often roasted and eaten by the handful, the way we eat pretzels or popcorn.

- Now That's a Dog Lover! A warlord named Tokugawa Tsunayoshi ruled in Japan more than 300 years ago. Tokugawa was such a dog lover, he passed laws that gave the death penalty for killing, injuring, or even *ignoring* a dog. (These were called the Laws of Compassion.) During his 30-year reign, up to 200,000 people were punished for these crimes. "Good dog! *Very* good dog!"

- Lions and tigers can mate and have cubs. The babies are called "ligers" when the father is a lion, and "tigons" or "tiglons" when the father is a tiger. But do you know what you get when you cross an aardvark with a platypus? Trust me, you don't want to know.

- Beetles are popular pets in Japan. Giant stag beetles have sold for as much as $30,000 there. One salesperson of beetles said, "They have different personalities. When I hold my beetle, I have real affection for it."

Why Are You Carrying Around a Stuffed Bunny? A tribe of people called the Celts who lived in Europe thought that rabbits had magical powers. One reason for this is because rabbit babies are born with their eyes *open*, unlike most other animals. For Celts, to have *any* piece of a dead rabbit (or the whole thing) was good luck. (It was good luck for the human, not the rabbit!) Over time, the piece that ended up on people's key chains was the foot.

Scientists have determined that human babies are usually less intelligent than chimpanzee babies.

FOLLOW-UP ACTIVITY

You may not have known this, but animals can talk. They are reluctant to do so in front of humans, however. Secretly watch your dog or ferret. (Remember to be patient, as this may take hours, or even days.) Eventually the animal will mutter something, possibly a complaint about its food. When it does, jump out and say *"Ah-ha!"* Once caught, the beast will be happy to have a conversation with you, probably about sports.

DUMB DIRECTIONS ON PRODUCTS!

Companies want us to be so careful with their products that their warning labels may take safety a little too far. Is it the *company* that is incredibly stupid or do they think *we* are the dopes? *All the warnings below are taken from real products!*

"Caution: The contents of this bottle should not be fed to fish." *On a bottle of shampoo for dogs.*

"Keep away from children." *On a bottle of* ***baby*** *lotion.*

"Do not use while sleeping." *On a hair dryer.*

"Never use while sleeping." *On a propane blowtorch.*

"Do not take if allergic to aspirin." *On a bottle of aspirin.*

"Do not use in shower." *On a hair dryer.*

"This broom does not actually fly." *On a Harry Potter toy broom.*

"Do not light in face. Do not expose to flame." *On a lighter.*

"Some assembly required." *On a 500-piece jigsaw puzzle.*

"Choking hazard: This toy is a small ball." *On the label for a rubber ball.*

"May be harmful if swallowed." *On a shipment of hammers.*

"Instructions: Put on food." *On a bottle of ketchup.*

"Do not attempt to stop the blade with your hand." *In the manual for a chainsaw.*

Dumb Directions on Products!

"These ear plugs are nontoxic, but may interfere with breathing if caught in windpipe." *On a pack of earplugs.*

"Warning: May contain nuts." *On a package of peanuts.*

"Warning: May cause drowsiness." *On a bottle of sleeping pills.*

"Do not put in mouth." *On a box of bottle rockets.*

"Remove plastic before eating." *On the wrapper of a fruit snack.*

"Do not drive cars in ocean." *In small print at the bottom of the screen during a car commercial that shows a car in the ocean.*

"Shin pads cannot protect any part of the body they do not cover." *On a pair of shin guards.*

"This product not intended for use as a dental drill." *On an electric drill.*

"Eating rocks may lead to broken teeth." *On a rock gardening kit.*

"This product may cause harm if eaten." *On an aluminum chair.*

"You could be a winner! No purchase necessary. Details inside." *On a bag of corn chips.*

"Directions: Use like regular soap." *On a bar of soap.*

"Serving suggestion: Defrost." *On a frozen dinner box.*

"Product will be hot after heating." *On a bread pudding package.*

"Do not turn upside down." *On the* ***bottom*** *of a dessert package.*

"Do not iron clothes on body." *On packaging for an iron.*

"Do not drive car after taking cough medicine." *On a* ***children's*** *cough medicine jar.*

"For indoor or outdoor use only." *On a string of Christmas lights.*

"Remember: Objects in the mirror are actually behind you." *On a bicyclist's helmet-mounted rearview mirror.*

"When operating the selector dial near your eye, take care not to put your finger in your eye accidentally." *On a camera.*

"Kills all kinds of insects! Warning: This spray is harmful to bees." *On a can of insect spray.*

"Do not use when temperature exceeds 140 degrees Fahrenheit." *On a wheelbarrow.*

"Caution: Risk of fire." *On an artificial fireplace log.*

"Contents may catch fire." *On a book of matches.*

"Warning: Cape does not enable user to fly." *On a Batman costume. (This is doubly dumb, because Batman can't fly either!)*

"Do not use as an ice cream topping." *On a bottle of hair coloring.*

FOLLOW-UP ACTIVITY

Create your own product. Give it directions in another language, like Swahili or Martian. Chuckle as your customers use it incorrectly.

EMERGENCIES!

Emergency! Emergency! An emergency is what we call a life-threatening situation. It is a big deal. What you are *supposed* to do in an emergency is stay calm and think clearly. But what your body and brain want to do in an emergency is scream, jump up and down, and run away.

Everybody knows that if you have an emergency (and *only* if you have an emergency) you should call 911. What you may *not* know is that the very first 911 call ever made was by an Alabama senator named Rankin Fite. He called 911, said hi, and then had coffee and doughnuts.

But ever since then, 911 is only supposed to be called for a real problem. Unfortunately, some people don't know what a *real* emergency is. They will call 911 about "emergencies" at the drop of a hat. For example, look at these real calls that have been made to 911:

- A woman living in Los Alamitos, California, called 911 to complain that a person was making "bird-type noises" outside of her house. The police came and found the source of the emergency: a bird in a tree.

- A Los Angeles resident returned home to find his wife lying down on the couch. He asked her if she was unconscious. She said, "Yes." He called 911. (He should have asked if she was conscious. Then if she said "No," he still could have called 911!)

But emergencies can happen in unlikely places. There are about 7,000 emergency room visits a year for injuries involving either pillows or indoor houseplants. (You know, pillows are dangerous because they are so soft and fluffy, and . . . *hey, wait a minute*!) In order to report medical emergencies so that a doctor anywhere in the world can understand what is wrong, doctors use a system called the International Classification of Diseases (ICD). The ICD is very specific. Just look at these codes from an edition of the ICD:

T18.2:	Victim has a hair ball.
V97.3:	Victim was sucked into a jet aircraft engine.
V96.1:	Victim was injured in a glider fire.
W56:	Victim was bitten by an orca.
W64:	Victim was pecked by a turkey.
W79:	Victim has a bean or marble stuck in their nose.
Y35.5:	Victim was beheaded by a guillotine.
Z89.419:	Victim's large toe is unexpectedly missing.

The sad fact is that emergencies do happen, and someday, one may happen to you. What should you do when an emergency strikes? Read on.

Here is the key to dealing with any emergency:

Step 1: Think!

Step 2: Do something (or nothing) based on your thinking!

Here is how you should NOT deal with an emergency:

Step 1: Do something without thinking first!

Step 2: Think what you did was stupid.

GENERAL TIP

Call 911 as soon as possible in any real emergency. Do this *before* beginning any other emergency steps. The emergency operator will need to know *who* you are, *what* happened, and *where* you are. If you're calling from a cell phone, make a note of what your closest street is before calling 911. This will help the authorities locate you.

"Calling Dr. Nurse! Calling Dr. Nurse!" At last count, there were three doctors in the United States with the last name "Nurse." And yes, there is always at least one Dr. Frankenstein out there practicing medicine!

HOUSEHOLD EMERGENCIES

Here are some of the common emergencies that a boy might run into around the house.

YOUR HEAD IS STUCK BETWEEN THE RAILINGS

At first you will panic when you realize that your head is stuck. Calm down. If your head went in, it will come *out*, just not as easily. Your ears might get a little crushed on the return trip, but that's a price you're going to have to pay for pretending that you were an animal in the zoo.

First, try facing straight forward, with your head even. Now slide your head as far to the *top* of the railings as you can. The width between the rails is a little wider there. Try pulling your head out. No luck?

Yell for help. If you still can't get out, have your assistant try rubbing mayonnaise on the sides of your head. Get your head back up to the top of the railing and try it again.

Still no good? Have your assistant find a crowbar and start thinking of a good excuse for your parents.

YOU HAVE A BEAN, MARBLE, OR OTHER ITEM STUCK UP YOUR NOSE OR IN YOUR EAR

For some reason, at least once in a boy's lifetime, he decides to do things backwards. Instead of pulling things *out* of his nose, he'll stick something *in* it. And now it's *stuck* in there!

Naturally, you want to get it out, but be careful not to shove it farther in! Try closing off one nostril and then "blowing" out the other one, just like you're blowing your nose. If you're lucky, that lima bean will pop right out, even greener than it was before.

No dice? Try gently pushing down on the outside of your nose to coax the marble out.

Still no good? If the object is a bean (or something soft) and it isn't stuck too far up there, you can carefully use some tweezers to try to pluck it out. But if you STILL can't get it out, it's time to call your doctor. You may feel silly, but trust me, they see the old "*bean in the schnozz*" emergency all the time. They have a small suction device that will take care of your problem right away.

YOU CLOGGED THE TOILET

So, you busted a grumpy, huh? (See "Poop Department" in the "Gross Stuff!" chapter, page 148.) The toilet clogs when there's too much, uh, toilet paper in it and the water can't drain away.

The key is to act quickly. Don't just stare at the toilet filling up saying, "*Uh-oh.*" You don't want that mess to overflow! As soon as the toilet backs up, get down on your hands and knees and look behind the toilet. You will see a valve there. This valve lets the water into the toilet. Quickly turn that valve to the right (*remember: righty-tighty!*). This will shut off the water to the toilet so that it can't fill anymore.

Now back out of the bathroom and close the door. Put up a sign that says, "*Don't use toilet.*" Wait for your parents to deal with it now. Trust me, you don't want any part of the rest of the solution.

YOU LEFT THE HOUSE WITHOUT A COAT, AND IT'S REALLY COLD OUTSIDE

Come on, do I have to explain every little thing to you? Either tough it out, borrow a jacket, or call your parents. Besides, how cold is it? There are parts of Siberia that regularly get to 50 degrees below zero (Fahrenheit). In 1983, Vostok, Antarctica, recorded 128 degrees below zero, a world's record. *That's cold!*

At that temperature, breathing is *fun* and *deadly*. When you breathe out, the water vapor in your breath freezes in the air like tiny ice cubes. That's *fun*. But your lungs are very wet on the inside; if you breathe in air that cold, your lungs will be covered in frost. This is *deadly* and it kills you. (That's not fun.)

 More Fun with Cold! If the temperature is ever down to about 10 degrees Fahrenheit where you live, go outside and blow some bubbles. If they don't pop right away, they may fly long enough to freeze and then shatter in the air. Very, *very* cool. (By the way, Hell is the name of a village in Norway. Hell freezes over in the winter.)

 Big Boys *Do* Cry! Let's say that you have an accident. Maybe you fell off your skateboard, or your parachute didn't open that time you went skydiving. Is it okay to cry? Sure! Surveys show that up until age 12, boys and girls cry the same amount. After that, boys (and men) cry between one and two times a month. (Girls and women cry about five times a month.)

 What's the most *dangerous* job in the nation? Police officer? Fireperson? How about *fisher*? More fishermen and fisherwomen die on the job each year than any other occupation.

The Consumer Product Safety Commission is in charge of making sure that children's products are not dangerous. One winter season, they had 80,000 buttons made up to be given away at toy stores. The buttons read "For Kids' Sakes, Think Toy Safety." Unfortunately, the buttons had lead in their paint, sharp edges, and could easily be swallowed by a child. They all had to be recalled.

SPECIAL FEATURE: THE WORST EMERGENCIES IN HISTORY

The worst emergencies and disasters often have a natural cause, like an earthquake, a hurricane, or a disease. For example, experts agree that one of the world's worst emergencies was the arrival of a disease called the "Black Death" in Europe in 1347. Eventually, 75 million people died from this disease, which was spread by fleas. More recently, in the 1920s and '30s there were massive food shortages in the Ukraine. More than 12 million people died of starvation, and living people had to eat dead ones to survive. Jellied meats and sausages made from human flesh were the only types of meat available.

One of the strangest man-made emergencies was the "London Killer Fog." You see, they get such thick fog in England, it is called "pea soup." Thanks to air pollution, this fog has sometimes combined with smog and turned yellow. In 1952, the city of London had a week of severe fog. The fog did not burn off or blow away as it usually does, and it trapped all the air pollution that was released from cars and factories. As many as 16,000 people died from breathing the pollution. This killer pea soup helped to wake up the world to the importance of taking care of our planet.

FOLLOW-UP ACTIVITY

Wait for a situation that is the *opposite* of an emergency. (This could be something like dropping your fork from the dinner table or seeing a plane in the distance.) Call a friend on your phone. Tell him that you have a *nonemergency situation*. Describe it carefully and tell him where you are, so that the men in the white suits know where to pick you up.

EXPERIMENTS!

"Back in the day," we used to experiment with Life Savers. We would get some mint "Wint O Green" Life Savers, go into a closet, and close the door. We would then chomp down on the Life Savers with our teeth, and watch the colored lights flash in each others' mouths! We didn't know that we were seeing something called "triboluminescence" (tri-bo-loom-in-ES-ens)—we just knew it looked cool. If you want to spare your teeth, just put the Life Savers in a plastic sandwich bag, go in the closet, and hit them with a hammer.

Try the same thing with a Curad strip bandage; don't chew on it, just wait for your eyes to adjust to the dark, then grab the bandage's tabs and yank them open. You'll see a flash of light!

Now it's time to get out your white laboratory coat, Russian accent, and test tubes, because we are going to have a few experiments around here! (If you want to try to present these as tricks to an audience, make sure to read the tips in the "Magic!" chapter, beginning on page 195.)

The following experiments are all pretty simple, with the easiest ones listed first. And remember, an experiment does not always work the first time. Think about what you did, check the instructions, and experiment again. That's why they're called *experiments*! Sometimes you have to experiment until you get it right.

 Here is the only math equation you will find in this book:
111,111,111 x 111,111,111 = 12,345,678,987,654,321

IT'S DIFFERENT FOR GIRLS

Girls and boys are different in many mysterious ways.

You Need: 1 male human *(over 11 years old; 10 might work)*
1 female human *(over 11 years old; 10 might work)*
2 lip gloss, ChapStick, or lipstick containers (*don't worry, nobody has to put it on*)

A simple experiment! Have your boy and girl volunteers kneel on the floor. Make sure that their legs are together.

Now, have both of them bend forward and put their elbows up against their knees. Their forearms should extend forward from the knees, with the palms flat against the floor. (Their legs should still be together.)

Place the lip gloss containers (or whatever you're using) upright at the end of their fingers. Okay, now you're ready. Have both of them now kneel up straight with their legs still together. Have them clasp their hands behind their backs, above their waists.

Now tell them this: "*Keeping your arms and legs in their positions, lean forward, knock the lip gloss over with your nose, and return to the kneeling-up position.*"

Watch them! The odds are very high that the girl can do it. The odds are very high that the boy can't!

The reason this happens is because girls tend to have more body weight in the lower half of their bodies than boys do. They can balance better!

OTHER STRENGTH AND BALANCE EXPERIMENTS!

These don't require girls—any human volunteer will do.

STAND UP

Have your volunteer stand with his feet together, four foot-lengths from a wall. Have him lean in to the wall with his hands at his sides, so that his forehead is on the wall. Now tell him to stand up straight. He can't! Ha!

WEAK IN THE KNEES

Tell your volunteer that in a moment he will be unable to lift his right knee while standing on his left leg. You will not interfere or touch him in any way.

Have this person stand with the outside edge of his left foot against a door or wall. Now tell him to put his left shoulder against the wall. After the person has done this, wave your hand over his right knee and say your magic words: "*Great Googly-Moogly!*" Tell the person to keep his left foot and shoulder against the wall and to lift his right knee. He can't. It's magic! (Plus, it can't be done!)

YOU CAN'T MAKE ME

For this experiment, find someone who is stronger than you. (I know, it's not easy.) Challenge him or her to a strength contest.

Now grab your head! Here's what I mean: seat yourself on the floor and put your open hand on top of your head, spreading your fingers as wide as you can. Now tell your opponent to try to lift your arm up so that it isn't on your head anymore. He cannot make any quick moves (or kick you or pull from an angle), he can only pull straight up. He can't do it, even if he actually picks you up! *You're stronger!*

STRENGTH-SUCKER

Tell your volunteer that you can take away all of his strength with one finger. First, have him sit back in a chair. Tell him to relax, to totally relax. Have him fold his arms and tell him to keep them folded. Step forward, sneakily put the toes of your shoes against his toes. Lean forward, say your magic words (I still like *Great Googly-Moogly!*), and gently but firmly press your finger against his forehead.

Tell him to rise. *He cannot.* Tell him to stand up! *He cannot!* It is impossible to stand up if you are leaning back in your chair, and can't use your arms, and can't move your feet (unless the person cheats and slips out the side.) But he didn't know that! Nice work!

OPPOSITES ATTRACT

Static electricity can make water bend!

You Need: an inflated balloon
a sink with running water
a wool sweater

This is so basic, it's ridiculous. Blow up your balloon and tie it with a knot. Turn on the tap water in the sink. Don't turn it up high; keep the water stream small. Now push the balloon near the running water. Nothing happens! Now rub the balloon on the wool sweater. *Really* rub it! When you're done, push the portion of the balloon you were rubbing toward the running water. Don't get too close, because you'll see that the water is more than happy to help! That's right, the water stream will bend as it tries to get at the balloon! Basically, the static electricity in the balloon (which is negatively charged) is attracting the positively charged part of the water.

NOTE: If the balloon gets wet, all charges are lost. Dry it off completely and try again.

JUMPING BEANS, SWIMMING RAISINS

I don't know about other dried fruits, but raisins are great swimmers! This is an easy experiment with a fun result.

You Need: any cold, clear carbonated drink: clear soda, mineral water, and tonic water all work
a glass or jar
a handful of raisins

Pour your drink into the glass. Bubbly! Now put a handful of raisins in the glass. They sink! Of course, that's because raisins are heavier than water. Wait . . . they're rising! They're at the top! Now they're going down again . . . *Dive, dive, dive!*

What happens? The raisins are initially heavier than the liquid, but as they sink, they get coated with bubbles. The bubbles form a "life preserver" for the raisins and raise them to the top! There the bubbles burst, and the raisin sinks again. The show is over when the bubbles run out!

Extra twist: Try turning this into a magic trick! Do the experiment the same way, but when the raisins sink the first time, start saying spells and acting like a spazz to get them to rise. (By the way, this trick also works with plastic pushpins.)

Extra, extra twist: Try doing the same trick with small, round pieces of Silly Putty. It should work! Now try this: If you put a ball of Silly Putty into water, it will sink. But if you shape your Silly Putty like a boat, it floats!

JOURNEY TO THE APPLE'S CORE

Tell a spectator what you're going to do and watch their eyes widen!

You Need: a piece of paper
a knife
an apple
a cutting board

Fold the piece of paper once and set the blade of the knife into the fold. You are now going to cut the apple in half, without cutting the paper at all!

Put the apple on the cutting board. Set the knife blade on top of the paper and begin pushing it down on the apple. (*Don't saw it; just push carefully down.*) After you cut through the apple, check out the paper: it's still in one piece!

BEWARE THE DEADLY STRAW

Sure you can suck liquids through a straw, but straws are also very dangerous!

You Need: plastic straws
an uncooked potato

This is a fun experiment to do as a magic trick! Just take the potato and try to stab it with a straw. The straw will bend and maybe stab into the potato a little bit if you're lucky.

Now say a magic word (*Hottentot tatertot!*) and hold your thumb over the hole at the end of the straw while you stab the potato with the other end. It should go right into the potato. The farther you push it in, the stronger the straw will get; as the air is trapped inside, the straw gets compressed, making the straw more powerful!

WATER MAGIC

You Need: a small plastic bag
sharpened pencils (*really* sharp!)

Bring your plastic bag and pencils over to the sink. Fill the bag about 75 percent full with water. Now tie a knot in the top.

Okay, you're ready!

Take one of the pencils, spear the bag with it, and leave it in place! Do this quickly, so that the pencil goes in straight and then pokes through the other side of the bag. You'll be surprised to see that if you poke the pencil through the bag fast enough, no water will spill out of the bag!

If you have the knack for this, poke more pencils into the bag. It's pretty impressive what a pincushion for pencils a bag full of water can turn into . . . without leaking!

I AM IRON MAN

You've got a lot of heavy metal in your body, and you don't even know it!

You Need: any breakfast cereal that has "100 percent iron" or "reduced iron" or "iron"
a plastic bowl
water
any magnet that you can hold in your hand and stir with

Your body contains many different metals. One of the most important of these is iron. This is the same metal that you sometimes see rusting; it is in buildings, cars, and *you*.

To prove this, pour cereal into a bowl, then add water. Let the cereal get soggy. Then take the magnet and start stirring the cereal with it. You're going to have to stir a lot; if you have a younger brother or sister, try to trick them into helping you. (It might take up to 30 minutes of stirring to make this work!)

After stirring for a while, check your magnet. You should start to see small black particles forming on it. *Keep going!* You will get more! You'll be rich! Actually, you'll just have a lot of iron. Those small black particles are pieces of metal. You don't usually notice them when you're eating food because they're so small. They have to be small for you to digest them. Believe it or not, there is gold in your body too!

Outer Space Metal! The next time you go to the beach, bring along that magnet. Once you get there, tie the magnet to a string and walk around, dragging it through the sand behind you. The magnet will collect metal particles as you walk. The coolest thing is that about 20 percent of those particles are from meteors!

I AM THE STRONGEST MAN IN THE WORLD (PART I)

Amaze your friends with your strength! Baffle your enemies with your putty!

You Need: Silly Putty
a hammer, rubber mallet, or any heavy, flat object

Roll your Silly Putty into a ball. Put it on something that can take a good blow like a cutting board or a smooth concrete surface. Now hand the hammer or mallet to one of your friends. Tell him to hit the Silly Putty and try to flatten it in one stroke! Your friend will hit it. Nothing. *Try it again!* Nothing. (Even just using the palm of your hand will do as long as the Silly Putty is hit with a fast, sharp blow.)

Call your friend a wimp. Push down on the Silly Putty with your finger and squish it. *Easy!*

The reason this happens is because Silly Putty is actually not a solid, it's a liquid. It reacts differently to slow pressure than it does to hard, sudden pressure. This is the same reason why water feels differently when you do a belly flop off of the high dive than it does when you take a bath.

I REALLY AM THE STRONGEST MAN IN THE WORLD (PART II)

You won't believe that this will work. It will!

You Need: 10 people
1 wall

Okay, there don't have to be 10 people, but that's a good number to use. Have your volunteers get in a row by height, with the shortest volunteer at the end of the line, facing you. (This person must be tall enough to reach your shoulders without jumping around to do it.) Make sure that the people are all spaced correctly and aren't cheating.

Tell these people to place their hands on the shoulders of the person in front of them. On your signal, they are to all push on the shoulders of the person in front of them. But even their combined strength will not be enough to push you against the wall!

Now you turn around and face the wall, extend your arms, and put them in front of you on the wall, palms against the wall, fingers pointing straight up. The shortest person then places his hands on your shoulders.

Now tell them to push with all their power. They will huff and puff, but they shouldn't be able to move you! They may fall, but you will stand!

(This is because all the energy they push with only gets as far as the person in front of them. This is called "inertia." As long as you can hold off the person right behind you, you'll be all right.)

RICE JAR DRIVER

The golf ball will rise! I command it to rise!

You Need: 1 golf ball (or other round object about that size)
a jar with lid
uncooked rice

Put the golf ball at the bottom of the jar and then fill the jar with rice. Leave about 1 ½ inches at the top. Screw on the lid of the jar and shake the jar from side to side. Shake it some more (not up and down, but side to side) while saying your magic words. Now watch the golf ball rise to the surface!

Some people say the *rice is heavier, which moves the golf ball up*. This is not true; a golf ball weighs more than a container of rice the same size. But the rice likes to settle together, and until the golf ball is out of the way, it can't do that, so it pushes the ball up!

THE YOLK'S IN YOU

If you've ever wanted to see an egg get sucked into a bottle with a bizarre "slurp," this is your experiment!

You Need: a funnel
an empty bottle with a semi-wide mouth (salad dressing bottles are perfect)
1 hard-boiled egg, peeled
water
a tea kettle
a potholder

This experiment happens very quickly! Put the funnel in the mouth of the salad dressing bottle. Put the egg next to the bottle.

Now, boil enough water to fill the bottle. When the water is ready, carefully pour it into the bottle. Take out the funnel and swirl the bottle around a bit. Now, pour the water out and place the egg on the top of the bottle. SLURP!

Now that the egg is in the bottle, what made it go in? Well, hot things expand and cool things contract. The bottle's air was hot, but it was rapidly cooling down and contracting when you put the egg over its only entrance. The bottle had no choice but to suck the egg in.

Now try getting the egg out! Hold the bottle upside down and blow into it for a while, covering the neck with your mouth. When you remove your mouth, it might come out! (But only if you blow hard enough to create enough pressure inside the bottle to pop the egg back out!)

GRAPE LIGHTNING

Who knew that grapes have a bunch of electricity?

You Need: seedless green grapes
a knife
a microwave oven that you can see into

Take a grape. Remove the stem and cut it in half, but not all the way. Leave a skin attachment between the two halves. Put the grape on a plate facing either up or down. Put them in the *center* of the microwave.

Put the microwave on "high" power and set it for 10 to 40 seconds. Now turn it on and watch! You should see sparks, and maybe even electric arcs between the grape parts! At some point, the grape will split all the way apart. When that happens, stop the microwave, because nothing else will happen after that. (For another cool grape/microwave activity, see "Grape Races" in the "Indoor Games!" chapter, page 111.)

 If you prefer your lightning without fruit, try this. Blow up two balloons and knot them at the mouth. Rub one of them against some wool (like a sweater or a sheep) and the other balloon against a wall. Turn off the lights and bring the balloons together. *Zap!*

RUBBER BONES

Nothing is funnier than a rubber chicken . . . bone!

You Need: any chicken bone that hasn't been cooked yet
a jar with lid
white vinegar

Clean and dry off the bone and leave it alone for a day or two. Then put the chicken bone in the jar and pour enough vinegar into the jar to cover the bone. Screw the lid back on the jar and leave it alone for a week.

After a week, unscrew the lid, pour the vinegar out, and grab the bone. It's rubbery! You may even be able to tie it into a knot. That's because the vinegar dissolved all the calcium from the bone, leaving it soft. A good trick is to do this with a wishbone, and then ask someone to break it with you. This won't work, of course, but you can act amazed!

You can also do this with an egg instead of a chicken bone. Place the egg in the jar and pour enough vinegar into the jar to cover the egg. Screw the lid back on and watch the eggshell slowly dissolve! The shell will be eaten away after a week, leaving only a squishy egg membrane.

OOBLICK'S TEST OF COURAGE

If you needed a good excuse to waste some perfectly good cornstarch, here it is!

You Need: 1 cup of cornstarch
a bowl
some water

Silly Putty is actually a liquid. But what about cornstarch? Put your cornstarch in a bowl or large pan. It's a solid. Add a little water. Stir it in. It will probably get clumpy. Still a solid. Add a little more water. Stir it in. What happened?

As you add and stir in water, you can get the cornstarch to the point where you're not sure what it is. If it feels sort of like mayonnaise, you have just made *ooblick*! Ooblick is awesome. Pick up some ooblick in your hand and squeeze it into a ball. Solid! Put it back in the bowl and watch it ooze back like a liquid! Now when you stick your fingers in it, it will squish right through them.

You can keep goofing around with the ooblick, or you can move on to the Test of Courage. If you have a few baking pans, make enough ooblick to cover the bottoms of two or three of them. Take the baking pans holding ooblick outside. Set them a couple of feet apart. Take your shoes off. (You can do this with your shoes on if you prefer.) Now walk through the pans! If you make each step quickly and with force, the ooblick will note your courage and leave you alone. If you chicken out and start gently putting your feet into the pans, the ooblick will stick to you!

 Because cornstarch is so fine, it can also be mixed with white glue to make a homemade version of Silly Putty!

DO ROBOT SHEEP MAKE STEEL WOOL?

This is a good way to put some sparkle in your life!

You Need: steel wool
1 "D" battery

Get a piece of steel wool about the size of your fist. Put it on a baking pan or other metal surface and touch the ends of your battery to the steel wool. The iron in the steel wool should sparkle and light up; this is because iron can burn as long as there is enough oxygen around!

MONSTER IN A BOX

A good experiment to run over several days.

You Need: a shoebox
a small flower pot with soil
tape
cardboard pieces
an uncooked potato, sprouted

Take your shoebox and cut a hole a couple of inches wide at one end. Set your flowerpot at the opposite end of the shoebox to measure how much room to leave for it. Then use your pieces of cardboard to make a simple maze between the flowerpot and the hole.

The maze doesn't have to be fancy; just tape the cardboard pieces to the sides of the box in a simple pattern. Put three or four walls with three-inch openings in different spots.

Now plant the potato in the soil. This experiment will work faster if you use a sprouted potato. You can then cut off a section with the sprout and plant it, but it doesn't matter if you just use a regular tater.

Water your spud, put the lid back on the box, and leave it in a window with some sunlight for several days. If it is hot and you think the plant is getting dry, take the lid off and water it. Otherwise, leave it alone until you see something coming out the hole at the end of the box! Then lift the lid . . . spooky!

FLAMING GREENBACKS!

WARNING: Only do this experiment when a responsible adult is present!

This money could burn a hole in your pocket!

You need:
- a responsible adult
- a dollar bill
- salad tongs
- rubbing alcohol
- dish or bowl
- a bigger dish or bowl full of water
- matches or a lighter

Perform this experiment near a sink or outside on a concrete surface.

Take a dish or bowl and pour some rubbing alcohol into it. Now mix the alcohol in the bowl with an equal amount of water.

Take your dollar bill and hold it with the salad tongs. Dip the bill into the dish and soak it for a moment in your mixture. Pull it out and hold it away from yourself. Have the responsible adult hold a flame next to the bill.

This is the great part. The dollar bill will catch on fire, but it won't burn! You will see a blue-colored flame surround the dollar, but the water will keep the dollar wet and safe, as the alcohol burns off. In other words, the water will put out the flame that the alcohol begins! (If anyone starts to "freak out" when the bill is surrounded by flame, you can always put the dollar in the big bowl of water or the sink.)

To be sure the bill is "out," put it in the bigger dish full of water before hanging it up to dry.

FOLLOW-UP ACTIVITIES

1. Rig the roof of your house with a lightning rod. Wire the electricity to go to your bedroom, where you can use it to reanimate dead bodies and also to make toast. (Adult supervision is required.)
2. Research time travel and then make your own time machine. Use it to travel back in time to answer the most important question that has ever faced the human race: *Where did I lose my pocketknife on September 14, 2015?*

FIREWORKS AND EXPLOSIONS!

One of the greatest pleasures of life is blowing up an old model of an airplane or a car with some firecrackers! So I'm not going to pretend that fireworks aren't fun, but the fact is that every day some kid blows off his fingers by not following proper safety procedures with fireworks. SO READ THIS NOW:

IMPORTANT INFORMATION

Nine of the 50 states don't allow people to use any fireworks at all, so if you live in one of these states, congratulations. You're safe from fireworks! Another nine states allow some fireworks, but do not allow firecrackers. Many cities and counties also have their own fireworks laws. So here's what you must do: *know and obey the fireworks laws in your area.* For information on the laws in your area, visit The National Council on Fireworks Safety website at www.fireworksafety.com.

Speaking of safety, when I was 12, my friends and I were waiting at the bus stop. An older kid started messing around with firecrackers. He would light the firecrackers and throw them in the street. *Bang! Bang!* The rest of us watched.

One of the firecrackers that he lit didn't go off. It just sat in the street, looking innocent. "That one's a dud," I said helpfully.

This kid looked at me and went and got the dud. After he picked it up, the "dud" went off with a nice "*Bang!*" in his hand. He screamed ("*Yeow!*") and started running around like a chicken with its head cut off. "I guess it wasn't a dud after all," I said helpfully.

That kid was lucky. He didn't blow his hand off, but he did get a nasty explosion burn on his hand, and his example taught us all a lesson that day. *There's no such thing as a dud.* Firecrackers and other fireworks are unpredictable. Once a firework has been lit, do not pick it up again unless it has been soaked in water for a long time.

Here are some other safety measures that will save you from injury. *Make sure* there are adults around when you set off fireworks. *Make sure* you are well away from any buildings or plants that could catch fire. *Make sure* there are no dogs or other animals around. *Make sure* you always have buckets of water ready to throw on any spark. Douse sparks immediately and ask questions later. I don't care if that spark landed on your Aunt Matilda's wig. *Get it wet!*

So let's say you have some legal fireworks, you're with some responsible adults, and you are in a safe area to set them off. (A cinder block in the middle of an empty parking lot or street would be perfect.) Now, move your fireworks supply 50 *feet* away from that spot. You don't want all your fireworks going off at once if a spark lands in there. The screams would be incredible!

What now? Do you have protective eyewear on? You should. Heck, I wear long sleeves, a hat, and gloves too. You can't be too careful! Anyway, now you're ready to light the fuse to some fireworks. Whenever you are lighting a fuse, keep your body away from the firework. Use a long-handled lighter or long match and *reach out* to light the fuse. (I turn my face away from it, too, just in case.) If this seems like overdoing it, just think: a regular little sparkler burns at a heat of 1,000 degrees Fahrenheit. It could burn your nostrils off!

That's it. Light one item at a time, and have fun. (And don't burn your nostrils off!)

YOUR SAFETY TEST

Okay, let's see if you can handle fireworks. Do this: Get a lemon. Cut off a piece of its rind. Now light a candle. Holding the outside of the rind with your fingers, get close to the flame and squeeze the inner parts together. Cool sparks, huh?

Did you burn your fingers? Explode your pancreas? Either way, read the next paragraph carefully.

WHAT HAPPENS IF YOU DON'T FOLLOW SAFETY RULES?

Every year, about 8,000 people arrive at hospital emergency rooms with fireworks injuries. And almost half of them will be *kids under the age of* 15. Don't let this happen to you! The parts of the body usually injured are the eyes, hands, head, and face. Since you'll want to use all of those body parts in the future, *be careful*! Finally, many of these injuries will come from *illegal* fireworks, so buy the legal kind. They're safer!

 Soak fireworks completely in water before putting them in the trash.

 If you are going to store fireworks, put them in a cool, dry place. Tape shut the container they're in, so that no moisture can get inside.

GUNPOWDER: THE "DEVIL'S INVENTION"

Gunpowder is what made early fireworks go BOOM! But who was the first genius to discover the magical properties of gunpowder? As with so many other things (yo-yos, compasses, cards, kites, pasta), it was an unknown person living in China. About a thousand years ago, this person (probably a cook) accidentally mixed saltpeter (potassium nitrate), sulfur (used to make a fire burn hotter), and charcoal together. *BOOM!*

The Chinese didn't call this stuff "gunpowder" because guns hadn't been invented yet. They called their invention *huo yao*, or the "fire chemical." It didn't take too long for the Chinese to figure out that if they attached bamboo tubes filled with the chemical to arrows, the arrow would go extra fast. After a while, they left the arrow out of the equation since the tubes could launch themselves and create a nice explosion up in the air! The Chinese used their new invention for many celebrations and events.

One Chinese man, Wan-hu, even tried to use these rockets to fly. He set up two big kites with a chair and 42 rockets. *Three, two, one, TAKE-OFF!* There was a loud explosion, and Wan-hu was gone! Was he up in the air? *Nope*. Was he in the ashes that were left where the explosion was? *Yep!* Wan-hu *was* the ashes that were left where the explosion was!

The Chinese used *huo yao* for celebrations and also for exploding arrows and other weapons. But when the Europeans and Arabs got their hands on this explosive powder, they began inventing cannons, guns, and other antisocial devices. This is when it got its nickname, the "Devil's Invention."

But gunpowder has had peaceful uses. Northern Italians were especially interested in fireworks for fun, and the famous traveler Marco Polo brought back firework recipes from the mysterious East for them to use. In 1292, Marco Polo wrote of his firecracker collection: "They burn with such a dreadful noise, they can be heard for 10 miles at night . . . it is the most terrible thing in the world to hear for the first time." (To this, I say: "*Marco . . . Wusso!*")

In early America, firearms and fireworks were very popular. Maybe you've heard the line from "The Star Spangled Banner" about *the rockets' red glare*? One unusual form of American fireworks was an activity called "Shooting the Anvil." A blacksmith's heavy anvil was set up in an open area. A bag of gunpowder with a fuse coming out was then placed on top of it. The people would then put another anvil on top of the bag, light the fuse, and run away! The colonists had to keep their eyes open, though. After the explosion, the top anvil would fly *way* up in the air, and what goes up could come down on them!

Back in those days, to discourage kids from shooting guns for fun, adults actually encouraged the use of firecrackers as a safe alternative. Boys came up with fun uses for their firecrackers, like attaching them to large weeds to knock them down, sticking firecrackers in tomatoes for juicy explosions, and of course, blowing up their toy soldiers.

FIREWORK TYPES

There are many different types of fireworks: pinwheels, Roman candles, rockets, squibs, gerbs, and so on. But there are really just two basic elements that most fireworks have in common: they either go "*Boom!*" like a firecracker, or they give off cool lights and sparks like a sparkler. Maybe they do both! You already know about firecrackers. Sparklers, though, are usually made by dipping a stick in a gooey mix of chemicals. Contained in the chemicals is a black powder (a gunpowder type of mix) so that the sparkler burns. Mixed in with the powder are flecks of metal dust, like iron, aluminum, or magnesium. When these get hit with a high temperature, they burn with a bright spark. For example, zinc burns with a green color, while aluminum burns with a white flame.

When you see fireworks going off in the sky ("aerial fireworks"), you can see both of these firecracker and sparkler elements. Aerial fireworks are usually shot out of a cannon-like device called a "mortar." All the ingredients needed for the fireworks are in a shell with a fuse. (The length of the fuse determines how high the fireworks are when they explode.)

When the aerial fireworks go off, you hear a loud BANG first. That sound comes from the explosive in the middle of the shell, which is much like a big firecracker. Then you see the starburst of color coming out of it. (By the way, blue is the hardest color to show with fireworks.) These colored starbursts are really just bigger chunks of the same stuff you find on a sparkler. The *pattern* of these starbursts is decided by how they are placed inside the shell.

If you see more than one explosion from the same firework, the shell may have other shells with different colors or sound-making devices hidden within it.

Different cultures like different aspects of fireworks. The Japanese word for fireworks is *hanabi,* which means "flowers of fire." The Japanese like fireworks that give off smoke clouds and starbursts in different colors. In Europe, many people enjoy the *noise* of fireworks the most—you know, that moment when the explosion goes off and you can feel the air press in on your eardrum: BOOM! (Sometimes it's so scary, the next thing you know, *Euro-peein'*!)

Gunpowder is not usually used much in fireworks anymore. Firecrackers usually have something called "flash powder" in them, which was originally made for photography. But one thing hasn't changed. Whether they whistle, screech, or bang, boys dig the sound of fireworks. (Unless they're duds!)

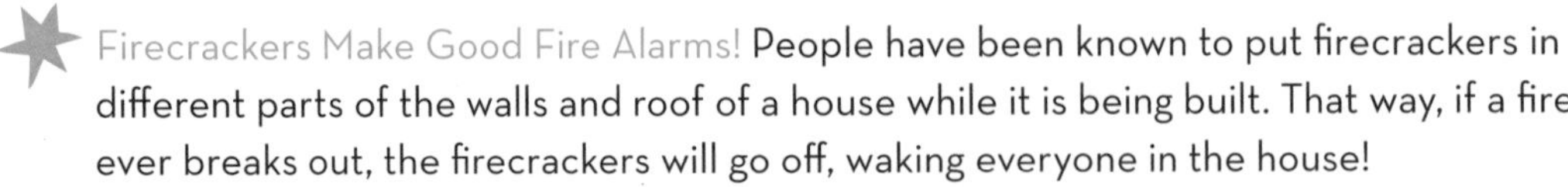

- Firecrackers Make Good Fire Alarms! People have been known to put firecrackers in different parts of the walls and roof of a house while it is being built. That way, if a fire ever breaks out, the firecrackers will go off, waking everyone in the house!

- The longest string of firecrackers ever set off was in Hong Kong in 1996. To celebrate the Chinese New Year, a string of firecrackers was lit that took 22 hours to completely explode.

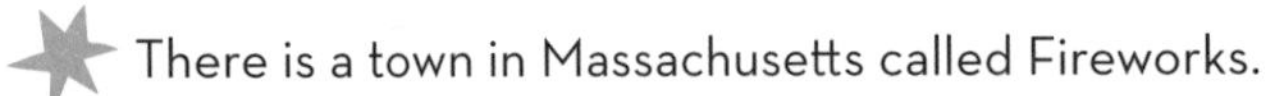

- There is a town in Massachusetts called Fireworks.

HAND GRENADES

Hand grenades are the only hand-thrown devices still used by armies. Like most explosions, a hand grenade blows up because of expanding gases. Here are two hand grenade designs that you can use that won't start a fire or blow off your hand!

HAND GRENADE 1

For this grenade, take any small plastic container with a plastic lid, like a film canister. Fill it one-third to one-half full with water, then throw a couple of Alka-Seltzer tablets in it. Quickly snap on the lid, and throw it! *Bang!*

HAND GRENADE 2

Get a ziplock sandwich bag. (Not the giant freezer bags, but one of the smaller models.) Also, get some vinegar and baking soda, and a paper towel. Then cut a 6-inch square off of your paper towel and put 3 tablespoons of baking soda in the middle of it. Now fold it up.

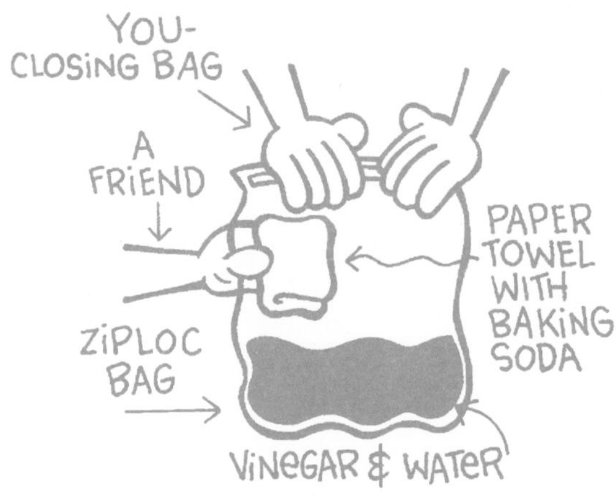

Over the sink, pour 3/4 cup of vinegar and 1/3 cup of warm water into the ziplock bag. Now comes the tricky part: you want to put the paper towel into the bag without letting it touch the vinegar! You may want to have someone help you, as they pinch the folded paper towel inside the bag while you carefully zip it tightly.

Once the bag is zipped, take it outside, drop the folded paper towel into the vinegar, shake the bag, and drop it on the ground. You should get a good bang out of it! (If not, try changing the amounts described above; I sometimes skip the warm water part.)

THE DRY ICE BOOMER

WARNING: THIS ACTIVITY CAN ONLY BE DONE WITH ADULT SUPERVISION AND EYE PROTECTION!

WARNING: Dry ice is frozen carbon dioxide. It is REALLY cold! Dry ice is usually colder than -75 degrees Fahrenheit, so if it touches your skin, you're in trouble. It will stick to you and cause freezing burns and frostbite! Only handle it with gloves and salad tongs!

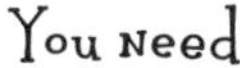

- a 2-liter plastic soda bottle
- dry ice
- the outdoors
- a wrist rocket or slingshot
- eye protection, long sleeves, a hat (paintball helmets are good), and gloves

YES, ANOTHER WARNING: Don't do this activity around strangers and innocent bystanders. It could be unsafe, and it will definitely freak them out!

This might be the simplest exploding device of all time. If you do it correctly, it is perfectly safe.

Take your *plastic* soda bottle and some dry ice. (Only plastic bottles will work for this. Do not use any other kind of container.) Decide what open, safe area you can use for the explosion. It must be a place where you can stand at a safe distance, and where someone wouldn't unexpectedly come upon the bottle or be disturbed by a loud boom!

Once you are in the area where you are going to explode the container, make sure that everything is in place. *You must be prepared to keep an eye on that bottle for up to half an hour.* Okay, now put some dry ice in the bottle. Add water until the bottle is about one-fourth full. Crush the side of the bottle a little. Screw on the lid tightly. Stand back.

The dry ice will go through what is called a "phase change." This means it is changing from a *solid* into a *gas*. As it does so, the gas will expand the bottle outward. Once the crushed part of the bottle fills out, you shouldn't go anywhere near it. If the crushed part of the bottle does *not* expand out, it SHOULD still be safe to approach.

RESULT

There will be a loud boom and the bottle will burst. If the container does not burst, WAIT! Like I said, it could take 30 minutes for it to blow. Do NOT approach the container; it could go off! If you get impatient and want to leave or try again, shoot rocks at the bottle with your wrist rocket (or throw rocks at it, or shoot it with your BB gun, or pop it with a 20-foot spear, or whatever) until you break its side. THEN (and *only* then) is it safe!

SPECIAL SECTION: M-80S AND CHERRY BOMBS

M-80s and cherry bombs are *illegal fireworks*. Both of them have been against the law to possess since 1966, and they are very *unsafe*. Do you want to know why they were outlawed? Because so many kids were blowing their hands and feet off with them. Don't buy them! If you see any, they are probably homemade, and if there is one thing you *don't* want homemade, it's fireworks.

M-80s were originally designed as "military rifle-fire simulators." In other words, they were used in the military for exercises when they needed the *sound* of gunshots. Although M-80s are not as powerful as a quarter stick of dynamite (a lot of people think this), they *can* hurt or kill someone. M-80s contain 60 times more powder than is legal for a firecracker. Lots of firecracker manufacturers try to make their product sound cool by calling them "M-70s" or "M-90s" or things like this. This is just a trick; these firecrackers are nothing like an M-80.

As for cherry bombs, they are usually round and are often dyed red. Just like with the M-80, you will sometimes see legal firecrackers that are called "cherry bomb type" or some baloney like that. Their makers are just trying to trick you into thinking you're buying the real thing. Avoid ANYTHING that is labeled something like "cherry bomb" or "M-80" to avoid getting ripped off or hurt (or both)!

NITROGLYCERIN AND TNT

Many people think a stick of dynamite is just a really big firecracker. WRONG! Dynamite (or TNT) is very different, and the difference is something called "nitroglycerin."

"Nitrogen" is everywhere; for example, it makes up about 80 percent of the air around you right now. And "glycerin" is a sweet syrup used in foods. In 1847, an Italian named Ascanio Sobrero was experimenting with glycerin in an attempt to find a cure for headaches. He mixed some glycerin with some acid and he ended up with what we now call "nitroglycerin." Ascanio learned that the combination of glycerin and acid is explosive when the glass tube it was in blew up in his face, leaving him badly scarred.

Ascanio was a good man. He tried to keep this terrible new explosive a secret because he was afraid of how it might be used in the wrong hands. But word of the explosive got out. Nitroglycerin was very unstable and dangerous, but that didn't stop people from messing around with it. Ascanio said, "When I think of all the victims killed during nitroglycerin explosions . . . I am almost ashamed to admit to be its discoverer."

A man from Sweden named Alfred Nobel worked at trying to make nitroglycerin safe for use in road building and mining. It took years of work, and his own brother was killed in an accident with it, but Alfred discovered that if he mixed nitroglycerin with a special kind of dirt and molded it into sticks, it would not explode by itself. He called this invention "dynamite."

Alfred Nobel was an unusual person. His father made guns and explosives for armies. But Alfred was an inventor and poet who spoke five languages and thought of himself as a loner. He made a fortune from his invention of dynamite, but like Ascanio Sobrero, Alfred had a conscience. So he set up a system of special prizes that would be given out every year to people who make a valuable contribution to the world in science or the arts or for peace. These are called the Nobel Prizes, and they have been given out yearly since 1901.

FOLLOW-UP ACTIVITY

There is an ultimate weapon so frightening and awful, only a crazy person would ever use it. Because this ultimate weapon is so terrifying to others, it can be used to bring peace to the world. I am, of course, talking about your dad's gas problem. Encourage your dad never to bomb unless he is punishing evildoers or trying to scare a salesperson away from the front door.

FLYING THINGS!

If you're interested in launching something into the air, you've come to the right place!

TURTLES

In 456 BC, a very bald man named Aeschylus was minding his own business when a flying turtle hit him in the head, killing him. (Aeschylus was a famous playwright in ancient Greece.) How bald was Aeschylus? He was so bald, an eagle that had caught this turtle flew up and dropped the shelled reptile on a shiny "rock" to break it open. This didn't work. The rock was Aeschylus's gleaming skull, and the turtle's shell didn't break. (But Aeschylus did!)

KITES

Kites were invented in China 3,000 years ago. These first kites were not for fun and games, however. They were used by soldiers to signal each other from far away. The color and type of kite as well as the way it was flown gave a message to another soldier.

Back then, boys imitated what the grown-ups did. (Oh wait, boys *still* do that!) So since soldiers were "playing" with kites, Chinese boys and girls started doing the same thing. (Hopefully they didn't foul up the army's communications.)

Anyway, kites are cool, but you don't really need this book to learn about them. I am happy simply to share with you the coolest kite of all time. It doesn't need a string, and it catches on fire! It is . . . the Kite o' Flame!

THE KITE O' FLAME

WARNING: THIS ACTIVITY CAN ONLY BE DONE WITH ADULT SUPERVISION!

When this is done properly, you will get "Oohs!" and "Aahs!" from all who see it!

You Need: a full sheet of newspaper
Scotch tape
4 people with matches or lighting devices
a cool or cold night
adult supervision

The idea of the Kite o' Flame is that it will fly up on its own while burning majestically, and then disappear into the air. You have to see it to believe it! There are no strings with this kite. Instead, *heat* does all the work. That's because heat rises, and so this kite will rise from the heat of its flames. Because of the heat factor, this kite will only work if it is cool or cold out. Because it looks better at night, fly this kite on a winter evening, especially if it's just snowed or rained.

WARNING: Because of its flame, ONLY do this activity with your parents present. Also, only fly this kite in an area far away from houses and plants. (A parking lot is perfect.)

OFFICIAL ADULT

Take the newspaper and lay it down so that the main crease forms a small mountain (not a valley). Bring the four corners together to meet in the middle; try to make the points line up perfectly. Carefully tape the four corners to each other. The puffy area of air that you will create is what makes this kite fly. Turn the kite over, then place a person with a match at each of the four corners.

1 LAYOUT NEWSPAPER.

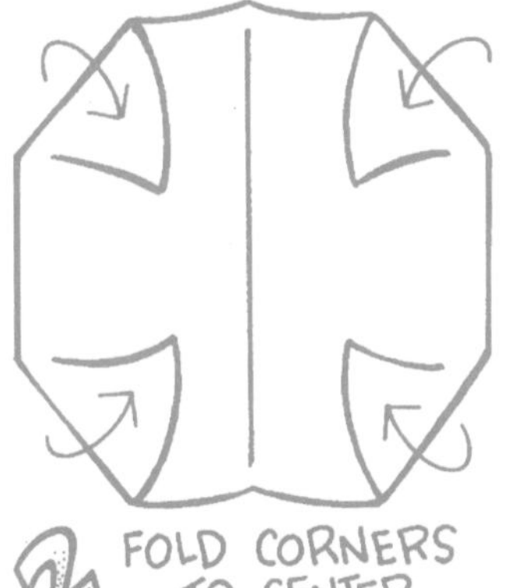
2 FOLD CORNERS TO CENTER.

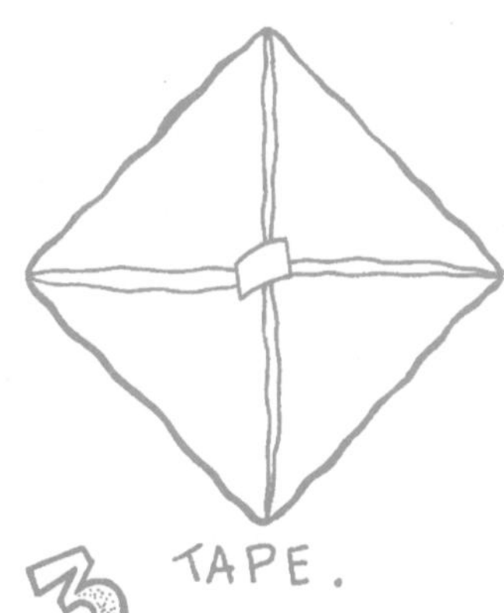
3 TAPE.

Have everyone light their match at the same time. On your command, they should all light the corner they are holding. The kite will begin to slowly rise if you have prepared it properly; you may need to try this a couple of times to get it taped and lit correctly, but it's worth it. The kite does not rise far or go fast, but it is awesome.

 There are competitive kite-flying games in some Southeast Asian countries in which the kites are equipped with sharp edges. Contestants then try to shred their opponents' kites!

PAPER AIRPLANES

The cool thing about paper airplanes is that they never need batteries. (You can try putting a battery into yours, but they don't usually fly as well.) Since a paper airplane has no engine, its design must take advantage of airflow and wind to keep it in the air. If it doesn't fly as well as you wanted, that just means that you should *experiment.* Try some different adjustments, wing folds, and stabilizers and give it another shot.

PLANE CONSTRUCTION

When you create your plane, fold on a flat surface. Use good straight folds, no rough edges, and try to make it perfect. It will really pay off.

PLANE FLIGHTS

Never judge a paper airplane on its first flight! Throw the plane gently, like a dart. Most planes climb and then stall if you throw them too hard. If your plane climbs and then stalls even if you throw gently, try putting more weight on the nose; sometimes just a small piece of paper taped at the nose does the trick.

If the plane turns (or "banks") in either direction, the wings have uneven angles. Check them and refold if necessary.

Some of the terms used in this section include the following:

crease: same thing as a fold.

valley: paper's fold looks like a valley, or the letter "V."

mountain: paper's fold looks like a mountain, an upside-down "V."

air-to-ground rocket: device installed on paper airplanes to eliminate targets, like the annoying neighborhood kid or the barking poodle next door.

elevator: adjustments that can be made on the back of the plane that adjust its flight. If the elevators are up, the plane's nose will come up. Generally, I make my elevators about ¼ inch deep and about an inch long.

You need: paper (duh!), standard 8½ by 11 inch sheets
a pen or pencil for marking
a ruler (good for folding and measuring)
transparent tape

HANGIN' WITH THE GLIDER

With just a few folds, this may be the fastest plane you can make!

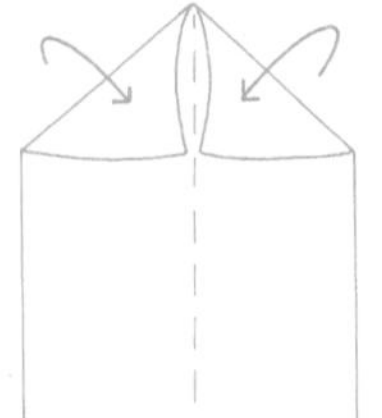

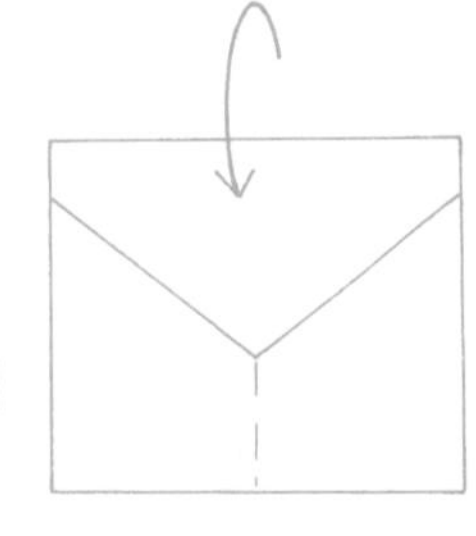

1. Fold the paper in half the long way, open it, and fold the top two corners in so that the edges are right on the center fold.
2. Take the top peak of the triangle that is formed and fold it down to the middle crease. (How far you fold is up to you; I stop at about 1 ¼ inches from the bottom of the paper.)
3. Now fold the top left and right corners down to the middle crease again just like you did in Step 1. Leave a tiny bit of room between them. (A small triangle will be sticking out below this.)
4. Fold everything down that center crease to make a mountain. (This will make your triangle rise up and fold in half.)
5. You're almost done. Turn your paper so that the pointy end is in your palm. Fold the wings on each side by folding from the point to the end and making the top align with the bottom.
6. Once you get that fold, open up the wings so they are flat and even. Give it a slow, steady throw. I like to tape the middle of the body together to keep it tight.

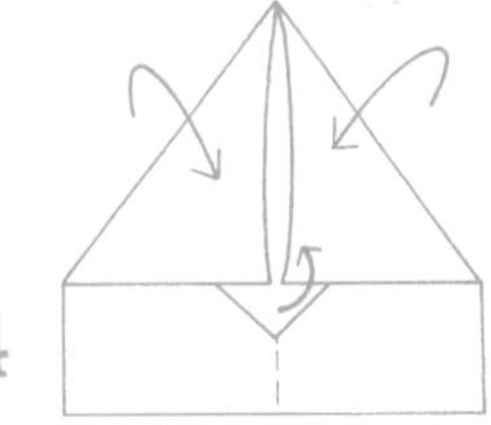

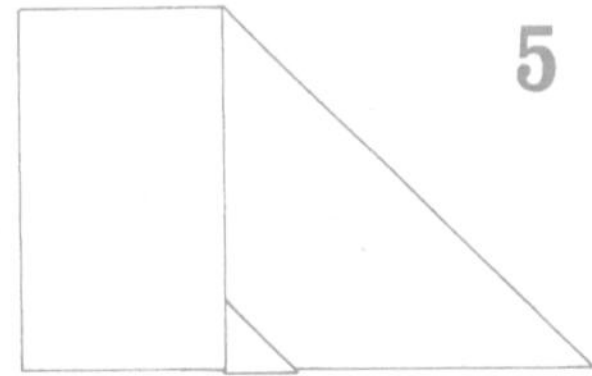

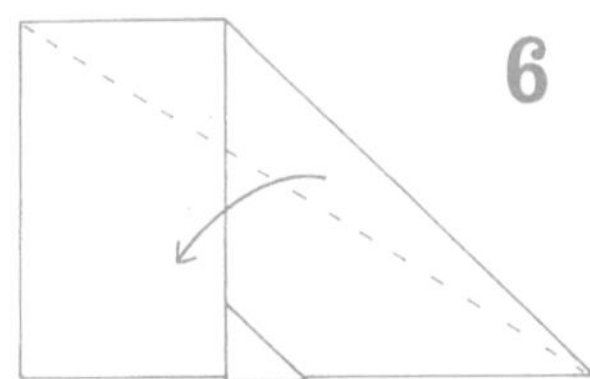

BULL'S-EYE: THE DART

Every boy needs to memorize this design. It is the best version of the most classic paper airplane ever!

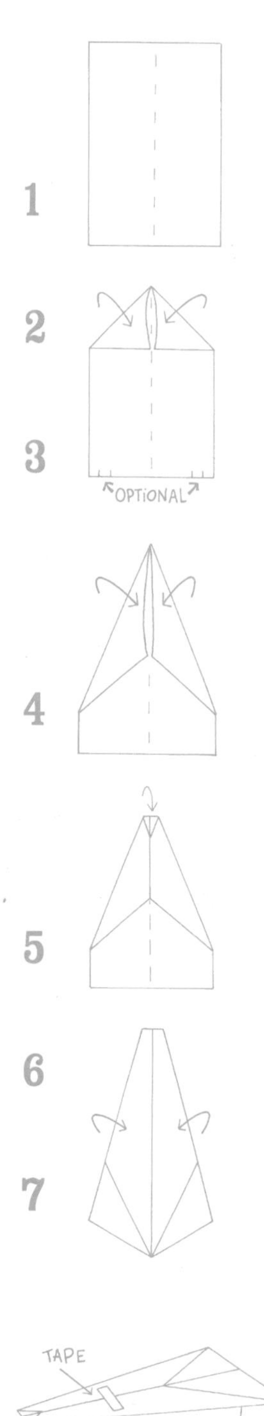

1. Fold the paper in half the long way.
2. With the paper like a valley, fold the top corners in so that they align with the middle crease.
3. *Optional:* Now that you have found your top, go to the bottom of the paper. Make a mark from the edge at ½ and 1 ½ inches from the left and right sides.
4. With those corners folded down, find your new top corners. Fold these down to meet the center crease also.
5. The only bad thing about the dart is, it has a sharp nose that gets crumpled fast. To avoid that problem, fold 1 inch of the nose over.
6. Now turn the paper over. Take the outside edges and fold them into the center.
7. Turn it over again. Fold it right down the center again in the reverse direction (the opposite way of the first fold).
8. Grab the middle and open the wings. Align the wings so they are at a 90-degree angle from the plane's body. Tighten up the body and put a small piece of tape about 2 ½ inches in from the nose to keep the wings together. Put another small piece of tape where the wings meet the body to keep it aerodynamic.

Depending on your paper, this design may be too nose-heavy. If your plane goes into dives, look at the marks you made in Step 3. With scissors, make a ¼-inch cut in from those four marks. Fold the paper up to make a flap. These will be the "elevators." These movable flaps will bring any plane's nose up if they are up. (If you've ever sat by the wing in an airplane, now you know what those flaps do.) Now throw the plane again. Awesome! Experiment with different flap settings to make your plane turn and fly differently. The same applies to all other planes.

THE TANK

Also known as the Tractor, this is a durable design that can handle a lot of crashing!

1. Take your top left edge and fold it back to the right side.

2. Do the same thing with the other side.

3. Now fold the paper in half.

4. Unfold it, and fold the nose of the paper almost back to the bottom of the folds you have made. (You can fold more or less back depending on whether you want the nose heavier or lighter.)

5. Take that fold in the half you made and fold it the other way. You are going to make a keel, which will make a "W" shape when you look at the plane from the front. I make my keel on this model about 7/8 inch. Once you get the fold right, you might want to slightly tape the front and back to keep it together.

6. Fold the wings out.

7. Turn the edges of the wings up. (I usually fold about 1/2 inch.)

8. Make any other tape adjustments needed to keep that keel together, then try a throw. You may want to add elevators and rudders to the wings to get the flight path you want.

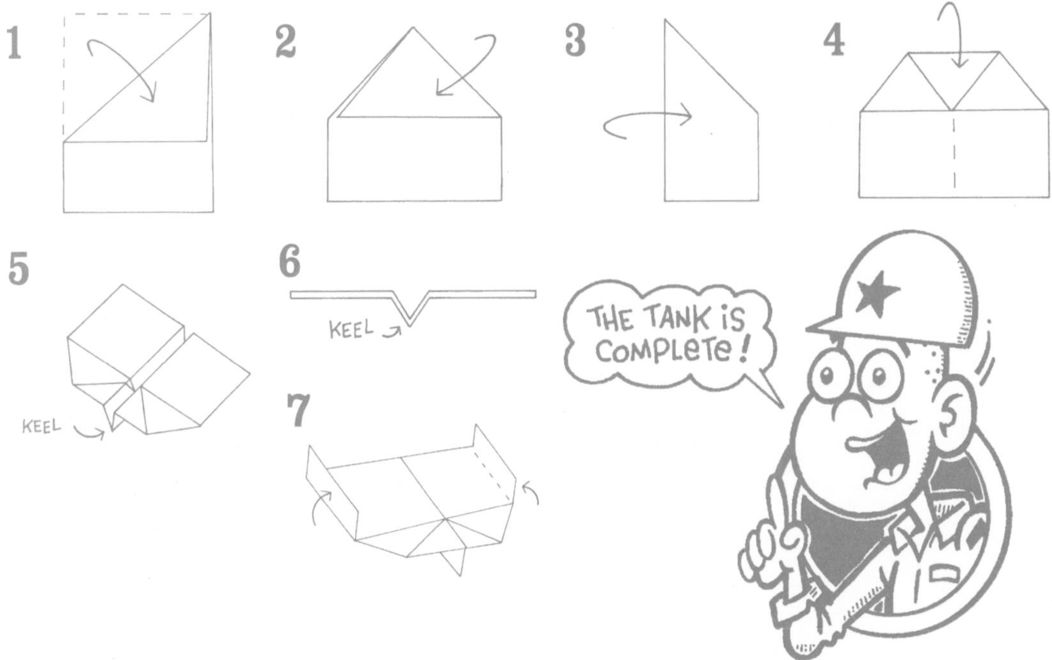

THE RING OF POWER!

It's not an airplane. It IS a flying circle!

1. You need a square of paper for starters.
2. Fold it in half diagonally.
3. Fold a little bit of the folded edge over.
4. Now fold that strip again.
5. Curve the two ends of the folded strip toward each other. Don't fold anything as you go! Now fit or tuck the ends as far as you can into each other. Get it snug.
6. To throw the Ring of Power, pinch the tail end between your thumb and forefinger. Then hold it up toward your head and push it away from you. A little experimentation will show you the best way to do this.

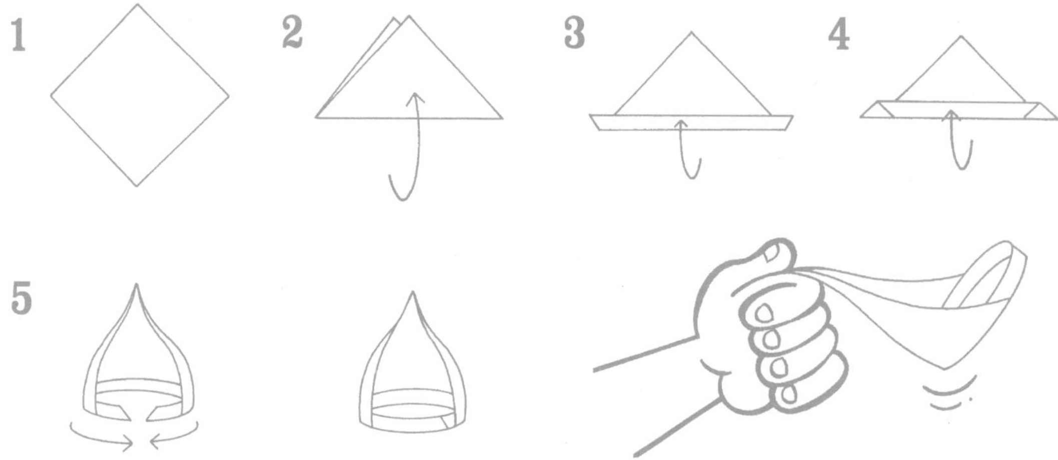

Don't Touch If You Don't Know What It Does! In March 1994, an Aeroflot flight with 75 passengers was flying from Moscow to Hong Kong. At more than 30,000 feet, the captain allowed his 11-year old daughter and 15-year-old son to sit in the pilot's seat. While there, the pilot's son apparently asked, "May I turn this?" The boy turned the plane's main control, disconnecting its autopilot. Nobody noticed this at first, but the plane then went into a spin and crashed with no survivors.

THE PLANE OF A THOUSAND FLIGHTS

This is a good design for stunts, but it can fly straight ahead as well.

1. Start with a *square* piece of paper. Fold the paper perfectly in half from top to bottom and left to right. Mark the exact center point of the paper. Now unfold it again.

2. Bring the whole bottom edge of the paper up to that center mark. Now fold it down there.

3. Take each of the double-layer corners and fold them in so that they align with the inside edge perfectly.

4. Look at the paper. You have a flat bottom that angles up to the sides. Do you see your *new* corners at the bottom? Take them and bring them up to meet the center mark you made. Now crease down, which will make a longer fold along the sides of the paper. (This will give the whole paper a "V" shape.)

5. Take the tip of the "V" and fold it behind the paper so the tip of the "V" touches the center mark on the back side. Now refold the whole thing along the crease that you have running from top to bottom.

6. Now fold the wings just like you did for the Glider: fold the wings on each side by folding from the point to the end and making the top align with the bottom.

7. Unfold the wings so they are flat.

8. This plane really flies differently with different modifications. To make the plane fly straight, tape the body tight on top and give it elevators folded up. To boomerang, curl the back outside edges of the wings and throw the plane upwards. And to do loops, hold the wings away from you and throw it with the nose straight up! Experiment away!

HELICOPTERS

The rotors on a helicopter are basically spinning wings. By spinning, they create lift for the machine, and if you tilt the spinning mechanism slightly, the helicopter can move in any direction. More importantly, a helicopter can hover!

QUICK COPTER

If you have some paper, two straws, and some Play-Doh or clay, you can crank out a copter!

You Need: some paper
2 straws
Scotch tape
some Play-Doh or clay

1. Cut two pieces of paper that are 2 ½ inches across and 4 inches long.
2. Tape one straw to the other to form a "T" shape. Put a little lump of clay at the bottom of the "T."
3. Gently fold the pieces of paper over the ends of the "arms" of the straw "T." Tape the other side of the paper to hold it together, and put a little tape between the paper and straw to keep it in place. Look at the diagram for how to do this properly.
4. Holding the vertical straw, slide or brush your hands together to create lift. The Quick Copter will rise up and away!

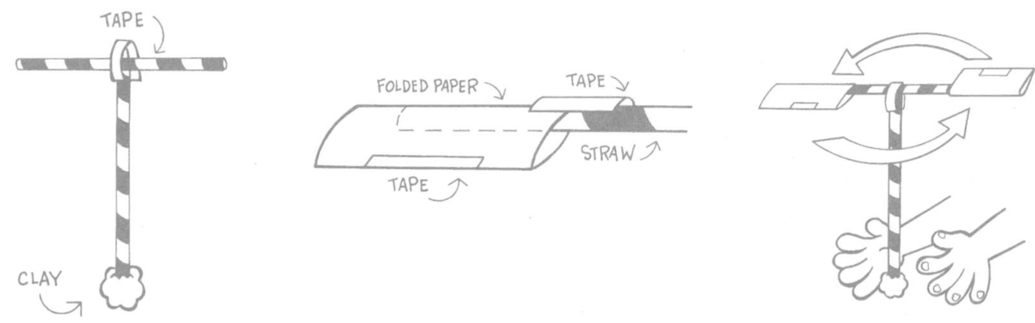

NO-ROTOR HELICOPTERING HOVERCRAFT

What makes helicopters unique is their ability to hover. Here's a futuristic design that eliminates the rotors!

You Need: glue
an empty thread spool
a CD (borrow one from your grandparents)
a button
a balloon

1. Glue the spool to the old CD so that the holes in the middle line up.
2. Let it dry and then glue the button to the top of that. (The holes should still line up!)
3. Now blow up the balloon and stretch its mouth over the top of the spool/button. (Don't let the air escape while you do this.)
4. Set the contraption on a smooth surface and let go of the balloon. The device will float along and hover over the table as it scoots!

ROCKETS

Many people will describe someone who is smart as a *rocket scientist.* This is weird, because a rocket is the simplest kind of engine there is. A car engine is much more complicated. From now on, if you want to say someone is smart, say that they are a real *auto mechanic.* It makes more sense!

You can become a rocket scientist pretty easily. First, let's look at how a basic rocket works. Rockets are powered with some kind of *force* that propels them upward. This force may be a liquid fuel that burns and turns into a gas, like kerosene. Some rockets use a solid fuel instead, like many fireworks do. Rockets can even use only air or water for their propellant!

 Gravity Stunts Your Growth! Rocket-riding astronauts grow from 1 ½ to 2 ½ inches while in outer space. Without gravity pulling them down, they get taller! Hey, what do you have if you tangle your shoelaces in outer space? *Astro-knots!* (Okay, sorry.)

ROCKET BASICS

 Have parent supervision for any rocket experiment.

 Launch your rocket in an open area away from as many roads, trees, and roofs as possible. (You should also take the wind into account.)

- Wear protective eyewear in case of a blowup on the launchpad.
- Follow directions, and don't change or skip steps!
- Finally, use your common sense! For example, don't ever put something (like your face) over the rocket once it is staged for a liftoff.

MODEL ROCKETS

Model rockets are also sometimes called "solid fuel rockets." Solid fuel rockets have a charge (or "grain") that burns smoothly once it's ignited. These rockets come in kits (found in any hobby shop or toy store) that supply the motor and the rocket. You can usually use the rocket again, but you have to buy more motors sooner or later. Although they can be expensive, model rockets are a blast.

Okay, it's not a model rocket, but here are the plans for making the world's cheapest and easiest solid fuel rocket.

MATCH ROCKET

It was a great day when I found that with two matches I could make a rocket that really zips! Some people say their match rockets have gone into orbit (though they're probably liars!).

You Need: foil
a couple of cardboard matches
2 needles (pins will work if you don't have needles)
some transparent tape

1. Do this outside with adult supervision in a place where a fire can't start.
2. Cut a piece of foil one inch square.
3. Tear out a match from a matchbook. (Wooden matches can also work, but I like cardboard ones.)
4. Lay the match near the edge of the foil. Half of the match should be sticking off the foil. (Optional: Now cut the head off of another match and lay it at the end of the head already in the foil.)

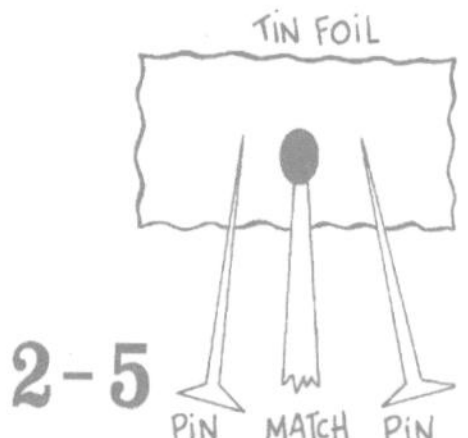

5. Put the needles on each side of the match, with the sharp ends near the match head.

6. Leaving a "pointy head" on the assembly, carefully roll the foil around the match and pins. Make sure to *completely* close the foil and get it as *tight* as possible around the match. Do a good job wrapping the needles! You should end up with an aerodynamic shape.

7. Pull the needles out, leaving two small holes on each side of the match. (Be careful not to crush these holes shut, or it won't work!)

8. If you have a launcher that you want to use, put the rocket in it, with the holes facing down. (I use a hollowed-out pen, but any piece of hard plastic or metal tubing will do. Keep one end of your launcher blocked off.) You can also just set the rocket on an incline with the head protruding and it might take off.

9. Stand to the side of the rocket, and hold a flame on the foil. A lighter actually works better than a match for this. Try to move the flame around a bit so you don't burn a hole in the foil; you just want to heat the assembly up enough to ignite the match heads!

10. Watch the Match Rocket fly away!

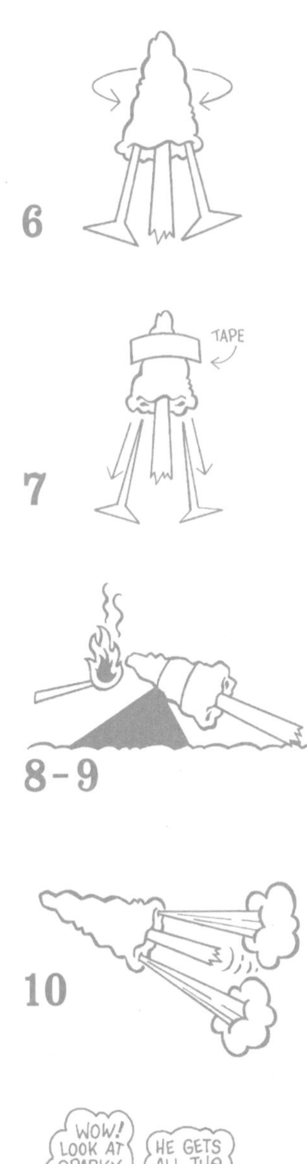

Problems? Make sure you're wrapping that foil as tight as you can. Try adding another match head to the mix. Try using one needle instead of two. Wrap a little tape around the foil to prevent blow-outs. Or, if you have another kind of foil, use that to wrap the match. (Some foils are thicker than others; heavier ones don't fly very well!)

Still no good? Write me at kingbart@comcast.net.

AIR ("PNEUMATIC") ROCKETS

Just like a blowgun shooter uses a puff of air to shoot his dart, air rockets rely on a fast jet of air to get liftoff. This kind of force is called a "pneumatic" (new-MAT-ic) force.

CHAPSTICK LIP BALM ROCKET

Here is how to make the world's simplest air rocket: the Lip Balm Rocket, made by using a ChapStick-brand lip balm tube! When your chapped lips have used up all the balm in the container, follow these steps for a hand rocket that can be fired at will!

You Need: an empty lip balm container

1. Remove the cap of the container. Save it.
2. Remove the end of the container by using a penny to pop the turning device off the bottom of the tube, which includes the plastic threaded dowel. (This has to be pulled out of the part that contains the balm.) Save it.
3. Remove the cup that holds the balm. Dig out any balm still in there.
4. Reverse the cup so that the hollowed portion faces the bottom of the tube and stick it back where it came from. Push it all the way down to the base of the balm tube.
5. Take the threaded plastic dowel and screw it back into the hole in the plastic cup. Leave it hanging out like a plunger. This is your firing mechanism.
6. Put the cap of the container back on.
7. Hold the tube firmly. Aim the cap at something. Pull your off hand back and strike the plunger mechanism sharply with your palm.
8. The cap flies off to parts unknown!

WATER ROCKETS

Water rockets (also called "hydro-pump" rockets) are my favorite kind of missile. Pressurized water is their fuel, and when these rockets achieve liftoff, water goes flying all over.

YOU'RE-GONNA-GET-WET ROCKET

This is a good basic water rocket for someone who likes to work on a project!

You Need: scissors
thin cardboard
duct tape
a plastic soda bottle
a couple of feet of plastic tube (aquarium shops have this)
an air valve (the pointy thing you shove in a ball when you blow it up with air)
a cork that will fit in the neck of the bottle
an awl or ice pick to drill a hole through the cork
a bicycle pump

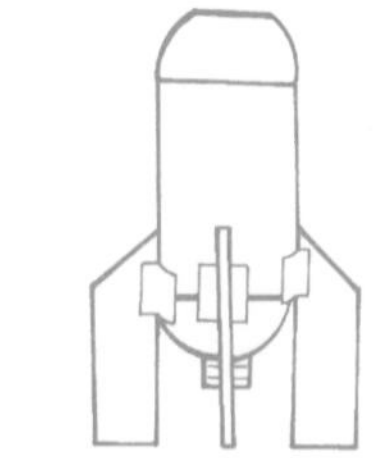
2

3

1. Cut out three or four fins from the cardboard in the general shape shown; make them between 7 and 9 inches long.
2. Duct-tape the fins to the bottle (with the fins at even distances) so the bottle can stand up on its own.
3. Take your tube and fit the air valve into one end of it. Have the fat end stuck in the tube and the pointy end sticking out. Now drill a hole through the cork that is just big enough to fit this end of the plastic tubing. Push the valve and tube through the cork so that the valve's pointy end comes out the end of the cork.
4. Turn over the bottle with fins taped to it and fill it about one-third to one-half of the way with water.
5. Now shove the cork into the bottle's opening! Get it in there good and tight, but not crazy tight. (It does need to be tight enough to keep water from coming out when you turn this upside down.)
6. Take the open end of your plastic tube and shove it into the tube from your bicycle pump. (If it isn't a tight fit, shove it in pretty far and duct tape the whole thing tightly.)

3

4

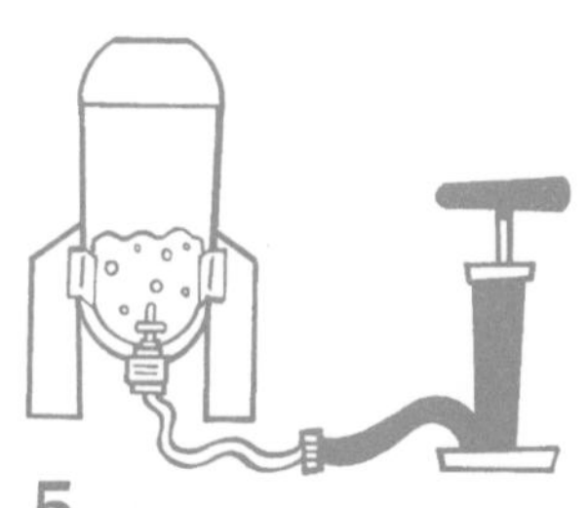
5

7. I sort of figured you were already outside, but if you weren't, take all your parts outside! Find a flat launch site away from anything that you might lose your rocket on. Turn the bottle over. Start pumping! You will see the pressure building up inside the bottle. At some point, it will be great enough to kick the cork out from its end and take off! Save all your parts and try experiments with different levels of water in the rocket.

FOLLOW-UP ACTIVITY

Get a sheet of paper that is 20 feet across. Using one of this chapter's designs, make a giant paper plane. Get it on your home's roof, climb on board, and have a friend give a shove. Remember to pack small bags of pretzels and peanuts for nutrition during the flight.

FUN IN THE OUTDOORS!

So you're thinking about hiking and camping, huh? That's a good call; you can roam around in the wilderness, have adventures, and sleep under the stars. (Sleeping *under* the stars is much more relaxing than sleeping *on* them.) And when it comes to camping, there are certain things that WE are most interested in. You know, like . . .

THE CAMPFIRE

Fire! Fire! Few things are as appealing about camping as the campfire. There is something about sitting around a warm, cheery fire, surrounded by the darkness and the woods, staring thoughtfully into the glowing coals and dreaming . . . *Hey, my shoes are on fire!*

But before you make a campfire, ask yourself this question: "Do I even *need* a campfire?" If it's warm out and you're not cooking anything, don't start one. A fire will "blind" you from seeing the activity of any nighttime animals around you. Bats are flying, animals are peeking at you, and the Moon is coming up. Without a fire, the stars in the sky are brighter and you can enjoy the sounds of the wilderness. Try a candle lantern or a small light source for a while and see if you like it.

If you decide to start a campfire, *you must be very careful*! All it takes is one spark or ember from your campfire to start a forest fire. Every year, some half-wit starts a huge forest fire that destroys thousands of acres of wilderness because he didn't follow these steps carefully. Don't be that half-wit!

1. Make sure that fires are allowed in the area you want to use. Also remember that campfires underneath trees are a bad idea. There should be nothing flammable hanging over the fire at all.

   Try to pick a campfire spot that is *downwind* from your campsite. Clear the ground of *anything* that can burn for a distance of at least 10 to 12 feet around the fire pit. If you can, use a fire pit that is already built, with large, flat stones around it. This keeps the fire contained and gives you a spot to prop up your marshmallow sticks!

Avoid using river stones for your fire pit. They can crack or even explode when heated. If possible, get a large pot and fill it with water. Keep it by the fire pit for any problems that might occur.

2. Gather twigs, dry bark, and small sticks as well as some larger pieces of wood. Only gather dead wood from the forest floor; never chop off live branches to start a fire. Then make a pile of your smallest, driest twigs in the center of your fire pit. Next, take your longer twigs and build a little teepee over the pile. If you have a match, strike it and hold it in the middle of the teepee. If you don't have a match or a lighter, just rub two Boy Scouts together for a spark.

If you think that the area you are visiting may be wet or may not have twigs, bring some paper and/or kindling with you. An old trick is to bring lint from the dryer to start your fire. (Hey, that rhymes!) Lint is lightweight and burns like a son of a gun. AND DON'T USE LIGHTER FLUIDS. They can start a fire too quickly . . . *a forest fire*, that is!

★ You should never burn poison oak. Burning it releases poisons into the air! Poison oak and poison ivy both have leaves that grow in groups of three. You know the old saying: "*Leaves of three, take a pee.*" (Wait, that's not it.) "*Leaves of three, let them be.*" (That's it!) Poison oak leaves are usually green and they look like oak leaves. (Duh!) They can grow as bushes or as vines.

3. As the fire gets going, add a few slightly larger pieces of wood. Start with a small fire; you can always make it bigger. On the other hand, if you make it too big, it is very difficult to make it smaller!

Now that the fire is going, you should notice something unusual: the wind direction has reversed and the smoke is blowing in your face! Rats! This always seems to happen. Since the fire is now going, remember that there always has to be someone there to watch it. You must never leave a fire by itself. So if you're leaving, *put it out.*

4. If you want to get fancy, make yourself a "keyhole fire." This type of fire has a rock perimeter in the shape of a keyhole. The handy part about it is that you rake coals from the main fire to the top of the keyhole, where you can do your real cooking without worrying about getting burned.

   Another way to cook over an open fire is the old "*double-Y-stick-crossbar*" cooking setup. If you can find two forked sticks, plant them well in the ground and put another branch across the top. Make sure the stick going across the fire is high enough not to catch on fire!

SPECIAL FEATURE: THERE IS NO MARSHMALLOW IN MARSHMALLOWS!

Yes, marshmallows are tasty; even better, they catch on fire when held over the campfire. Try toasting a marshmallow and then sucking out its melted insides, leaving only the cooked skin.

This magical food used to be made by the ancient Egyptians from the marshmallow plant (*Althaea officinalis*). For them, marshmallow was a honey-flavored candy thickened with the sap of the marshmallow plant. Today, marshmallow plants grow in the eastern United States near salt marshes and on banks near large bodies of water.

But the modern marshmallows you buy are just a mixture of sugar and gelatin. (The gelatin replaces the marshmallow sap.) How sad! This fluffy mixture is pushed through long tubes, like a Play-Doh Fun Factory. The long white tube that comes out is then cut into pieces, which usually end up on the end of a stick over a campfire. But whether you like them lightly toasted or as black as the night, remember: there is no marshmallow in marshmallows!

After you finish cooking your meal, put two pots of water on the fire. One will be for washing the dishes and one will be for washing yourself. By the time you're done eating, the water will be warm and ready to use.

5. When it is time to put out or "douse" the fire, sprinkle water over the whole fire area. Once the flames are down, then stir the ashes and embers and pour more water on it. Drown it! Pour *extra* water on it to make sure it is out! You'll know the fire is out when you can walk on it barefoot. Then bury all the remains of the fire under dirt. Don't accidentally cover the fire with sod, old leaves, or pine needles. This can cause it to smolder for hours, and even to start again.

POOPING AND PEEING

Some people think that you should not poop in the woods because there are plenty of logs there already. Nevertheless, when you have to go, you have to go, and Nature calls a lot louder when you are out *in* it. So here's a good rule of thumb: poop and pee at least 100 feet from camp!

PEEING

Here are the most important words you will ever read: don't pee into the campfire! The smell will be awful and everyone will hate you. Pee where nobody will be disturbed by you . . . but don't get lost out there! Think of how embarrassing that would be.

Father: How did you get lost, Timmy?

Timmy: I was going to take a pee, and the next thing I knew, I was lost.

Forest animals: Timmy is a doughhead! Timmy is a doughhead!!

Some male campers just keep a wide-mouth jug near their sleeping bag in case they have to go during the night. (Thank goodness you were born a boy.) Just make sure that nobody wants any lemonade in the morning.

POOPING

Taking a good dump in the wilderness requires you to *hunker down*. This means that since you don't have a toilet to sit on, you're just going to have to pretend. So find your spot, drop your drawers, and start to squat: now you're hunkering!

But before you get that far, you need to prepare for "cat sanitation." That means burying your poop, like a cat does!

You need:

1. *A small shovel.* Dig a hole at least 6 to 8 inches deep. Then hunker down and poop into it! (Obviously, you can't do this on rock.)

2. *Toilet paper.* If you have ever had to wipe using bark or leaves, you'll know it is not very pleasant. It's even worse if you accidentally grab some poison oak! Be sure to clean up well. You don't want to leave any "dew on the lily," if you know what I mean. This could lead to bacon strips in your underwear instead of in the frying pan where they belong. As for your used toilet paper, be friendly to the environment. Either burn it or bring a ziplock bag and pack it out with you.

If you're camping in the same spot for a while, just sprinkle some dirt over your poop so that others can use the spot. And when you're all done with your poop hole, cover it up completely and run away!

HIKING

Hiking? How hard could it be? Don't you just put one foot in front of the other? Well, yes, but there are many other things to think about.

ATTITUDE

Camping is for people who like to "rough it." Luckily, most boys don't mind getting a little sweaty and dirty in the great outdoors. Boys know that *something* will go wrong during a trip; you can count on it! This gives us a chance to show that we're not afraid of a challenge. Be a *hardcore positive thinker.* Nothing is good or bad, unless you *think* it is good or bad, so whenever you go on any trip, remember, *nothing* can get you down.

Father: Son, I'm sorry that the squirrel stole your pocketknife.
Son (cheerfully): That's okay, Dad, he probably needed it more than I did.

Father: Son, it's starting to rain.
Son (happily): I love the sound of the rain hitting the leaves, don't you, Dad?

Father: Son, I'm stuck in quicksand.
Son (not worried): Don't worry, Dad! I'll use my pocketknife to cut a pole and then I'll pull you out! Oops, I forgot about that darn squirrel! Sorry, Dad!
Father: Glub, glub.

CLOTHES

Yes, you need to wear them so you don't scare the animals.

SPEED

If you are like most boys, you will want to go *fast*! But hiking fast is a good way to get lost, sprain an ankle, and miss all the views. You should figure on going about two miles every hour. *Try this:* Don't walk more than a quarter-mile without coming to a complete stop and looking around. You will see a lot more this way, and you won't get as tired. (You should stop *less* as you get *more* tired, because then it's harder to get moving again!)

DRINK

As you're hiking, if you can't remember the last time you drank some water, *then drink some water*! Don't wait until you're thirsty to drink. If you do, you will tend to drink too much all at once. This can lead to bloating, cramps, and flash floods when you pee.

GETTING LOST

People often think that they're lost when they aren't. And when you're hiking somewhere you've never been before, it's especially easy to think you are lost.

To avoid getting lost, pay attention to where you are going. Have your trail map handy and notice landmarks as you go. Stay on the trail! Good hikers don't even go 10 steps off a trail unless they know exactly what they are doing. So although it's tempting, don't go off the trail to chase a leprechaun. Do not follow deer trails; these are for deer, and deer never get lost. (Plus, these trails tend to just vanish if you actually do follow them.) Also, don't take shortcuts!

Now let's say that you actually *are* lost. You are separated from your party and now you really don't know where you are. Guess what? You'll be fine. People are already looking for you.

Don't panic. If you don't have a very good idea of which way to go, get in some shade and stay put. Do you have a whistle in your first-aid kit? Get it out. Then blow on it every five minutes or so. Get a drink of water. Stay calm. Don't start a fire unless it's freezing and safe to do so. Do tie a brightly colored piece of cloth to a stick and wave it around. And keep blowing that whistle every five minutes. You can yell "Help" too, but not continuously, or your voice will give out.

WHINERS

A whiner (also known as a "wussy") is someone who *doesn't* like a challenge. What they like to do is *complain*! If it gets hot, a whiner lets everyone know it. If the whiner is hungry or tired, he will repeat it over and over without realizing that everyone feels the same way. Whiners don't have a sense of humor and they don't know how to have fun. *Luckily, you do!*

Whiner: I'm so tired . . . Are we almost there?

You: Cheer up! Only 10 more miles of hiking to go!

Whiner: Ten miles?! Is it uphill?

You: Yes, it's actually uphill coming and going!

Whiner: Oh no! I'm so hungry . . . when are we going to eat?

You: We are going to suck on some delicious rocks in about half an hour!

FUN AND GAMES AFTER DARK

There's nothing better than lying in the woods at night, hearing the mysterious stirrings of nature all around you.

But I can get scared just being by myself in a dark *room*, much less the dark woods! If I get scared when camping, I try to figure out what each sound I hear *really* is. For example, that mysterious rustling sound is just the wind in the leaves. And that quiet swoosh is probably an owl swooping down on an unfortunate mouse. As for that scratching sound outside the tent, it is most likely a raccoon, or maybe a huge mutant cricket that is going to cut my head off and use it for soccer practice.

Wait, this isn't helping!

Remember that storytelling is one of the best things to do while camping. (See the "Storytelling!" chapter, page 264.) It's easy for our imaginations to get the better of us in the dark. So just remember that things are the same in the dark as they are in the light, but they're *darker*. (I'm a genius!)

Telling scary stories to other kids can really get them frightened, so do it as much as possible. Pranks are also fun in the dark, but of course the jokester has to first learn that there's nothing to fear in the darkness. If you give yourself a chance, you'll find you can use your senses of hearing and touch in the night to help offset the darkness.

THE CAMP ATTACK

Running through a camp in the dark and pulling all the tent stakes out, and then running away, is not a very clever thing to do. Try it sometime and you'll see what I mean.

THE CREATURE IN THE SLEEPING BAG

Another trick that appeals to some people is putting a live animal like a frog or a grizzly bear in someone's sleeping bag for a joke. Don't do this! Read ahead and you will see why.

Bill (getting into his sleeping bag): Well, goodnight, Sam.

Sam (smiling): Good night.

Bill: I'm so tired . . . AAAAHH! . . . Hey, what's that?

Sam: What?

Bill: There's something furry in my bag! AAAAHH! It's biting my leg! Help!!

Sam: I reckon that's the grizzly bear that I put in your sleeping bag as a joke! Heehee!

Bill: Oh, I see. Good one, Sam! Hahaha, ouch, AAAAAGGG!!

GETTING TO SLEEP

Well, it's finally time for a little shut-eye. You've made sure that the fire is safe, and you're zipped up in your sleeping bag. Say, you don't have any food in your tent, do you? If you're in bear country, that's the fastest way to get a bear in your tent with you. If you're *not* in bear country, it's a good way to get ants in your tent with you! Now all you have to do is close your eyes and go to sleep.

Wondering how cold it is? If you count the number of chirps a cricket makes in 15 seconds, and then add 40, you will have the current temperature, within a degree or two.

ANIMALS

It's good to know about the plant and animal life that you'll see in the outdoors. That way, as you're hiking along, you can proudly point to a mysterious creature in a tree and announce, "*That is a Ring-Tailed Fuzzwart. Run for your lives!*"

Wild animals have excellent senses of smell and hearing. They can sense you coming before they see you because you haven't showered in a while and you are making a lot of noise. So it's possible to walk through a wilderness area *full* of animals and see *none* of them. They either left or hid long before you got there.

If you want to see animals in the wild, be patient. You may have to hold still for a period of time, and then move slowly. This will force you to *concentrate*. If you are hiking or moving, walk *into* the wind if you can. This means you are *upwind*. An animal in front of you won't smell you before you arrive because your scent is being blown in the opposite direction. The animals *downwind* can smell you, however. (You stink!)

Try to move as slowly and quietly as possible. If the animal you are spying on looks your way, don't move! Many animals only look for movement, ignoring everything else. Also, remember one important thing about wild animals: they're *wild*! You cannot expect them to behave like a dog or a cat, even if the bear seems very friendly or if the chipmunk is really cute.

BEARS

I am an expert on bears. (I have been to the Bear Country Jamboree at Disneyland several times.) As for you, you should be somewhat afraid of any bears, but more importantly, you should respect them. They will probably leave you alone if you play it smart and leave them alone. Just remember the words of Robert Penman of the Alaska Department of Public Safety: "*Bears usually will only kill humans when surprised or super-hungry.*"

"Usually"!

MOSQUITOES

You're lucky! *Only half* of the mosquitoes in the outdoors are hunting for you. That's because only female mosquitoes bite. They are drawn to you by the carbon dioxide that you breathe out, so if you stop breathing, they will leave you alone.

Mosquitoes spread many diseases and are found from the equator to the Arctic tundra, so there is no escape from them. When a mosquito lands on you, it saws into your skin and then basically sucks your blood through a big straw. While the bug is doing this, it is also spitting into your wound. Mosquito spit prevents your blood from clotting, so that it can be sucked up easier. You are allergic to mosquito spit, so that's why the bite itches and irritates you later.

You can protect yourself by spraying on insect repellent. Good repellents contain a substance called DEET. But if you want to go natural, try a citronella-based spray. Other methods include wearing garlic (really!) and running around like an idiot, waving your arms and slapping your body everywhere skeeters land.

 Whatever you do, never get bitten by a million mosquitoes! That's how many it would take to drain all the blood out of you.

THE MOOSE

It turns out that moose might be the biggest troublemakers of the animal world. First of all, that name is confusing. One moose, two *moose*? *Mooses*? *Meese*? Forget about it!

Also, moose sometimes lie in wait to trample unsuspecting people like you. According to moose safety experts, if a moose charges you, it is okay to run. *So do it!* You also might want to hide behind something and then peek out to see if the moose is still after you. If the moose is, don't try to argue with it. Instead, place this book gently on its antlers. This will make it happy and the moose will leave.

SKUNKS

Skunks are *nocturnal*—that means that they come out at night. They like to forage around for food, and should steer clear of you. But if you happen to surprise a skunk, back off! If you're not too close, the skunk will warn you before spraying. First, the skunk will pat his front feet on the ground. (You should run away at that time.) Then the skunk will shake his head from side to side. (You should now be running.) Finally, the skunk will raise its tail and spray you! (If you're stupid enough to still be there!) Oh, and *don't ever get any skunk juice in your eyes*. It can cause temporary blindness.

Once the skunk's stink is on you, it is almost impossible to get off. Some folks say that tomato juice can get rid of it. They're wrong. All that will do is make you smell like tomato juice *and* skunk. Exposing yourself and your clothes to campfire smoke helps, as does a bath in water with baking soda mixed into it, followed by a vinegar rinse. But if you really want to stop a skunk from smelling, hold its nose! (That's a joke.)

"Who Let One?" Besides humans driving cars, the skunk's only enemy is the owl. That's because owls don't have a sense of smell.

FOLLOW-UP ACTIVITY

Go to a park and ask one of the rangers some of the following questions. Then make up some of your own.

1. Are there any secret, unexplored parts of this park? If so, what is in those areas?
2. I was bitten by a mosquito last night. Is it possible to spray the entire park to destroy these pests?
3. A coyote came into the campsite last night and ran off with my baloney sandwich. Who do I see about getting paid back for that?

GADGETS, TOOLS, AND TOYS!

Here is the story behind some of the devices that every boy should be familiar with.

COMPASSES

From where you are right now, there are four directions: north, south, east, and west. *And you should always know where these directions are!* If you aren't sure which way is which, think about where the sun rises and sets where you live. If you are north of the equator (but not too far north!), the sun will rise in the east and set in the west.

But what if the sun is directly overhead or if it's overcast? Go get a compass. The compass is a handy tool because it will almost always point to the north. Look at your compass dial; if the needle is pointing north, then the opposite direction of north will be south! West will be to the left of north and east will be to the right.

Compasses are handy tools because of this. You know how one end of a magnet will attract another magnet, but if you reverse its end, it will repulse the other magnet? The planet Earth is a huge magnet, and the north end of the planet attracts other magnets. Your compass needle responds to this magnet and always shows you the way to the north. "Compass" north and "true" north are not quite the same thing. The magnetic north pole of the Earth is actually about a thousand miles away from the "real" North Pole. This has to do with the fact the Earth is tilted on its axis as it rotates. The difference between true north and the compass is known as *magnetic declination,* and many maps show what the declination is.

DUCT TAPE

You may not have known it, but duct tape has magical powers; for example, it can get rid of warts! Army doctors have found that if duct tape is cut to fit over a wart, and then replaced once a week, the body's immune system is stimulated. This means that the wart is attacked by soldiers from the body's germ warfare system . . . *Wart be gone!*

Duct tape was first made in the early 1940s to keep ammunition dry during World War II. It was originally olive green, not silver. But these days, duct tape comes in all the usual colors, plus hot pink, and one brand that comes in camouflage! Since this tape is waterproof, it was first called "duck tape."

It was so useful, soldiers were quickly using the tape to fix jeeps, weapons, clothing, you name it. And after the war, heat experts saw that the tape was a handy thing to use on heating ducts. So the new name of "duct tape" stuck!

There are stronger tapes, like filament tape. But when duct tape is doubled over onto itself, it can pull a 2,000-pound car out of a ditch. Yet even so, you can still rip a piece of it off with your bare hands. Amazing!

Try an experiment: Throw your friend in a ditch, then wrap some duct tape around him. Now, with the help of some other people, see if you can pull him out. If this doesn't work, just wrap him up completely in duct tape and make a duct tape mummy! It's also fun to wrap up school binders in duct tape. (And teachers!)

FRISBEE

The world's earliest Frisbees may have been used for weapons. Some stories tell of how Roman soldiers over 2,000 years ago fought against enemies by throwing their small, round, sharp shields at them.

> ***Roman soldier:*** Hey, barbarian! Catch!
> ***Barbarian:*** I've got it! I've got it! I—I—*Aaaiiii!*

The next thing that led to the invention of Frisbees was *pies*. In the 1920s, a Connecticut baker named William Russell Frisbie stamped his last name onto the tin pans in which his pies were sold. And at some point, college students who'd eaten the pies started throwing the pie tins through the air. Crazy kids!

Meanwhile, a man from California came up with the idea of a plastic "flying saucer." He tried to sell his saucers with names like the Pluto Platter, the Sailing Satellite, the Sputnik, and the Flying Saucer.

These sold okay in California, but not nationwide. The flying disc idea just couldn't get off the ground from coast to coast.

And then one day, the president of the Wham-O toy company was at an East Coast college. And he saw those college students throwing around Frisbie's pie-tin lids!

The students told him they called the sport "Frisbie-ing" (after William Russell Frisbie). So Wham-O took the name (yay!) and misspelled it as "Frisbee" (boo!). And in 1959, the toy company released their new product, the flying Frisbee.

A man named Ed Headrick perfected the Frisbee's design so it would fly better, and the toy became a popular classic. As for Mr. Headrick, after he died in 2002, he was cremated. Then his ashes were molded into some flying discs for his family and friends. May he fly high forever!

G.I. JOE

You're a boy, and that means you don't play with dolls. You play with *action figures*. And if you do, you've at least heard of that granddaddy of all action figures: G.I. Joe. This soldier came out in 1964. Hasbro, the company that created him, thought about calling him Skip the Navy Frogman or Rocky the Marine Paratrooper. They finally came up with Joe's name from the World War II slang term for American soldiers: "**G**overnment **I**ssue."

G.I. Joe was something new: a doll with his own flamethrower and bazooka! This made him a little too warlike for some people. In 1993, a group called the Barbie Liberation Organization switched voice boxes between the talking G.I. Joe and the talking Barbie. The result was a Barbie that said things like, "Eat hot lead, Cobra!" and "Take this Jeep and get some ammo fast!" As for Joe, he got lines like, "Math is hard" and "Let's go to the mall!"

 The very first G.I. Joe ever made was put up for auction in 2003 with an opening bid of more than $200,000!

 In a scientific survey of three boys at my school, it was agreed that G.I. Joe could beat up Barbie's friend Ken.

LEGO

These building blocks have been called "the toy of the century" and they can fascinate a boy throughout his entire life. Between the fun colors and the perfect shapes (over 1,700 of them), anybody can become an architect of the future! Heck, if you just have six of the eight-studded bricks, you can combine them in over a million different ways. This is why Lego bricks are so neat: they encourage creativity.

The man who invented Lego products was a furniture maker named Ole Kirk Christiansen. He enjoyed making wooden playthings for neighborhood children, and because he was good at this, Ole started making more money from his toys than from his "real" business. So Ole started a new business with a new name: Lego. This word was formed by two words getting shoved together: *leg godt*. This means "play well" in Danish. (Coincidentally, it also means "*I put together*" in Latin!)

Ole Kirk Christiansen started making his building bricks in 1949, and 12 years later, they were marketed in the United States. Today, the Lego Company has sold so many building bricks, that there are more than 60 Lego bricks for every human on the face of the planet. (And they're all lost under the couch.)

 The bestselling Lego set ever is the Lego Mindstorms Robotics Invention System.

PEZ

Although cigarettes are always bad for you, it is because of them that we have the wonderful invention of Pez! Yes, it's true! A man from Austria named Eduard Haas III made a brick-shaped candy from peppermint oil and sugar. He called it "Pez"; the letters came from the first, middle, and last letters of the German word for peppermint, ***P**feff**E**rmin**Z***.

Mister Haas noticed that a lot of cigarette smokers used his candy as a breath mint to help cover up their disgusting habit. This gave him the idea to make a Pez holder shaped like a cigarette lighter. The first holders came out in 1948, and they made eating candy fun. But the Pez holder didn't sell well in the United States. Haas thought about the problem, and decided to put a cartoon character's head on top of the dispenser. (The first head was either Mickey Mouse or Popeye, depending on whom you talk to.) You tilted the Pez head back and a single candy popped out. Haas also began making fruit-flavored Pez.

These new ideas worked like a charm. Pez added to the fruit and peppermint types some unusual choices for flavors, like flowers, menthol, vitamins, and chlorophyll.

The heads on top of the Pez are also sometimes a little strange. The Kooky Zoo series had Roar the Lion, as well as a Cow, Yappy Dog, and Monkey Sailor. (*That's a kooky zoo, all right!*) The Pals/Jobs series had a Doctor and a Fireman (*makes sense*), and also the Shell Boy (*huh?*), the Bride (*is she a pal or a job?*), a Knight (*nice work if you can find it*), a Maharajah, and a

Pirate (*who is a crummy example of both a pal and a future job!*).

 My all-time favorite Pez heads are Coach Whistle and the Psychedelic Eye.

POCKETKNIVES

What is it about pocketknives that we like? They have a sharp blade and they fold up and fit into our pocket. They're fun to hold and to goof around with. (Of course, pocket tools like the Leatherman Pocket Survival Tool are also cool!)

Folding pocketknives were made 2,000 years ago for Roman soldiers. These old knives had folding blades and many attachments, including a spoon and a fork. Even so, most people throughout history have preferred to carry around big knives on their belts. They were more impressive and they scared troublemakers away! It wasn't until about 400 years ago that the pocketknife got really popular (especially in America) because of its convenience for all kinds of people.

Here are some things to be aware of with your pocketknife. Whenever you are sharpening or cutting something with the blade, always move your stroke away from you! This will reduce the chances of cutting or stabbing yourself. It would be embarrassing to talk your parents into buying you a pocketknife and then have this happen.

> ***Timmy:*** Mom, I have something to tell you.
> ***Mother:*** Timmy, I see that you have a pocketknife sticking out of your chest.
> ***Timmy:*** *That's* what I wanted to tell you.

WHITTLING

This is an easy and fun thing to do with your knife. You simply pick up a piece of wood and start cutting it down to size. Some people wear leather gloves when they whittle, so that they don't end up whittling their own hands by accident. To prevent a painful cut, make sure that the wood you pick up is not too hard and/or dead. That will make your blade stick, making an accident more likely to happen.

Remember to carefully wipe the blade of your knife clean after cutting anything with it.

SHARPENING THE KNIFE

There are good sharpening stones available at most cutlery stores. Follow the directions that come with yours.

PUTTING THE KNIFE AWAY

The problem with pocketknives is that it's possible to cut your finger while folding the blade into its "closed" position. To avoid this problem, make sure that all of your fingers are safely on the sides of the body of the pocketknife before folding the blade in. (Or just remove your fingers for safekeeping beforehand.)

Every so often, put a little oil (WD-40 works) on your blade and in the body of the knife to keep it working smoothly.

Swiss Army knives were invented in 1891 by a Swiss knife-maker named Karl Elsener. During World War II, U.S. soldiers in Europe loved his knife called the *Offiziermesser* ("Officer's knife"). Because *Offiziermesser* was a little hard to pronounce, the G.I.s just called it the Swiss Army knife, and the name stuck. Nowadays, the biggest Swiss Army knife is the "SwissChamp" model, which has 33 features, including a small spatula and a ballpoint pen.

SILLY PUTTY

Silly Putty was invented during World War II (1939–1945). The United States was in the greatest war the world has ever seen, and supplies were tight everywhere. Gas, meat, rubber, and metal all had to be rationed.

At that time, most of America's rubber came from rubber trees in Asia. Since this was not a good source anymore, the call went out for a new synthetic kind of rubber. An engineer named James Wright took on this challenge. He managed to invent a "fake" rubber that was 25 percent more bouncy than real rubber. It could also stretch further, and it did not fall apart over time. This new rubber could take both extreme heat and cold, and it could even lift the ink off a newspaper! It was amazing!

It was *useless*. Despite all its magical powers, this new rubber had no practical purpose! If it couldn't be used for a tire, the U.S. Army had no use for it. After the war, there was a large supply of this rubber that nobody really wanted.

Wright's invention was called "nutty putty," and it was mailed out to many people to see if they could find a use for the product. A toy store manager named Paul Hodgson saw some nutty putty at a party. (A nutty putty party! *Whoo-hoo!*) In 1949, Hodgson bought a big chunk of nutty putty, and stuck little pieces of it into colored plastic eggs. These "Silly Putty" eggs sold like hot cakes! They sold *better* than hot cakes! History was made!

As for Hodgson, he became a millionaire.

Cool Trick: Shape your Silly Putty into a ball and then put the ball in the freezer for about an hour. Pull it out while it's cold and bounce it. You should notice a difference!

SLINKY

Like Silly Putty, the Slinky was invented during World War II. It was 1943 and the U.S. Navy needed help. See, the instruments that help a ship navigate are very delicate, and the rolling motion of the ocean can mess them up. So a man named Richard James was working on a spring to help fix this problem. Richard had many springs set up on different shelves in his laboratory. One day, he accidentally knocked one of the springs off of its shelf. Then Richard watched in amazement as the spring "crawled" from the shelf, to another shelf, to some books, to his desk, and to the floor!

Richard showed his discovery to his wife, Betty, and she knew immediately that it could be a great toy. She spent two days coming up with the right name for the toy: *the Slinky*!

The couple began production of Slinkys, and in 1946 they brought 400 Slinkys to a toy store. Would the strange springs made with 80 feet of wire sell? Within 90 minutes, all the Slinkys were gone! Luckily, Betty and Richard made more, and the toy is still around today. Does it have batteries? No. Do you plug it in? No. Does it have a video game that comes with it? No! And that is why I love the Slinky.

 The Slinky is the Official State Toy of Pennsylvania. *Whoo-hoo!*

SUPER BALL

The Super Ball has been bouncing out of backyards and into the street since 1965. A chemist came up with the idea of squishing a rubbery substance under thousands of pounds of pressure to make it "super" bouncy. Then the Wham-O company helped perfect the recipe and get the ball into the hands of kids. The ball bounces back with 92 percent of its original force, so get out of its way unless you want a black eye! Today, everyone knows how much fun it is to pick up a bat and smash a home run for hundreds of feet. It makes you feel like Superboy! (Okay, okay, Super*man*. Are you happy now?)

 If you like football, you have to like the Super Ball. Back in the days before the Super Bowl, professional football's biggest game was called the "World Championship Game." The owner of the Kansas City Chiefs didn't like this name much. He was watching his daughter play with a Super *Ball* and he got an idea: the Super *Bowl*!

 It won't quite be a Super Ball, but if you take one rubber band and wrap another one around it, and then wrap another one . . . and do this a thousand times, you'll have a pretty good rubber band ball.

INDOOR GAMES!

Games are fun, but you shouldn't get too hung up on winning or losing. Winning is not the most important thing in life, it just seems like it is sometimes. What would life be like if you won every game you played? You wouldn't even bother playing any games at all because there would be no point to it.

Learning how to win and lose teaches us how to be *good sports*. A good sport knows that the most important part of any game is this question: *"Am I having fun?"* If the answer to that question is "No," you may want to rethink whether you should be playing at all.

If you are having fun, it does not matter whether you lose a game or not. If you are having fun, it is impossible to be a sore loser because you enjoyed yourself! If you do lose a game, congratulate the winner. If you win, compliment the other player and don't rub it in. I guess the key is to not be a big baby.

He Really Was a Big Baby! Thomas Everitt was born in England in 1779. By the time he was 9 months old, he weighed over 100 pounds, bigger than kids 8 times his age. He was described as "lively and well-tempered." You'd have a smile on your face too if you knew that you could beat up all the bullies (and their big brothers) in your neighborhood.

The following games may be ones you are not familiar with; that doesn't mean that the good old games aren't any good! Darts, poker, chess, or dodgeball are all great, but you know how to play those. So give these other games a shot! (They are arranged roughly in order of how complicated their setup is, from simple to complex.)

STARE DOWN

You know how this one goes . . .

You Need: 4 eyes
2 players

How to win: Don't move your face or head.
How to play: Begin a staring match with someone. Here are four ways to do it:

1. Whoever blinks first, loses. This can be painful. (*No fair trying to make the other person flinch!*)
2. Whoever smiles first, loses.
3. Whoever looks away first, loses.
4. Whoever's eyes fall out of their sockets from staring so hard, loses.

Sweden has an unusual athletic event: the National Sauna Championships. This event takes place in a 212-degree Fahrenheit steam bath. A woman champion, Hilkka Loimi, lasted four minutes and 28 seconds in the sauna. When asked for a comment, she said, "It was hot."

HA, HA, HA!

Ha, Ha, Ha! is the stupidest game that exists. Give it a shot!

You Need: laughs
3 or more players

How to win: Don't laugh.
How to play: Have a prize for the winner. This helps. Then get in a circle or around a table. Figure out who's going to go first. Go clockwise from there.

The first player says, "Ha." The second player says, "Ha, ha." The third player says, "Ha, ha, *ha*." (I know this sounds stupid. It is!) And so forth. Keep going around, adding one "Ha" to each turn.

Say the word "Ha" as *seriously* as possible. Any player who laughs or gets the wrong number of "Ha"s is out. You can make faces or act weird to try to get someone else to laugh. You may not touch them or say anything.

ARM WRESTLING

Yeah, you know how to arm wrestle. But do you know how to WIN?

You Need: arms, hands
2 players, but having a third person as a referee is a good idea

How to win: Push the other person's arm down.
How to play: First of all, the key to winning in arm wrestling is *not* who is stronger. It's who knows what they're doing. You can beat boys much bigger and stronger than you with these tips. Impress your friends! Impress some girls! Read this!

If you are going to arm wrestle, you may be standing or kneeling at a table or lying down. If you are standing or kneeling, remember: have the foot (or knee) that is on the *same* side as the arm you are wrestling with more forward than the other. In other words, stagger your feet to the side you're wrestling on. If there is a table leg, try to get this foot up against it on the inside. Brace your leg against the table leg.

Okay, now it's time to wrap hands. Grab your opponent's hand, palm to palm. Get your thumb in there nice and tight. Many champions "wrap" their thumb, which means your fingers cover your thumb. You may want to experiment with this. (Also, with your off hand, you should link hands with your opponent on the tabletop right underneath this hold.)

Brace your body and get a good grip. Try to keep your upper arm as close to your body as you can. Have a referee hold the fists of you and your opponent and count to three. No pulling until then. On "three," quickly twist your opponent's hand around so that the back of his hand faces you *and then pull*! He is now out of position.

After you get your twist, keep your hand, wrist, arm, and body moving together. Many people make the mistake of using their *arms* to arm wrestle. Your arm and body working together are much more powerful than just your arm. Keep your fist inside the line of your shoulders. Even if you start to lose, keep your arm against your body. In other words, lean back with it. The moment you let your arm fight by itself, you'll lose.

The match is over when you can press your opponent's hand down against the table or when he "gives." If you can get a good start and wear him down, you can win even a long match. Use these techniques. They work!

ROCK, PAPER, SCISSORS, VICTORY

You need: a hand
two players

How to win: Outsmart your slow-witted opponent!
How to play: You should already know! You may have heard of this game under a different name, like "Roshambo." Anyway, look your opponent in the eyes. Each of you hold out a fist. Together, you raise and lower your fist three times as you count out "One, two, three!" or "Ro, sham, bo!"

As you bring down your fist the third time, you either keep your fist clenched (ROCK!), spread it flat (PAPER!), or make a sideways "peace sign" (SCISSORS!). Who wins? It's pretty basic. Rock crushes scissors, but scissors cuts paper. And paper covers rock!

The key to winning? Throw your opponent off with your creative moves. Try doing three rocks in a row. (That move is called the "Avalanche!") Or make the game more interesting by betting a million dollars on the game.

 The World RPS (Rock, Paper, Scissors) Society once held yearly tournaments. Thousands of people competed in them, and the winner got a thousand dollars!

THE ACE OF SPADES

The Ace of Spades is a simple game that involves catching a secret assassin!

You need: a deck of cards
6 or more players

How to win: If you are the "assassin," you want to assassinate everyone.
How to play: The ace of spades is sometimes called the "death card," and that's what it is in this game. Remove the ace of spades from your deck of cards and set it aside. Now count out as many cards as there are players; put these cards on top of the ace of spades (including the ace of spades as one of the cards). In other words, if there are six players, put down the ace of spades and then put five more cards on top of it.

Mix the cards and have the players sit in a circle or at a table where they can see each other's faces. Deal each player one card, facedown. The players then look at their cards, but each player must keep their card a secret.

The player who got the ace of spades is the assassin. The players look into each other's faces, but nobody knows who the assassin is except for one person: the assassin! And here's the key: the assassin "kills" people by winking.

The assassin doesn't want to be caught, so he tries to carefully wink at another player so that only that player sees it! If a player sees someone wink at him, he says, "I've been assassinated!" and drops out of the game. If the assassin can get all the other players out but one, he wins. (If there is only one person left for the assassin to wink at, it is a little too easy for him to guess who the assassin is.)

If a player can correctly guess who the assassin is before that, he wins. But if he guesses wrong, then he is out. Finally, if another player who is not being winked at can catch the assassin in the act, he is the winner.

WARNING: Only the assassin can wink! Also, there should be a built-in time limit so that the assassin doesn't take too long between his winks.

EDUCATED ELWOOD

Simple Simon is a little too . . . simple. This game was taken from an alternate universe where everything is reversed! In this universe, they do not play Simple Simon (a.k.a. Simon Says); they play Educated Elwood. When Elwood says to do something, the players are supposed to do the opposite *of what he says.*

You need: your brain
4 or more players

How to win: Be perfectly *dis*obedient to Elwood.
How to play: This is a simple game, but one that requires Elwood to be very watchful.

Pick a leader. He is Elwood. Elwood will give everyone directions. If he says, "Jump in the air!" the players shouldn't do anything. The leader has to say, "Elwood says, 'Jump in the air!'"

Then the players *still don't* jump in the air. Instead, they stand still, because standing still is the *opposite* of jumping. You have to be creative as you think of what the opposite of a direction is. If the leader says, "Elwood says, 'Puff out your cheeks and meow like a cat,'" then the players should suck in their cheeks and bark like a dog!

Remember: in this game, you are knocked out for *following* directions.

When Abraham Lincoln was shot in 1865, Vice President Andrew Johnson had to be notified that he was now the new president of the United States. When they found Johnson to tell him this very important news, he was playing with marbles.

ESKIMO-INDIAN GAMES

The World Eskimo-Indian Games are held regularly. They have kept alive American games that have been around for many years. Here are some of them.

THE BUMP

In this game, you will destroy your opponent! (Or at least make him take a step!)

You Need: 2 players

How to win: Knock your opponent off-balance.
How to play: The Bump can be played two ways. In one version you stand side by side with your opponent, facing the same way, about 6 to 8 inches apart. When the signal is given, you try to knock your opponent off-balance by hitting him with your hip. (If you play hockey, this is a "hip check.") If you can get your opponent to lift or move a foot, you win.

The other version of the Bump is played the same way, but you stand back to back at the same distance. On the signal, use your butt to knock him off-balance! Size and weight are less important than you think; often you can fake out your opponent by bending out of his way when he is trying to butt-bump you, which throws him off-balance.

MUKTUK EATING

"Muktuk" is raw whale skin. It is very rubbery! Contestants try to be the first to chew and swallow a 2-inch cube of muktuk in the least amount of time.

MOUTH PULL

Standing side by side with an opponent, the contestant reaches around his opponent's shoulders with his hand. He then puts his hand in his opponent's mouth. (The opponent does the exact same thing.) Play begins as they try to pull each other off-balance. (Hand washing is required and no tongue pulling is allowed!)

EAR WEIGHT

Loop a piece of twine around your ear. At the other end place 16 pounds of weight. Now start moving and see how far you get before the pain gets the better of you. (Good contestants can go over one-half mile.)

NAME THAT TUNE

It is pretty amazing how quickly a person can identify a song; sometimes in just a note or two, you know what song is being played.

You need: a stereo or computer with decent speakers
3 or more players; teams can also be used easily for this game

How to win: Name that tune!
How to play: One player (called the "Tune Master") selects a song that the other players will probably know. The Tune Master then decides which of the other contestants will "Name That Tune" *first*. Only the one player (or team) selected guesses on the song. The more obvious the song (for example, "Happy Birthday"), the less of it should be played, sometimes only a second or two.

What that means is that the contestant will listen to a short part of the song. This might only be the first note or two! Then he tries to "Name that Tune" by naming the song. If the selected player identifies the song correctly, he gets a point, and the Tune Master picks a new song for the other contestants.

If the selected player *doesn't* get the song right, the song is "pushed" to the next contestant. If this player gets it, he gets the point. The same amount of the song should be played; no more! Still no dice? The song can go back to the first player, and a little more can be played. And so forth! If no player can identify the song, it is discarded, and the Tune Master moves on to new songs.

The role of Tune Master should be rotated every complete round.

Scrabble was invented by an out-of-work architect named Alfred Mosher Butts in the early 1930s. Butts called his game "Lexiko," and he eventually sold the rights for his game to someone else. In 1948, his game was renamed Scrabble and it sold well. As a matter of fact, 150 million Scrabble games have been sold since then. It's the best-selling board game in the world.

TABLETOP FOOTBALL

A classic! Here's how to make the football and the rules.

You need: 1 piece of paper
2 players, but you can have a tournament with more
a table
something with a straight edge (like a book)

How to win: Score by flicking the ball so it overhangs the edge of the table.

How to make the football: Get a piece of paper. Fold it in half the long way. Cut along the fold. (You should now have a narrow strip of paper.) Hold the paper up (the tall way) and fold the top right corner down to the other side to form a triangle. Continue to fold in this way, making triangles until you run out of paper to fold. Tuck the extra paper into the "pocket" on the top of the ball. I like to put tape on the edges; it makes the football heavier and more deadly.

How to play: Decide how many points you and your opponent will play to (I like to say 35 points). Now face your opponent across the table. The table should be narrow enough that you can at least *almost* reach the far side of it. Put the football down at your side of the table (within 4 inches of your edge) and flick it toward your opponent's end zone (the edge of the table).

If your shot is short of the edge of the table, it is now your opponent's turn to flick the ball at your end zone. But if your shot goes over *the edge and off* of the table, your opponent picks it up and flicks the ball to your side of the table.

Ah, but what if your shot *overhangs* the edge of the table *without going over*? That's a touchdown (six points)! If there is any argument over whether the ball is hanging over, use the book. Slide it straight across the edge of the table; if it hits the ball, it's a score.

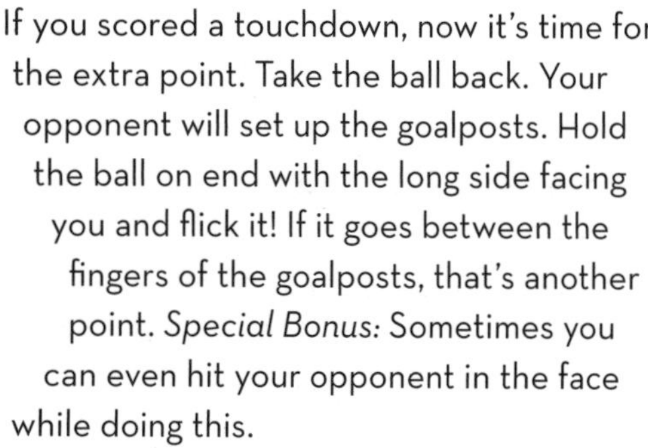

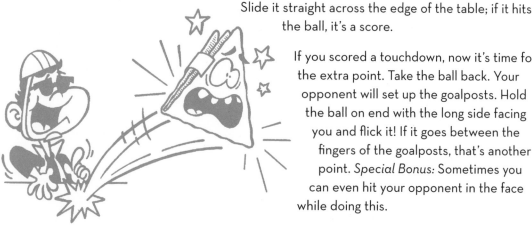

If you scored a touchdown, now it's time for the extra point. Take the ball back. Your opponent will set up the goalposts. Hold the ball on end with the long side facing you and flick it! If it goes between the fingers of the goalposts, that's another point. *Special Bonus:* Sometimes you can even hit your opponent in the face while doing this.

You can change these rules! One common change is allowing four chances (or "downs," like in real football) when driving the ball. Also, you can try giving the opponent a chance to cancel a touchdown: When the ball is overhanging the table, the defender (person scored on) flicks the corner of the football hanging over. If the ball flies through the air and hits the other person, the touchdown is canceled!

Ping-Pong (or table tennis) was invented by an engineer named James Gibb in the 1880s. He wanted a lively game that he could play inside when it was raining. Gibb called his game "Gossima." It was originally played with balls made from champagne corks and paddles made from cigar-box lids! After Gossima was renamed "Ping-Pong" in 1901, it became a big hit.

LIARS' DICE

If you can lie, play this game. If you can't lie, you're a liar, so play this game!

You need: 5 dice
a cup that isn't glass
3 to 12 players

How to win: Lie or catch someone else in a lie.
How to play: First, you need to know that "dice" is a *plural* (meaning *more than one*) word. The word "die" means just one of these rolling cubes. Second, you need to know the winning dice rolls. They are similar to poker, but easier, because unlike playing cards, there are no suits or face cards to worry about with dice.

On the next page is a ranking of dice rolls from weakest to strongest; remember, you can't just tie the previous hand, you must beat it!

Rolls	**Lowest Possible**	**Highest Possible**
High die! (one number only)	*One*	*Six*
One pair! (a pair of numbers)	*Pair of ones (snake eyes!)*	*Pair of sixes*
Three of a kind! (three of the same number)	*3 ones*	*3 sixes*
Two pair! (two pairs of numbers)	*Pair of ones and twos*	*Pair of fives and sixes*
Straight! (five numbers in order)	*One, two, three, four, five*	*Two, three, four, five, six*
Full house! (three of one number, two of another)	*3 ones and 2 twos*	*3 sixes and 2 fives*
Four of a kind! (four of the same number)	*4 ones*	*4 sixes*
Five of a kind! (five of the same number)	*5 ones*	*5 sixes*

Seat your group around a table. Figure out what direction you're going in and pick someone to go first. Player One rolls the dice, covering the cup with his hands as he turns the cup over. Player One looks at the dice. Since he is going first, he doesn't have to beat anyone else's roll. He says "A pair of fours." Player Two takes the cup. Player Two has a decision to make: If he thinks Player One is a *liar,* he says "Liar!" and lifts the cup up to show everyone the roll. If it IS what Player One said (a pair of fours), then Player Two is *out.* If it ISN'T what Player One said, then Player One is out! He's a liar and he got caught. But he's not out because he's a liar; he's out because he got caught. (Just like real life!)

But if Player Two thinks Player One is telling the truth, he says, "I believe you" and picks up the cup and the dice. *Now it doesn't matter if Player One was lying or not.* Even if he was lying, Player Two must now roll and beat what Player One *said* his roll was. (In this case, he must beat a *pair of fours.*)

Player Two rolls the dice and secretly looks at them. *Rats!* He only rolled a pair of twos. It's time to lie! Player Two looks at Player Three and says, *"I have a pair of sixes."* This is a lie, but Player Three doesn't know this. He now has to decide what to do.

And so it goes. Each player must decide if the player before him is telling the truth. If he thinks the player is lying, the dice are revealed and *somebody* is out. If he thinks the player is telling the truth, he must then roll and beat the roll. Just remember that *there are no ties.*

You can't get the same thing as the person in front of you. (If you do, change the roll in your mind and lie.)

Last thing: if someone is knocked out, the next player to get the dice does not have to beat anything. Your best strategy in this game is to be a good liar and to spot other people when they lie. Work at it and you'll improve.

 Always Guess Tails! If you toss a penny 10,000 times, it will not be heads 5,000 times, but more like 4,950. The "heads" side of the coin weighs slightly more, so it ends up on the bottom more often. Dice work on a similar idea. You are very *slightly* more likely to roll a "six" because of the six indented holes on the side of the die. The side opposite of the six is the "one," which is the heaviest side. Maybe that's why "snake eyes" are bad luck; it is the least likely dice roll there is.

TAPE BALL

This game for a large group has a lot of catching, throwing, and treachery.

You Need: 2 or 3 tape balls
a large room (or someone's yard)
6 to 36 players

How to win: Don't drop the ball.
How to play: Tape Ball is a great group game that can be played indoors. First, make yourself a couple of tape balls. It only takes a moment. Take a sheet of newspaper and loosely crumple it into a ball shape about the size of a big orange or a small cantaloupe. Take some masking tape and without breaking the tape, begin to loosely wrap the newspaper ball. Don't try to squish it down or make it tighter.

Continue wrapping the paper until it is completely covered and there is no paper showing. The beauty of the Tape Ball is that it can be thrown with all the force of a regular ball, but if it hits someone, it doesn't hurt any more than being hit by a crumpled up piece of paper.

Once the balls (at least two) are ready, have your group arrange themselves around the room. If you have a lot of people, make sure that everyone can at least stick their elbows out without hitting someone.

Have two people start with a ball. The idea is that they will throw the ball to another person. (Wow!) It should be a good throw, meaning that it is catchable. The throw should be in the general area of the person's chest; if he held still and the ball hit him, it's a good throw. If the person catches the ball, he then throws it to someone else. But if he drops the ball, the person who dropped it is out until the game restarts. (However, if it was a *bad* throw and the ball is dropped, the thrower is out.)

Keep in mind that there is more than one ball being thrown around. (I've seen groups play with four balls at once; pretty amazing!) While you are watching one ball, another one could hit you! If you don't catch it, you're out. Because there is twice as much action as most games, it is good to have a referee or two who can watch the action and make calls. If it is too hard to decide who should be out, just keep both players in and continue the game.

At some point, the game will get down to two players. Then it is time for the duel. They each take a ball and face each other about 15 feet apart. On the count of three, they start throwing the balls back and forth between each other. Whoever drops the ball or makes a bad throw first loses.

OTHER RULES

1. No burning it in!
2. You can't throw it right back to the person who threw it to you. (*No back-and-forthies!*)
3. If the person is right next to you, you should throw it to him underhand.
4. You have to get rid of the ball within 2 seconds; no waiting to throw it till someone isn't looking.
5. On the other hand, if someone isn't looking, throw it at him. If you can do the "no-look" pass, this also catches people by surprise. Just make sure it's a good throw. (It's better to make a good throw and stay in then to try something fancy and be eliminated.)

GRAPE RACES

If you haven't experienced the drama and thrill of microwave grape racing, you haven't lived!

You Need: your parents' permission
seedless green grapes
a little oil (sunflower oil is best)
a microwave oven
1 glass pan to use in the oven that doesn't rotate
2 to 6 players

How to win: Pick a fast grape.

How to play: Pick a grape or two and remove the stems. This will leave a tiny hole at the back of the grape. Now get your pan and put a small film of sunflower oil on the bottom of it. Spread it around.

Line your grapes up against one side of the pan. The holes of the grapes will face the pan side closest to them. Carefully set the glass pan in your microwave; don't roll the grapes around. Set your microwave on high. Remember, the pan cannot rotate while the grapes are heating up!

Depending on the power of your oven, the grapes will either quickly or slowly get hot. Since a grape is mostly water, the liquid inside of it will start to turn into a gas at some point, and it will look for a way out. The easiest way out will be at the stem hole.

If you have some good racing grapes, some of them will start to slowly make their way across the pan. Their gas is escaping them and pushing them forward, like a balloon. (If you have bad racing grapes, they will just tremble and explode, so keep a sponge handy.) Experiment with your own techniques.

OUTDOOR GAMES!

It's time to head into the great outdoors. You probably already know a lot of great outdoor games, so I won't bore you with games you already know, like baseball or skydiving volleyball. Just remember when playing any game that nobody likes to play with a bad sport. A bad sport (also known as a *sore loser*, a *bad winner*, a *jerk*, etc.) is someone who ruins the game for everyone. Bad sports can't follow the rules, or they can't shut up, or both.

A bad sport is also someone who will follow the *letter* of a rule instead of the *spirit* of a rule. For example, let's say you're playing dodgeball and the rule is that if you hit someone in the head with a ball, you're out. You throw the ball at someone in the waist area and they deliberately duck so that the ball hits them in the head! Should you be out of the game? Of course not, but the bad sport will say that you *should* be out, even though it wasn't your fault.

Don't be a bad sport, and don't play with someone who is one. That goes for all the games in this book and for all the games that *aren't* in this book. Below are some games that you may not have tried before that can be a lot of fun.

Mud Football? Mud Anything! Remember, even though your mom may not like it, ANY game is more fun in the mud. (That's why the Mud Olympics take place in Germany every year!) You might want to play football in the mud, or you may just want to find some big muddy puddles and go sliding into them! Just hose yourself off before coming inside again.

EL GLOBO

A good summer game!

You Need:
- balloons
- water
- a Wiffle bat
- a tree or pole
- 2 or more players

How to win: Get wet!

How to play: If you know how to play *piñata,* you know how to play *El Globo*! First, put on your swim trunks. Next, start making some water balloons, and hang one of them from a tree.

Then blindfold one of the players, spin him around, hand him the bat, and put him within reach of the balloon! (It's better if the bat is plastic in case he loses his grip.) When the batter hits the balloon, it's time for everyone to cool off! Or, put up more than one balloon to improve the odds of a cooling shower.

Practical joke alert: This is a great trick to play on someone who *thinks* they are swinging at a piñata. Show them the *piñata,* then blindfold them and switch the *piñata* with a water balloon! Imagine the fun!

★ Quick, name the only major outdoor sport that has more officials or referees than players. Give up? It's tennis.

SARDINES

In this game, you really pack them in!

You need: night
3 to 50 players

How to win: Don't be the last one left out!

How to play: Okay, this is basically a nighttime version of hide-and-seek, even though you can also play it in the daytime. The catch is that one person hides from everybody else. The hider gets 3 minutes to hide, and then the searchers start to look for him.

Once a searcher finds the hider, *he doesn't say anything.* He silently joins the hider in the hiding place. Now two people are hiding! More searchers will find these two, and as they do, they quietly join them in the hiding place. There may not be much room, so everyone has to cram in together like sardines. Whoever finds the rest of the group last is the first hider for the next game.

Golf Cup News! Over a thousand gym teachers were asked what outdoor sport is the most difficult to play. Almost all of them answered "Golf." By the way, the odds of hitting a hole in one for an average player are 33,000 to 1. (Once, a golfer in Massachusetts hit his tee shot over the green on a par 3, where it hit a passing Toyota, bounced back, and rolled into the cup.)

FLYING SHOES

Keep your feet on the ground . . . or the sheet!

You Need: a bedsheet or blanket
1 shoe (or more) per player
4 to 8 players

How to win: Keep your shoe on the sheet.
How to play: Lay the sheet on the ground a decent distance away from any low roofs. Everyone should put a shoe on the sheet. Then everybody picks up an edge of the sheet and tries to bounce someone else's shoe out of the sheet by waving and shaking their edge of the sheet. Careful! You might make your shoe fly by accident! Careful again! Don't get hit in the head by a shoe coming down from orbit! If your shoe gets knocked out, keep playing and try to remove an opponent's footwear.

In 1908, a man named Jack Norworth and a friend wrote a song called "Take Me Out to the Ball Game." This song is now sung at all professional baseball games in the United States. The funny thing was that Jack Norworth had never actually been to a baseball game before he wrote his song. And when he finally did go to one, many years later, he wasn't very impressed!

POISON BALL

This is an active game that involves running and throwing the ball.

You need: 1 large, soft ball (Nerf balls work great)
4 or more players

How to win: Don't get poisoned!
How to play: Form a loose circle with your group and count off so that everyone has a number. Then Player One goes to the center of the circle with the ball. He calls out a number of a player and throws the ball straight up in the air. (He must throw it up at least 10 feet, which is the height of a basketball rim.)

At this point, all players (including Player One) run away. But the player whose number was called runs to the middle of the circle and grabs the ball. As soon as he has the ball, he yells, "Freeze!" All players must then stop running.

The player with the ball is allowed three steps toward any other player he chooses. He then gets to throw the ball at that player. *No burning it in!* It is easier to throw accurately when the ball is not thrown at top speed. The player being thrown at must hold still; no dodging. (It's usually best if they just turn their back to the thrower.) Any balls hitting the other player in the head do not count.

If a player is hit by the ball, they will start play in the next round by throwing up the ball like Player One did. The first time a player is hit with the ball, they get a "P." The next time, they get an "O."

This continues until the player gets "P-O-I-S-O-N," at which point, they are out!

Tip: As with any game, it is important to include everyone equally. Make sure to call out numbers evenly and to throw the ball at people equally. In other words, one player should not have their number called a second time if there is another player whose number has not been called at all.

If you're at the pool with three or more people, have a Nose-Nudge Relay. For it, you have to use your nose to nudge a Ping-Pong ball across the pool. This is fun, funny . . . and surprisingly hard!

WATER BALLOON JOUSTING

The Middle Ages on two wheels!

You need: balloons
water
a grassy field
2 bikes
bike helmets
4 players (2 riders, 2 assistants)

How to win: Nail the other rider with a water balloon.
How to play: Back in the Middle Ages, knights would ride on horseback toward each other and try to hit the other person with a long wooden spear called a *lance*.

In this version of jousting, you will ride your bike at your opponent and try to hit him with a water balloon.

You and your *squire* (your assistant) should fill six water balloons. Your opponent does the same thing. Find a grassy field somewhere that you can ride your bike on. Set up your water balloons about 30 yards from your opponent. Take one in your hand; the other knight will do the same. Make sure you're wearing your helmet.

On a signal, you should both start riding toward each other. As you pedal toward the other knight, remember to stay to the right side of him. He will do the same, so that you don't have a head-on collision.

You can only pedal so fast with one hand, so try to go slowly enough that you can make an accurate throw. When he's in your sights, it's bombs away. After throwing the balloon, whether you hit or miss, circle back to your squire to get another balloon.

Be sure to let the squires in on the fun too; switch spots with them so that they can throw at each other. And by the way, did you know that jousting is the official game of the state of Maryland?

THE STALKER

It's time to hunt the ultimate prey . . . man! Animals look for movement in the forest . . . can you hold still?

You Need: any quiet, outdoorsy area (like a clearing, woods, or meadow; even a soccer field could work, as long as it's a quiet day)
3 or more players

How to win: Silently hunt your prey.
How to play: One person goes about 30 feet away from his companions, closes his eyes (no peeking) and kneels, sits, or squats down. (A blindfold can be used to cover the eyes if there is a problem with trust.)

The other players try to silently stalk this person without being heard. As soon as the "prey" hears a sound that he thinks is a stalker, he quickly stands, turns in that direction, dramatically points, yells something ("Keep back!") and opens his eyes. (If he has a blindfold on, he raises it to see.) If there is a stalker there, the stalker must completely freeze. *That* stalker is now the prey. The person who *was* the prey is now the stalker. If there is *no* stalker there, the prey is also now a "loser."

The new prey must sit down where he is, close his eyes, and the game starts over.

NOTE: If a stalker can get to the prey and touch him before being spotted, he is the Ultimate Hunter. All other players must give him a yo-yo or something of equal worth.

It's Good to Root for the Home Team! The most deadly game ever played in modern times is soccer. In 1964, there was a soccer game between Peru and Argentina. The winner was to go on to the Olympics. The game was held in Peru (bad idea!), and when Peru lost the game in the final minutes due to a referee's call, 45,000 fans in attendance went out of control. In the riots and craziness that followed, 318 people died, making this perhaps the worst sports disaster ever.

PRISONER'S BASE

No one knows how old Prisoner's Base is. Depending on whom you talk to, it is 700 or 2,000 years old. Either way, this game has stood the test of time.

You Need: a field or playing area; if you're on pavement, you could use some chalk
8 or more players

How to win: Capture all members of the other team or take over their prison.
How to play: If you can mark off a 30 x 50 foot playing area, that's about how much space you need for this game. The opposite corners of the field are the "prisons." (If you play in a street, the curb could be the boundary and the sidewalk could be where you put the prison.)

Two equal armies are formed, and each army takes half of the field. There are no prisoners at this time. The leader of one army steps forward and dares someone from the other army to meet him. (This is a great game for trash talking.) Now the fun starts.

The key of this game is tagging. You can only *get* tagged when you are on the *other* army's side. You can only *tag* an opponent when they are on *your* side. Only physical contact made on another player's body is a tag. Clothing doesn't count.

Players begin to sneak into the territory of their opponent. If they are tagged when even one foot is on enemy territory, they go to their enemy's jail, where they must stay until they are rescued or the game ends. (If they *all* get put in prison, the game's over.) But why would a player try to sneak onto enemy territory?

1. If someone from your army is in prison, you can set them free by getting to the prison untouched and tagging them. If you can do this, you are all guaranteed safe passage back to your side of the field.

2. It's fun to taunt your opponent by going into their territory and leaping back before getting tagged.

3. It's best to play with a built-in time limit. So after, say, 10 minutes, which team has more prisoners? It wins! And in one version of this game, if you can enter the enemy's prison *without* getting tagged, you win the game!

The Worst Round of Golf of All Time! A man playing golf for a charity event in Riverside, California, supposedly hit 14 spectators, two caddies, a chipmunk, and a blue jay. Those were his *good shots*. His *bad shot* was the one that flew off the golf course onto a nearby highway, smashing a car's windshield and creating a six-car accident.

COWBOY POKER

If you know how to play poker, you know how to play Cowboy Poker . . . if you have the guts.

You Need: a deck of cards
a large fenced-in field or other enclosed space
1 raging bull
3 to 10 players

How to win: Don't run!

How to play: Set up a table in the middle of your enclosed area. Have a "pot" in the middle of the table that is already set up. (Every player can put in money, candy, whatever.) Have the dealer deal the cards, and then release an aggressive bull into the area. Keep playing! The bull may rush the table. Keep playing! The bull may toss you into the air. Keep playing! After 4 minutes, the winner is the player who remained in his chair and didn't run away.

Variations: Instead of a bull, you may wish to substitute a friendly dog, an assertive guinea pig, or a large stuffed animal.

ULTIMATE FRISBEE

When played correctly, the second-greatest game of all time. Lots of exercise and excitement!

You Need: 1 ultimate Frisbee
1 field
6 or more players; in regulation Ultimate Frisbee, there should be 7 players per team

How to win: Throw the Frisbee down the field to a teammate for a score!
How to play: You need a field to play on. This field could be as large as 70 x 40 yards, or as short as 100 feet long and 80 feet wide. Make the end zones deep; 25 yards deep is just right. Decide on your field size based on how far your players can throw the Frisbee and on how many players there are.

At the start of the game and after each score, both teams line up on the front of their end zone (or closer if you need to). The defense throws the Frisbee to the offense. The receiving team can let the Frisbee land and then pick it up, or they can catch it and start passing it downfield.

The offense moves the Frisbee *in any direction on the field* by completing a pass to a teammate. *Players may not run with the disc.* If they catch the Frisbee running, they should stop as soon as possible. The person with the disc (the "thrower") has up to 10 seconds to throw the disc. The defender guarding the thrower can count out loud to 10 if they like. The defense gets the disc if the opposing thrower doesn't throw it in 10 seconds.

The person passing the disc can use a swivel or pivot foot, just like in basketball. *If a pass is dropped or not completed* (for example, it goes out of bounds or is blocked or intercepted), *the defense takes the Frisbee and goes on offense.*

There is no physical contact allowed between players! Picks and screens are not allowed. A foul occurs when contact is made. If a foul is called on one team, then the Frisbee goes back to the other team.

Each time the offense completes a pass into the defense's end zone, the offense scores a point. They then line up at their end zone and pass it to the other team. See which team can get to a certain score first, or play for a certain time period.

Tips: There are no downs like there are in football. Also, there are no referees in real Ultimate Frisbee, so good sportsmanship is important. Respect the other players and have fun!

SPECIAL FEATURE: THE FIVE RULES OF FRISBEE (ADAPTED FROM DAN RODDICK'S *TEN COMMANDMENTS OF FRISBEE*)

The most powerful force in the world is that of a Frisbee trying to land under a car, just out of reach. (This is called "car suck.")

The better the catch, the higher the odds the person will then make a bad throw.

Never say, *"Watch this!"* before doing something cool. Whatever you were going to do now won't work.

The best catches are never, ever seen. ("Did you see that? Anybody?")

In any group of people, someone will always say, "Hey, you could attach razor blades to the edge of this and maim and kill people!"

OTHER FRISBEE GAMES

Decapitation

Two teams line up and face each other 15 yards apart. They take turns throwing the Frisbee as hard as they can at each other. Points are awarded for any catch made with one hand by the defense (point goes to defense), any drop or two-handed catch by the defense (point goes to offense), or any bad throw by the offense (point goes to defense).

Boomerang Frisbee

Players throw the Frisbee boomerang style and run to catch it themselves. The winner is the person who can throw and catch it while covering the most distance.

"Play Ball! Zzzzzz . . ." The actual *playing* time in a Major League Baseball game lasting 2 ½ hours has been clocked at under 10 minutes.

ROUNDERS

This is the greatest game of all time! Everyone plays! This is terrific for large or even huge groups of people.

You need: a large space
a Nerf football, or any spongy, irregularly shaped ball
1 bat
3 sanctuaries (Sanctuaries can be baseball bases or almost anything. I use traffic cones with PVC pipes stuck vertically in their ends so that a "striker" can grab them.)
8 to 100 players

How to win: Score!
How to play: Rounders has been around for hundreds of years. It has influenced the modern games of baseball, cricket, and Death Match 3000.

In Rounders, someone is picked to be the "striker." He hits the ball and starts to run. He wants to score. Each time any striker successfully completes a journey around the "sanctuaries" and returns to his or her "castle," that is a score for their team. At the end of the game, the team with the highest tally (the most runs scored) wins. The only way to prevent a striker from scoring is to "peg" him or to catch the ball struck on the fly or on the first bounce.

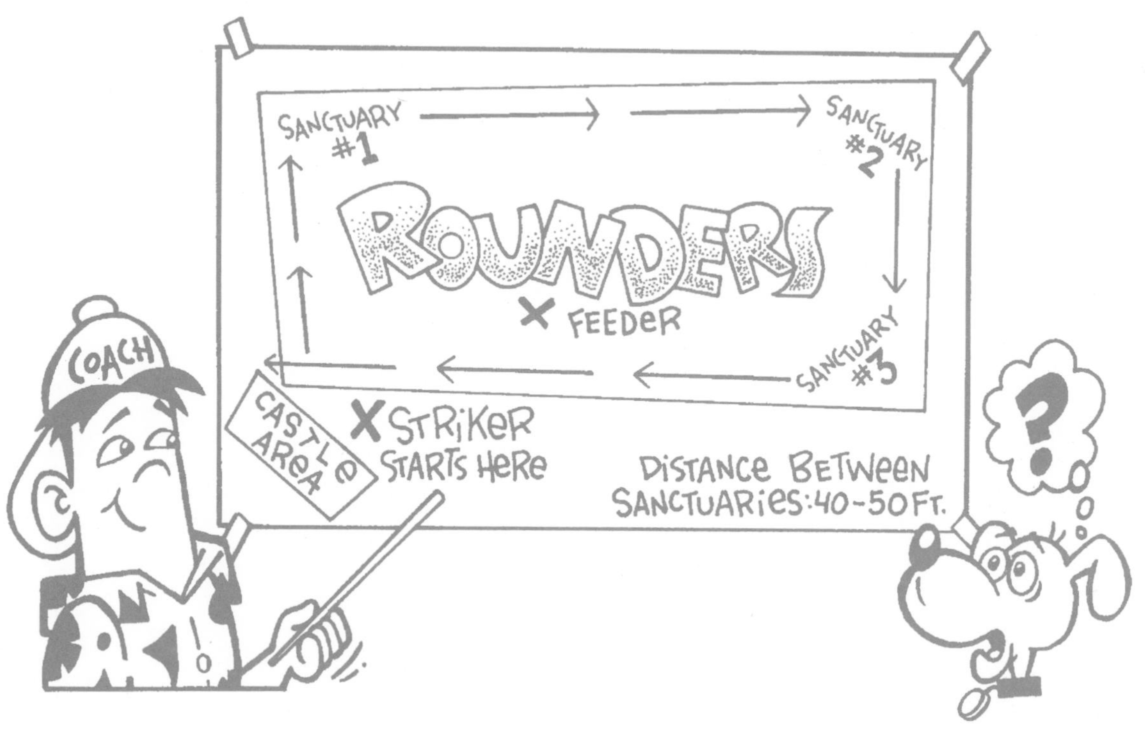

AMAZING ROUNDERS RULES!

1. **Infinite swings.** The striker (the person hitting or "striking" the ball) has no limit on the number of tries he needs to hit the ball. There is no striking out. The striker keeps trying until the ball comes in contact with the stick. (The striker must take an actual swing at the ball!)

2. **The ball must be fed where the striker wishes.** The "feeder" is the person from the other team who throws (or "feeds") the ball to the striker. The feeder must throw the ball where the striker wants it. If the striker is unhappy with a feeder, the striker asks for a new feeder from the other team. The feeder should try to give the striker a good throw; no rolling the ball or burning it in. (The feeder doesn't have to worry about someone "stealing a base." You can't do this in Rounders.)

3. **Run on any hit!** Remember, the striker must take *a real* swing at the ball! Any time the stick hits the ball (unless it's a "tip" that does not make any forward progress), it is a hit and the striker must run! The ball may be struck anywhere. *There are no out-of-bounds!*

   Important: Any strikers already at the sanctuaries do not have to begin running when the ball is struck. (There is no need to tag up, like in baseball, on fly balls.) However, once they begin to run, they have to keep going at least to the next sanctuary.

4. **Run clockwise.** Upon hitting the ball, the striker then must run clockwise around the sanctuaries. The striker does not need to touch any of the sanctuaries and may run anywhere on the field as long as he eventually passes outside or around each sanctuary. (That's why they call it Rounders; you run *around* the sanctuary!)

5. **Striker is out.** The striker is out if the hit is caught in the air or after the first bounce. Also, any striker is out if he is plugged (hit with a thrown ball) while running. He is *not* out if he is on or holding a sanctuary (one that wasn't used before—see rule #7) before he is plugged.

   A note on plugging: The throw must hit the striker below the neck. If it doesn't, the thrower goes to the dungeon.

6. **Sanctuaries only work once.** Once a striker has touched a sanctuary, he may not let go of it and then grab it again—it has been used up for that striker. More than one striker can use a sanctuary at the same time. Also, one striker can pass other strikers as he runs.

7. **No blockades.** No defending team member may touch or get in the way of a striker in an attempt to prevent him from getting to a sanctuary or going around the sanctuaries.

8. **Freezing play.** If the feeder gets the ball in the pitching area and touches the ball to the ground while yelling, "*Freeze!*" then the strikers on the field must go to the closest sanctuary that they haven't used yet and hold play.

9. **Everybody out!** The teams change sides when the castle's team has gone through their whole striking lineup. That means that *every* person on that team has either scored or gotten out. *Strikers may not be stranded on a sanctuary.* Play continues *until the last person in the lineup is either out or scores.* (Subsequent strikers who already batted can be stranded.)

10. **Master Rounder.** The last striker can become a "master rounder" if he decides to try and circle the bases twice. After leaving the third sanctuary after his first trip around, *he may try to make the full trip around again without stopping and get back to the castle.* If he makes it, his whole team gets to bat again; if not, the inning is over and the other team comes up. (You might want to keep your fastest person till last because of this.)

11. **The dungeon.** If a defender plugs a striker above the neck, or blocks a striker's route, they go to the dungeon. (This is like a penalty box.) Also, any poor sports go to the dungeon as well.

12. **The king is always right.** It's best to play this game with a "king." The king is an adult or other respected person who is the referee. Once the action gets going, it can be almost impossible for the king to see the whole playing field. It doesn't matter: *the king is always right.*

13. **Do you think the king is wrong?** See rule #12.

FREQUENTLY ASKED QUESTIONS

Q. The striker hits the ball toward a defender near the first sanctuary. The striker then runs away. Is this legal?
A. It's not only legal, it's smart. The striker would get pegged if he ran toward the player with the ball! If he runs away, he has a much better chance; of course, he will need to eventually run back to the first sanctuary, and stay there or go around it.

Q. A striker runs *around* all the sanctuaries without touching them, gets confused, runs to the second sanctuary, and holds it. Is this legal?
A. Actually, it is legal. The sanctuary hasn't been "used up" for him because he never touched it.

Q. A defender tries to "peg" a striker. The ball bounces and then hits the striker. Is the striker out?
A. No. The ball must be "on the fly," not "on the bounce" when it hits the striker.

Q. A striker is being chased by someone with the ball. The defender tries to peg the striker, but the striker ducks, which results in the striker being hit in the head with the ball. What is the decision?
A. The striker is out; there is no penalty.

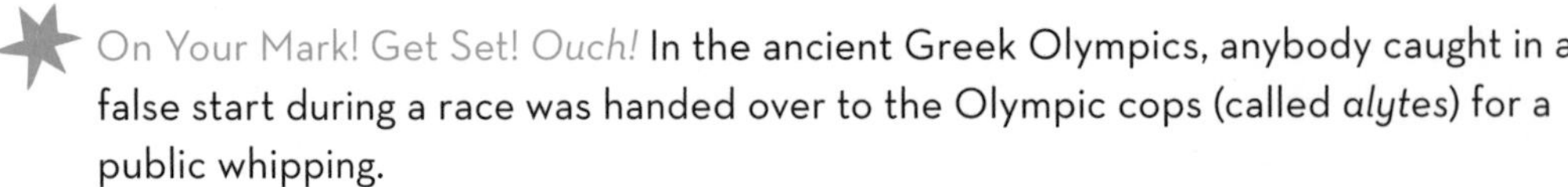

- On Your Mark! Get Set! *Ouch!* In the ancient Greek Olympics, anybody caught in a false start during a race was handed over to the Olympic cops (called *alytes*) for a public whipping.

- On Your Mark! Get Set! Go! *Keep Going!* Maybe the world's longest race is the Sri Chinmoy Marathon in New York. At 3,100 miles, it takes the best runners more than 40 days to complete.

- Want more games? Take a look at *The Pocket Guide to Games*!

GIRLS, BULLIES, AND PARTIES!

GIRLS

I guess girls are okay, but the cooties, good grief, the COOTIES! Anyway, I don't know how to break this to you, but one day you will start looking at girls as more than just pests. You'll start noticing how girls smell good. You'll have your whole life to puzzle over what makes girls special, but for now, let's look at some of the common questions boys have about girls.

1. *Where do girls come from?*

   Nobody knows.

2. *There's a girl that I like. How do I let her know that I like her?*

   There are many ways to let a girl know that you have a crush on her. The gutsiest way would be to walk up to her and say, "*I like you.*" Few boys have this kind of courage.

3. *Okay, so I'm a coward. What else can I try?*

   Make eye contact with the girl in class or by her locker and smile. Try to catch the girl when she is by herself for a moment. Try saying "Hi" and see if you can get a conversation going. Try complimenting her hair or clothes, or asking her what she thinks about a certain movie, music group, teacher, whatever!

   She might be surprised or nervous, so be prepared to *bail out*! This means that you made your initial contact and then you move on. You can try a slightly longer conversation the next time you see her. But if she doesn't seem interested, leave her alone. Nothing's worse than liking someone and then hating her because she doesn't seem to like you back.

4. *Should I get other people involved?*

   Sure! If you want the whole world to know that you like a girl, get other people involved. Let's say there's this girl named Krista who you like. One of your friends could tell one of Krista's friends that you like her. Then those two friends will tell about a hundred other people first. Pretty soon, total strangers will be coming up to you in the hallway saying, "I hear you like Krista!"

Of course, once this news gets out, you will have to deny everything. You will deny all rumors ("I don't like her!") and you will never be able to look that girl in the eyes again because of your hideous embarrassment.

5. *So what's the best way to do this?*

   I have a brother named Kris who always seemed to have girlfriends when we were kids. I once asked Kris how he got girlfriends.

   "I'm nice to them," he said.

   This is still pretty good advice.

6. *Okay, this girl knows I like her, and I think she likes me too. What's next?*

   This is the toughest part of all. First, you need to talk to her. (Or at least text!) And since you probably can't drive yet, see if you can get together on the phone or online after school. Or try meeting her at a movie, party, game, or mall.

   If you are allowed to actually "go out" with her, don't try to do anything too big on the first "date." It would be a lot easier to get together with a group, so there's less pressure. Plus, you don't want to make her feel uncomfortable. So keep it casual! No big presents, flowers, or cards. Just get to know her a little. Try to be positive and upbeat; don't try too hard to be funny or cool. Girls can spot guys who are "TTH" (*Trying Too Hard*), and they don't like it.

7. *How long should our first get-together or date last?*

   No more than a couple of hours. Like I said, don't overdo it. Just get to know each other. Don't have so much time that you're bored or uncomfortable.

8. *What about holding hands, kissing, and all that?*

   Heck, if you think I'm going to write about that, you're nuts! Let me put it this way: be sure that when you say goodbye, the girl you like knows you *still* like her. So make plans to do something again!

   OKAY: "That was fun. Want to get together again sometime?"

   BAD: "Catch you later." [Farts and runs off]

   WORSE: "Will you marry me?"

9. *Any final tips?*

   Yes. Don't put gum in a girl's hair. They hate that. Also, stay on the good side of the girl's parents by being polite. And you may think I'm insane, but consider reading *The Big Book of Girl Stuff.* I know, your reputation will be destroyed if anyone sees you with it. But what's more important—your rep or great wisdom?

★ Cooties Are Real! Humans didn't wash themselves or their clothes very much in the old days. As a result, most people had lice in their hair! (A louse is a small insect that makes its living by hiding on your head and biting you.) A hundred years ago, it wouldn't be that unusual for a boy to sit in class and see a white critter crawl out of his table-partner's hair, and then back into the forest again. *Cooties!* (Of course, boys had them too.)

★ Yo, Short Stuff! The only age when the average girl is as tall or taller than the average boy is 12.

BROTHERS AND SISTERS

Maybe you have brothers and sisters. If so, look for a good book on anger management. And remember, even though your brothers and sisters might drive you crazy, almost no "only children" have been elected president of the United States.

SCHOOL

Do you think that the school year is too long? Please! You have it easy! The odds are that you don't go to school more than 185 days a year. Compare that to the school years of these other countries: Thailand, Scotland, and the Netherlands have 200 days in their school years. Switzerland has 207, Russia and Germany have 210, Israel has 215, Korea has 220, and Japan has 243. But the winner is China, with 251 days in the school year!

GOING TO A PARTY

Hey, you got invited to a party! Go to the party. Eat, talk, goof around, and dance if you feel brave. Play some games. If it's a party where you should bring a present for a boy, get them a pocketknife, kazoo, chattering teeth, or nerd glasses. These gifts are always a hit. If the party is for a girl, ask someone else for ideas.

There are a lot of ways to greet someone with body language. You can smile, shake hands, wave, or even bump heads. In some cultures, like Japan, bowing can be a way to communicate this greeting. A bow at a certain angle has a certain meaning:

A bow at an angle of 5 degrees is a simple greeting. "Hi!"

A bow at 30 degrees is a respectful bow that shows gratitude.

A bow at 45 degrees is used for an apology or to show great respect.

A bow at 75 degrees is used to check the shoes for mud.

THROWING A PARTY

A party can be heavy, so throwing one isn't easy. (That is a joke.) The first (and sometimes the hardest) part of throwing a party is deciding whom to invite. Wise men for centuries have said that there are three kinds of people you should invite to a party:

1. Your good friends.

2. Kids you don't know well but who seem nice.

3. Kids you don't know, but who you think would have fun.

Before people arrive, think about if you want to have dancing, games, or activities in different parts of the house. *Then get organized!* Also, make sure to take lots of pictures; kids love to ham it up for the camera!

Naturally, there should be lots of munchies once people arrive. I'm getting hungry just thinking about all the pizza, chips, sandwiches, and soda you'll load up your guests with.

Once people do start to arrive, remember: you're the *host*. That means that it's your job to make sure that everyone is having fun. You can't just talk to your best friends; you need to talk to EVERYONE.

Make sure that music is playing and everyone can hear it. If you have a friend who is responsible, have them be the DJ. Most people love to be the DJ, but other people will try to give the DJ suggestions for music. Pick someone for this job who can handle the pressure.

By the way, make sure that your parents are present. Although that sounds crazy, you know that kids (especially boys!) act differently if there are adults around. To prevent the possibility of fires, broken dishes, and broken bones, your parents need to be in the house. They might be squirreled into a back room, but just knowing that they're there will give you peace of mind.

Finally, I'll remind you again to make sure that people are having fun. Talk to everybody; don't stay in any one place too long. If you see someone who doesn't seem to know anyone, introduce them around or get them involved in an activity.

BULLIES

When I was a kid, everyone was always trying to convince me that bullies were actually *cowards*. If you just stood up to the bullies, they would chicken out and leave you alone.

What a bunch of baloney!

Bullies *can* be cowards, but don't bet on it. They can also be over-confident jerks with an itchin' to pop you a good one upside your head.

Because every bully is a little different from the last one, you can't deal with them all the same. Some bullies just want you to avoid them. So if you do avoid them, life is good. Other bullies will notice that you are *trying* to avoid them, and this makes them look for you. So what should you do then?

Use your *head* and use your *feet*.

Use your head to keep away from bullies. It is useful to "tell on" some bullies. Once they get in trouble with an adult and/or their parents, they know that you will stick up for yourself, and they will leave you alone.

The more hardcore the bully is, the less this strategy works. Decide how tough your bully is before turning them in. Use your *head*. And don't put yourself in situations where you are by yourself or in areas where there is no escape.

What if it comes down to a fight? It's you and the bully! Use your *head:* Is this kid your age or size? Do you think a fight will solve the problem? Are you ready to stick up for yourself?

If it doesn't look like fighting is a good idea, don't wait around to get pummeled. Use your *feet*. Your best weapons in a fight are your feet. No, not to use for kung fu kicks! Use your feet to run away. (This martial art is called *nogethitsu*.)

By the way, everyone asks themselves this question when bothered by a bully: "Why me?" Remember, although bullies may not always be cowards, they are almost always jerks with personal problems. So if it wasn't you, they'd just be bothering someone else. Try to think of it that way; you are providing a valuable service to society by keeping your bully off of someone else's case! And don't take it personally.

 Experts agree that if you can remove a bully's lungs, he will be less likely to bother you.

FOLLOW-UP ACTIVITY

Make friends with the toughest girl at your school. If a bully ever messes with you, politely ask the girl to pull out the bully's lungs. When she is done, keep the lungs in your locker as a souvenir.

GROSS STUFF!

The title of this chapter says it all. If you are ready to learn about disgusting, nauseating, and otherwise gross items, batten down the hatches and read on!

BARFING DEPARTMENT

Have you ever eaten something rotten? Or maybe you rode in the car too long, and your last meal wasn't sitting well? Your body has a solution to the problem! You can *retch, backwards bungee, vomit, make stew, hurl, blow, upchuck, heave, throw soup, feed the fish, puke,* or even *regurgitate*! But no matter what you call it, it's never any fun.

You barf when your stomach decides that a mistake has been made. Barfing is usually caused by motion sickness (boats and roller coasters are prime offenders), eating food with a lot of bacteria in it, or eating too fast and/or too much all at once. Now *everything must go*! But your body is very thoughtful. It sends you some signals before you blow chunks so that you can get ready. You get a horrible feeling that something bad is going to happen. Your mouth starts producing a lot of spit.

You're in a cold sweat. And then . . . *blauuuug!*

Your stomach is a big muscle. It heaves and contracts and brings up a whole mess when you barf. Barf is full of stomach acid, which is why it leaves a rotten taste in your mouth. Be sure to brush your teeth after barfing because the acid can stain your teeth; besides, you'll feel a lot better. (The *worst feeling in the world* is when your mouth isn't all the way open when you barf and some puke squirts out your nose! Aaagg!)

Don't feel bad if you puke in public. After all, an American president gave the most famous barfing performance of all time! In 1992, President George Bush Sr. was in Tokyo at an important dinner. He wasn't feeling well, and he ended up spewing into the lap of the Japanese prime minister and then falling on him. Nasty. It was all caught on television cameras, and the Japanese invented a new word in honor of the moment. *Bushuru:* To vomit in a public place.

If your puke is ever green, congratulations. You managed to throw up something that's not from your stomach at all. Green barf has *bile* in it, and bile comes from a spot way down near your small intestine. That means you had to dig down deep for that one. Good work!

The scariest barf is called "projectile vomiting." This is what happens when a baby heaves cheesy stuff that lands on the other side of the room. Sometimes a wad of projectile vomit can go right out the window.

It is possible to vomit on purpose. By sticking a finger or other small item (like a feather) down the throat, a person can gag and vomit. Why would someone do this? In ancient Rome, the custom was to have huge feasts with many different kinds of food. If a person wanted to continue eating but was too full to do so, he visited the Vomitorium. This was an area to barf, where servants would clean up the mess. A philosopher from that time named Seneca once wrote that the Romans "vomit so that they may eat and eat so that they may vomit."

To avoid barfing, try pushing down on your wrist an inch or two up from your palm. (There are wristbands that do this for you.) This works well for motion sickness. A sip of ginger ale can mellow out your stomach, as can a saltine cracker if you're not feeling well.

There is a jet owned by NASA nicknamed the "Vomit Comet." It is used to create "zero gravity" so that astronauts can train for outer space. The aircraft climbs and dives over and over, sometimes as many as 50 times.

FUNNY THINGS TO SAY WHEN SOMEONE BARFS

"Thar she blows!"

"Abandon ship!"

"He's got the urge to regurgitate! Throw up all that food he ate! Vomit! Vomit! Yeahhhh, vomit!"

FUN BARFING FACTS

You Make Me Want to Puke! Sea cucumbers can squirt out some or all of their guts when threatened. This is so disgusting, their would-be predator leaves. The puke is also sticky and tough. Some island cultures squirt sea cuke puke onto their feet like a pair of water shoes to protect their feet while they walk around in the water!

When a cow chews its cud, it's basically chewing its own barf!

After an owl eats an entire mouse or other rodent, it barfs up the skin, bones, and other tough-to-digest parts in a nasty little ball called an "owl pellet." Collect them all!

BELLY BUTTON LINT, TOE JAM, AND EARWAX DEPARTMENT

Here is a strange fact to consider: You used to breathe through the hole in your stomach called your belly button. When you were in your mom's womb, all of your oxygen went through the *umbilical cord* that connected to where your belly button is now. You couldn't breathe with your lungs then; there was no air to breathe.

Now that your "cord has been cut," you use your lungs to breathe, leaving your belly button to gather dirt, dead skin, and cloth fabric. If you put all those ingredients together, you have lint! You might want to take a look in your belly button if you haven't done so lately, because it can get pretty nasty if you don't clean it out every so often.

Paramedics once answered a 911 call about an "abdominal evisceration." This means someone's guts were falling out! The paramedics went to a home and found a 13-year-old boy on a bed. When asked why he called 911, the boy said he had "stuff" coming out of his belly button. The paramedics investigated and found what the "stuff" was: belly button lint.

Lint can gather other places too. Your feet are constantly sweating, so dirt, dead skin, and cloth (from your socks) make a nice little surprise for you between your toes. We call this toe jam, although some people actually have toe jelly. Whatever you call it, don't save it up for a peanut butter sandwich. If you don't know why not, just read the "Barf" section in this chapter.

There is a place in Dawson City, in Yukon, Canada, where adults can try a drink that has an actual human toe in it. It is called the Sour Toe Cocktail. The toe is a real human toe that has been preserved in alcohol and is put into drinks. As the story goes, the first toe came from the frostbitten foot of a trapper. That original toe was accidentally swallowed when someone drank the cocktail too fast. Since then, the toe has been replaced a few times, most recently in 2013.

As for earwax, it is also easy to make. Just take some dead skin and mix it with the oils that are naturally in your ear. Throw in a little of the dirt that floats in your ear, and you have earwax! (I wonder why nobody ever makes candles from the stuff?) There is a woman in New England who uses earwax on her lips as a cheap alternative to lip balm, but you're probably not interested in that.

Earwax can sometimes build up to the point where it clogs the whole ear. There is nothing as surprising as innocently putting your finger in your ear and coming out with a brown chunk of gunk. Some people suffer from *ceruminosis* (see-ROO-min-O-sis), or too much earwax. I once had a friend named Ben who thought he was going deaf in one ear. The doctor stuck a small metal instrument in his ear and pulled out an orange cork that had plugged up his hearing hole. He could hear again! The first thing he heard was the doctor saying, "That is disgusting."

Ben got off easy, though. Cockroaches like to find small, dark, greasy hiding places to hide out in. Guess where they sometimes go? "*Noooooooo!*"

BURPING AND BELCHING DEPARTMENT

Burping and belching are the same thing. You know how to burp, right? Heck, you've been doing it ever since you were born; you would swallow down air while sucking on your bottle, and then your parents would burp you. Why is belching so cool? Because everyone does it and it makes a fun noise.

In some cultures, a good belch after a meal is a sign of good manners. Of course, you don't live in one of those cultures, but never mind that.

TIPS ON BELCHING

Belching is simply a way of relieving excess gas in your stomach through the mouth. Some people can belch on command; these people have a belching superpower! However, most of us need a little help to belch. Fizzy drinks are always a good source for that extra gas.

Get a fizzy drink. *Do not shake it!* This will cause the can or bottle to burp on you when it opens! Instead, open it normally. If you have a straw, use it. Straws put more air in your system. Or just slowly drink a few mouthfuls, swirling the drink around in your mouth before swallowing. When you've built up enough gas, let 'er rip!

One good thing to have when you burp is gravity. This allows only the air to come up from your stomach. Astronauts in outer space have learned to try and never burp; if they do, there's a good chance that EVERYTHING in the stomach will come up at once.

There are many different things that one can do with a burp. Try some of the special belch varieties below.

Volume: How loud can you belch? Can you scare the dog? Can you make your grandmother's wig jump off her head?

Grossness: Can you make it sound wet?

Length: How *lonnnng* can you burp? Keep going till you run out of breath.

Tricks: Can you say something while you are burping? Try saying a funny phrase; it will be that much funnier if you're belching when you say it! How about a belch that sounds really low or high? Try saying the "ABCs" with one burp!

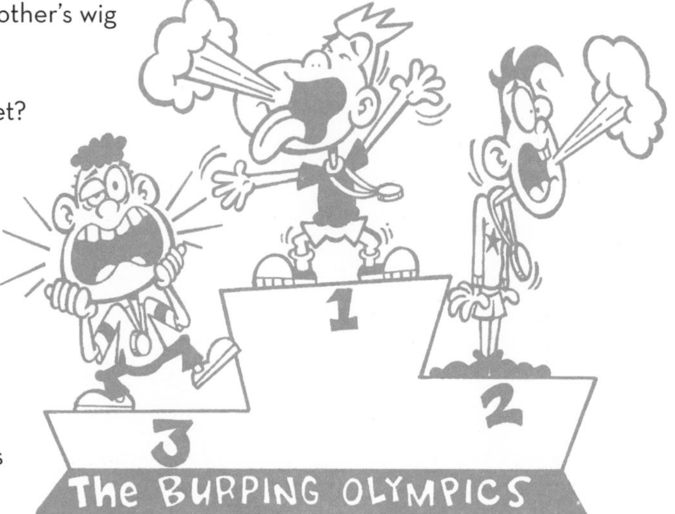

WARNING: Do not do this in front of visiting relatives, important visitors, or the president of the United States. Also, never try *too* hard to burp! You may bring up something besides gas. (See "Barfing Department," page 133)

And remember . . . Always say "Please pardon me" after a good belch!

FUN BELCHING FACTS

 A good belch can escape your body at 50 miles per hour!

- If you would like to use a fancy word for belching, try "eructation" (ee-ruk-TAY-shun).
- People belch, even when they are asleep! *"Zzzzzz . . . buuurrrrpp!"*
- Back Off, Monkey Boy! Orangutans use loud belches to warn intruders away from their territory.

B. O. (BODY ODOR) AND SWEAT DEPARTMENT

I've got some bad news for you: men sweat about 40 percent more than women. Heck, your feet alone sweat out a quarter cup of sweat a day. Dang it, you are *disgusting*! If you don't sweat much now, don't worry. You will. Once you become a teenager, you'll be a sweaty beast with reeking pit stains. The good news is that sweat doesn't stink. Hurray! The bad news is that bacteria that grow in your sweat do stink.

Germs called bacteria live all over the outside and inside of your body. As soon as you sweat, bacteria start swarming all over your skin. Then you reek! But remember, it is not your fault.

The skin of your face has about two million bacteria on it. That's actually pretty good compared to your armpits. The skin on your pits is home to 516,000 bacteria per square inch. But both your face and your armpits have to take the backseat to your mouth. More than 10 billion creatures live in there. Can you taste them? They can taste you! If you have bad breath, they are the reason why. Now go buy some mouthwash.

WHOA, DUDE! YOU STINK!
I DO NOT STINK. THE BACTERIA THAT LIVE ON ME ARE CREATING THAT UNFORTUNATE ODOR.
NO SWEAT

You may bathe or shower every day, but different cultures have different ways of looking at bathing, body odor, and bacteria. In France, over 50 percent of the people *don't* bathe every day, 50 percent of the men *don't* use deodorant daily, and 40 percent of the men *don't* change their underwear daily. You add up all those "*don'ts*" and someone smells like "*doo-doo.*"

 It is possible to give off three gallons of sweat on a hot day.

 In outer space, your B.O. doesn't leave your body; it surrounds you in a tight, stinky cloud!

BOMBING DEPARTMENT

Some people call this tooting or farting. In this book, I will call it *bombing*. This is what happens when gas comes out your back end: you drop a bomb! Sometimes it is noisy and sometimes it is quiet, but it's usually stinky. Bombs are like belches; they are funny because they make a weird sound and everybody does it. And I mean everybody. Benjamin Franklin, founding father of the United States, even wrote a book called *Fart Proudly*!

So where do your bombs come from? Part of a bomb comes from swallowing air while you suck on candy, chew gum, and eat. People who gulp their food usually bomb more than those who don't. But your body also makes gas naturally. As you digest food, gases are created in your intestines and will exit your back end faster than 30 miles per hour.

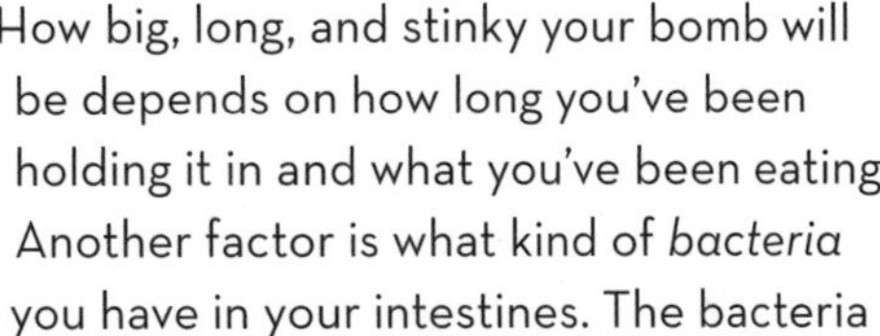

How big, long, and stinky your bomb will be depends on how long you've been holding it in and what you've been eating. Another factor is what kind of *bacteria* you have in your intestines. The bacteria are what give your bombs a gas called *methane*. (Methane is an important gas because it can catch on fire!) Bacteria bombs with a lot of methane tend to be hot, stinky, and silent! A bacteria bomb is known as an "SBD"—"*Silent But Deadly*."

The most embarrassing thing known to mankind is to bomb and have the whole world know it was you. Long ago, a gentleman was in the court of Queen Elizabeth I (1533–1603) of England. He bowed to her and accidentally bombed loudly. Everyone heard! The man was so humiliated, he traveled away from England for seven years before returning to the queen's court. Once he returned, Queen Elizabeth smiled and said, "My Lord, I had forgot the fart."

TIPS ON BOMBING

If you want to bomb, enjoy a helping of raisins, corn, white bread, cheese, bell peppers, turkey, onions, broccoli, cabbage, or brussels sprouts. Then sit back, relax, and watch the sparks fly. *Want loud bombs?* Eat some beans! You know what they say: beans on Saturday, bubble bath on Sunday. *Want stinky bombs?* Eat prunes, bran, cauliflower, or a lot of meat. Hard-boiled eggs are good for these bombs because an egg yolk contains sulfur, which is what creates the terrible smell of rotten eggs. (If you want to just make the *sound* of a bomb without the smell, go to "Making Sounds" in the "Making Faces! Making Sounds!" chapter, page 212.)

Good News: Farts usually break up pretty quickly, so if nobody has smelled yours within a few seconds, you've gotten away with it. (This is *not* true if you are in a small space like an elevator, a classroom, or Rhode Island.)

Bad News: Your nose will never be more sensitive to bad smells than when you are about 10 years old. So if you're in a small space like an elevator, a classroom, or Rhode Island, breathe through your mouth just in case.

How to Avoid Blame: Okay, you feel a bomb coming on and you're in a public place. What to do? If you're seated, don't innocently lean over to the side to let it out. Take it from me, this has never fooled anybody. Way back in 1530, a man named Erasmus wrote, "*Do not move back and forth in your chair. Whoever does so looks like he is trying to bomb!*" (That's almost an exact quote.)

Let's say you're at school and you accidentally drop a bomb in class. Try coughing or dropping a book to cover up the sound. If you can't do that, *blame the dog*! Oh wait, the dog's not in your class! Oh well, you will have to act innocent. If you have a friend nearby, give him an accusing glance to suggest he did it. If anyone accuses *you* of bombing, remember the classic comeback line: "*He who smelt it, dealt it!*" Or, if there is no denying that it was you who bombed, just smile and wave at the people around you and say, "Just trying to make you feel at home!"

Remember: Politeness is important, so try to avoid bombing in public if possible. Say, "*Please pardon me,*" if you do bomb in public. You're lucky to have that right; in China 2,500 years ago, it was illegal to bomb in front of other people. Finally, never try too hard to push a bomb out. You might be *very, very sorry*. You've heard the old expression, "Where there's smoke, there's fire"? Well, where there's a bomb, there's poop! Your body can tell the difference between poop and gas, but it has trouble with liquid. So if you have diarrhea, sit on the toilet every time you think you have to bomb.

OTHER TERMS FOR BOMBS

flatulence

backdoor trumpets

air biscuits

morning thunder

cutting the cheese

barking spiders

depth charges

butt bongos

wind beneath your wings

laying an egg

stink-tail

THE MOST AMAZING ACT IN THE WORLD

Joseph Pujol (1857–1945) was a French stage performer whose nickname was "Le Pétomane"—*The Fartomaniac*. As a child, Joseph was told that he must avoid swimming. The problem was that the water would go into Joseph's back end, and he would begin to sink! Joseph soon found that he had the rare ability to bring air in through his rear end. He could then let the air back out and make sounds while doing so. In other words, he could make butt bongos any time he wanted to, and they didn't smell! Joseph could bomb in many different sounds and for incredible lengths of time. Some of his imitations included cannons, thunder, all types of dogs, different birds (including ducks and owls), bees, frogs, and pigs. As a show closer, Le Pétomane would blow out a candle. He almost always got standing ovations, and during his peak, he earned more money per performance than any other entertainer in Paris.

FUN BOMBING FACTS

 Boys and girls bomb the same amount, but girls hold them in more to be polite, so their bombs are probably bigger.

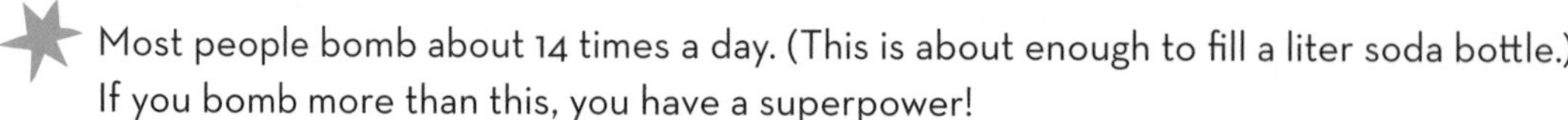

- Most people bomb about 14 times a day. (This is about enough to fill a liter soda bottle.) If you bomb more than this, you have a superpower!

- The Dog Did It! If your dog has bad gas, you aren't feeding it the right kind of food; its intestines can't digest the food properly, creating gas.

- The Beaver Did It! Native Alaskans enjoy a delicious dish called "stinky tail." It's not what you think; it is fermented beaver tail, which is made by burying the beaver tail in a pit for weeks or even months.

- The Elephant Did It! Elephants do drop huge bombs, but luckily they don't smell too bad. The *worst smelling* bomber in the animal kingdom (besides your dad) might be the turtle. The *loudest* bomber in the animal kingdom is the donkey. But the animal that bombs the *most* is the termite! Their bombing is actually causing global warming. (Hey, if you ate wood, you might have some digestive problems too.)

CREATURES DEPARTMENT

There are some gross animals out there and the leech is definitely one of them. Leeches are relatives of earthworms; they live in very wet environments and they want to suck your blood. Leeches range in size from tiny to more than 2 feet. Leeches may clamp onto your legs, but they also like to swim to a dark crevice where you won't find them, like your armpit, your butt, or worse! (No, I did not make that up. Luckily, these types of leeches are usually only found in Africa, Asia, and islands in the Pacific and Indian oceans.)

Leech "bites" are painless, so you probably wouldn't notice if a leech has attached itself to you. If you find a leech on you, don't cut it off. You could cut it in half, and it would keep sucking. In the movies, adventurers often put the lit end of a cigarette on the leech to make it let go, but since you don't smoke, this won't work. Instead, put salt, lemon (or lime) juice, or an ice cube on the leech. Then it will let go.

Inside of you may be another foul creature. Tapeworms anchor themselves deep in the guts of animals (like you!). They then hang out, eating the food that is passing through you. Don't worry, though, they don't get very big . . . just up to 100 feet long or so! (See, your guts go around and around inside of you . . . and so does the tapeworm!)

Probably the most disgusting creature in the water is the lamprey. This is a fish that looks like a combination of an eel and your worst nightmare. Baby lampreys live under mud and ooze out mucus and phlegm that traps victims long enough to be eaten. When baby lampreys are big enough, they swim after their food. They have a mouth that is round and a tongue that will saw through the skin of its victim. See, when a lamprey sees another fish that looks like good suckin', it attaches itself to the fish and sucks out all of its life-juice. That's right, lampreys suck.

As gross as the lamprey is, it's not much worse than the slime eel, or "hagfish." This delightful denizen of the deep is covered in mucus, which discourages other fish from coming near it. The slime eel is made up entirely of intestine; it has no stomach. It swims along the bottom of the sea floor and looks for fish that are either dead or sick. The slime eel then goes in the fish's mouth or gill or eye and eats it up from the inside out, using its tooth-covered tongue to scrape the food to bits. *Blech!**

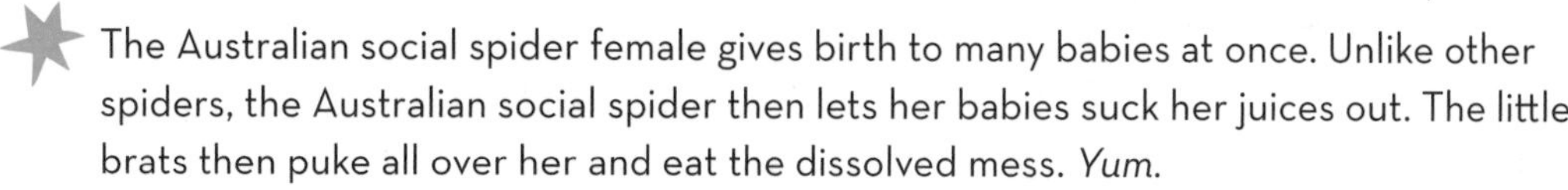

- The Australian social spider female gives birth to many babies at once. Unlike other spiders, the Australian social spider then lets her babies suck her juices out. The little brats then puke all over her and eat the dissolved mess. *Yum.*

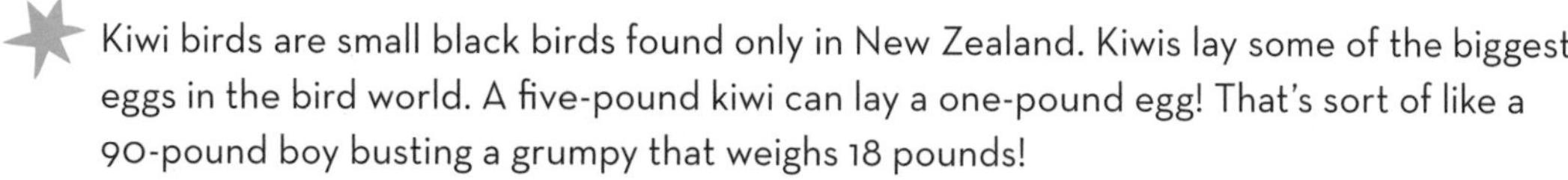

- Kiwi birds are small black birds found only in New Zealand. Kiwis lay some of the biggest eggs in the bird world. A five-pound kiwi can lay a one-pound egg! That's sort of like a 90-pound boy busting a grumpy that weighs 18 pounds!

- A Spanish visitor once saw a number of bags in the palace of Montezuma, the ruler of the Aztecs (an ancient Native American people). The visitor thought the bags were full of treasure, and opened them up. The bags were full of squirming lice! The Aztec people believed that even if they were broke, they could still show respect to Montezuma by picking lice off their bodies and giving the creatures to him.

DANDRUFF AND HAIR DEPARTMENT

Dead skin is falling off of you all the time. About 80 percent of the dust in your house comes from dead skin cells. If we added up all of your dead skin and dandruff, more than a half pound of it falls off of you in a year. Try saving yours up and then using it for confetti at a party!

Bald people are lucky. Not only are they more intelligent than most people, but we (oops, I mean "*they*") usually don't have the dandruff problems that people with hair do. That's because hair keeps dead skin cells from falling away from the body. Instead, the dead cells get clustered together and break off in bigger chunks of dandruff, or "*seborrheic scruff,*" as the doctors call it. Hurray for bald people!

---

* And remember, the third Wednesday of October is the time to celebrate Hagfish Day!

People have been shampooing, dyeing, clipping, and shaving their hair ever since humans have been around. It seems silly to spend so much time on it. Three out of five American women color their hair, but men can be just as foolish. In ancient Rome, men combed earthworm paste into their hair to keep from going gray. (They also rubbed bear grease on their heads to keep from going bald!)

 Hey, Fat Head! In your room are tiny dust mites that eat your dandruff. But your dandruff is so high in fat that the mites have to wait for a fungus to lower the fat content before they chow down. "*Mmmm . . . dandruff!*"

FOOD DEPARTMENT

I can remember coming into the kitchen one morning and seeing my mom frying something up in a pan. It looked like scrambled eggs, but it was sort of *blue*.

"What is that?" I asked.
"Scrambled calf brains," my mom answered. "Want some?"

Yech! My mom also liked to make *headcheese*. To make this, she would take a pig's head, remove all of its meat (you know, the lips, eyes, tongue, cheeks, snout, etc.), wrap it in a cloth, boil it, stick it in the refrigerator, and leave it there. When she came back to it later, a clear gelatin had magically formed over the whole mess. She would then stick the headcheese on a cracker and eat it with a smile. Not good!

Different cultures enjoy different foods. In the American Southwest there is a low-fat meat that tastes a lot like crab called "rattlesnake meat." Over 60 million guinea pigs get fried up in Peru each year, and they eat cats there too. (They say it tastes like rabbit.) But eating cat might be preferable to some Chinese foods like worm soup or sun-dried maggots.

I think you can see where I'm going with this: foods can be scary or ugly or disgusting. One of the scariest foods on the planet might be a snack that natives of the Amazon Basin sometimes enjoy: tarantula! Tarantulas can be barbecued or roasted on the coals of a fire in a large leaf. Those in the know say it tastes like shrimp, not chicken.

There are many ugly-sounding foods. For example, there is a cold Polish soup called "Chlodnik" ("*Another bowl of delicious Chlodnik, dear?*"). Other favorites of mine are "bladder wrack" (an edible seaweed), "bloater" (a dried fish), "Skum Saus" (a scummy sauce from Norway), and "Bratklops" (German fried meatballs). But it is hard to beat "*Wiener Krapfen*" for a bad name. Is it a combination of wieners and, uh, you know? Nope, it's a doughnut in Austria.

One of the *ugliest-looking* foods in the world might be a fungus called *smuts*. Smuts is a parasite that grows on corn or other grains. It looks like a sooty, gray tumor. Some say that it also *tastes* like a sooty, gray tumor. Another dish that isn't very pretty is an Icelandic meal called "Svid." To make Svid, cut off a lamb's head. Boil it. Eat it. You don't mind your meal looking back at you, right?

But for the world's most *disgusting* food, our judges have narrowed it down to four contestants. Coming in fourth place is a Vietnamese food called "Nuoc Mam." It is made by burying fish in salt until they digest themselves with their own stomach acid and then turn into fish sauce. Yummy!

In a tie for third place, we have two similar recipes. From Iceland is a dish called "Hakarl." To make it, take a shark and remove its guts. Then hide the shark in a wooden barrel for three years. When you come back, it should feel like cheese and smell like, well, like a fish that you left in a barrel for three years. Now eat it! Another crowd-pleaser from China is called "Pi-tan." Soak some chicken eggs in a liquid made of tea leaves, lye, and a couple of other ingredients for about three months. Then bury them for four years. After you've built up your appetite for that long, dig the eggs up, peel them, note the green yolks and delicious odor, and swallow 'em down!

Coming in second place is a French meal called "Yeux de Veau Farcis." You may have noticed that cows have fairly big eyes. Well, for this recipe, you'll need two of them. Boil the cow eyes for a minute, cut out any part that isn't white, and stuff them with mushrooms. Now you're ready to fry up a couple of eyeballs!

In first place (drum roll, please) is the Scottish New Year's recipe for "haggis." Get a sheep's stomach and fill it with oatmeal, fat, and a sheep's cut-up liver, heart, and lungs. Let it simmer for four hours, and then pour Scotch whiskey over the whole thing. (If you're smart, you'll then set the whole mess on fire.) The poet Robert Burns described haggis as "gushing entrails" (and he was trying to be nice!). Scots usually eat haggis with "neeps and tatties"—mashed turnips and potatoes. Once, a shipment of haggis was not allowed into the United States because it was considered "unfit" for humans to eat.

Read My Lips: I Don't Want Any! Once upon a time in Vietnam, orangutan lips were considered a delicious snack.

You know that waxy smell that you get when you open a box of crayons? That smell is *beef fat*. Processed beef fat (called *stearic acid*) is an ingredient in many crayons. A study found crayons to be the 18th most recognized odor in the nation; as for the taste, crayons are somewhere between wax, soap, and beef fat.

PEE DEPARTMENT

If you are average, you pee about 1 to 2 quarts of urine a day. Did you know that all of that fresh pee you're making is actually "cleaner" than your spit? That's because no bacteria can live in pee. And to think that you *swallow* spit . . . hmmm. Actually, because fresh pee is mostly water (with some salt and unneeded proteins) it is so clean, you *can* drink it. (I'm not saying you *should* drink it.) Believe it or not, you have drunk pee before. We all drink pee before we are born because the fluid we float in contains our own baby pee! The famous world leader Mahatma Gandhi drank a bit of pee each morning to get his day off to a p-p-perfect start.

An interesting thing about pee is that it has no odor. Even if you take vitamins and eat asparagus, your pee won't stink until it begins to break down. Of course, as soon as your pee hits the air, it breaks down, so that's why it can be smelly when you're pretending to be a firefighter.

A sensitive subject for many boys is bed-wetting. Don't feel bad if this has been a problem for you. One out of every seven kids is a bed-wetter! (One percent of all 18-year-old boys still wet the bed.) If you are worried about bed-wetting, try eating some crackers or having a spoonful of honey before going to bed. Either of these items will help you retain your water. (In ancient Rome, they used to make bed-wetters eat boiled mice, so we've come a long way!)

One last thing: your pee is also as warm as you are when it comes out. This means that whenever you are in cold weather, you should try to write your name in the snow in big yellow letters!

 Love Is a Prickly Thing! Male porcupines look for their mates in the autumn. When the male porcupine sees a female, he sprays her with pee to see if she's interested in him. If she stays, she likes him. Now that's love!

USEFUL ADVICE

You're in class and really need to pee, but you don't want to say "I need to go to the baffroom" in front of other students. Instead, raise your hand and say, "I need to micturate." All teachers know that this means you have to go pee, and will give you a hall pass!

IMPORTANT WARNING

If your pee is a dark brownish-yellow color, you need to drink more water. Your body needs lots of clear fluids to flush itself out properly, and soda doesn't cut it.

A MORE IMPORTANT WARNING

Never pee on an electric fence! You see, water conducts electricity, and . . . oh, it's just too awful to think about.

COLORFUL SAYINGS

"*Full of pee and vinegar*": This means "full of life."
"*Go pee in your hat*" or "*Go piss up a rope*": These mean "get lost."
"*Pee into the wind*": This is used to describe anything foolish or futile.
"*It's a pisser*": This means "it's amazing."
"*Pissing and moaning*": This means "complaining."

FUN PEE FACTS

 Average pee times—girls: 80 seconds; boys: 45 seconds. Wee-wee win!

 Birds don't pee at all. Their pee mixes with their poop, sometimes turning it white.

 Ancient Romans brushed their teeth with pee and also used it as mouthwash. They thought pee kept teeth firm in their sockets and white. (Talk about "potty-mouth"!)

 That's What I Call "Holding It!" When bears hibernate during the winter, they never get up to go pee in the woods. Their body simply reuses the fluids.

That's What I Call "Holding It" Too Long! Tycho Brahe (1546–1601) was a famous astronomer from Denmark who was very polite. It was customary to not get up from the dinner table to pee until the meal was finished. Some people believe that Tycho "held it" too long at the dinner table one night, and his bladder burst. Pee is poisonous, and Brahe apparently died of pee poisoning days later.

POOP DEPARTMENT

Did you know that some of your strongest muscles are deep *inside* your body? These muscles are there to keep your digested food moving along. That's right, you have a Play-Doh Fun Factory inside of you! The muscles squeeze in a wave-like motion called *peristalsis* (pear-ih-STALL-sis), so that poop is always moving through your system.

After your digestive system has taken the vitamins and water from your food, what's left over is what scientists call "poop." About one-third of the food you eat becomes poop. This includes a lot of vegetable and grain fibers. Most of the rest of it is bacteria. (Up to one-fourth of your poop can be bacteria!) It eats at the poop as it goes through your intestines, and the bacteria leaves behind chemicals that make your poop stink. The more bacteria in your poop, the more it stinks. Add some "bile" from your gall bladder, which helps break down fats and gives your poop a nice brownish-green color, and you're ready for a very special delivery.

But your special delivery may never arrive if there is not enough water in your body. If you are dehydrated, your poop will dry out and slow down in your guts. (Some people call this

a *plugged drain*, a *logjam*, or *clogged plumbing*.) It's like dry plaster is inside of you; it will move slowly, and when it comes out, it will be hard and painful. If your poop doesn't come out, try jumping up and down, eating some prunes, and drinking a lot of water to break up that plaster!

If the food you ate is not agreeing with you, something weird happens: your body tries to get it *out* of you as soon as possible! Instead of water being taken *from* the poop, water is *added* to it to make it run through your guts fast, like water through a pipe. When it comes out the other end, we call it DIARRHEA!

POOP TALES!

Diarrhea caused one of the best scenes in the film *Indiana Jones and the Raiders of the Lost Ark*. In one part of the film, Indiana Jones is attacked by a swordsman who is doing amazing tricks. Indy just pulls out his gun and shoots him. This scene was supposed to be much longer and would have taken three days to film, but actor Harrison Ford *really* had to go. (He had picked up a bad case of diarrhea on location.) Ford and director Steven Spielberg came up with this much shorter solution to the swordsman scene.

FUNNY THINGS TO SAY WHILE POOPING

"Look out below!"

"Captain, we have a message from the poop deck."

"Get out the chain saw, 'cause here comes a tree trunk."

"I busted a grumpy!"

SOME CATEGORIES OF POOP

Diarrhea: It can burn!

Floaters: They float!

Sinkers: Guess what they do?

Two-flusher: That's a big one!

Water Breaker: A log that starts at the bottom of the toilet, and in one unbroken piece, breaks the surface of the water.

OTHER TERMS FOR POOP/POOPING

night soil
voodoo butter
bowel movement
hazardous material
doody
doo-doo
caca
Lincoln logs
number two
answering nature's call
unhitching a load
dropping kids off at the pool

 Historical Poop Removal! If you are Scottish, you should feel proud. Your ancestors were the first people who could go to the bathroom indoors. Hurray! The earliest plumbing systems ever found are in Scotland. They're 10,000 years old, and yes, they still smell a bit.

 Modern Poop Removal! When astronauts bust a grumpy in outer space, the poop is dried and brought back to Earth for scientific analysis. The astronauts have to store it carefully; they wouldn't want to see a dried log floating around in zero gravity.

 Disgusting Item! Vultures enjoy eating rotting meat, but they worry about standing on a dead animal and getting their feet infected. To solve the problem, they poop on their own feet before perching on a corpse. Apparently vulture poop can kill even the toughest germs!

 Even More Disgusting Item! Eating your own poop is pretty nasty, but some animals do it; this is called "coprophagy" (kop-PROF-ah-jee). Beavers have a fairly high-fiber diet, and they have to digest their food twice. Here's how it works: The beaver eats its food (tree bark) and digests it. The beaver then poops out what looks like a gelatin/oatmeal mix. What next? The beaver then eats its poop and digests it a second time. When it comes out this time, it looks like sawdust. *Sawdust!*

 Historical Poetry! Toilets and good sewage systems make life healthier for the people who use them. In historical times, getting rid of sewage was not always done very well, as this 600-year-old poem shows us.

In days of old, when knights were bold
And toilets had not been invented,

They laid their load by the side of the road
And went away, contented.

SCABS, SCARS, AND BRUISES DEPARTMENT

You got a charley horse on your thigh and now it is turning greenish blue. It's bruise time! The bruise usually starts out purple and ends up a strange type of yellow as your body tries to deal with the injury. The problem is that you're bleeding on the *inside* of your body. What you are seeing is blood that has burst out of the blood vessels inside of you.

Maybe you actually got a cut or some "road rash" from falling off your bike. You bleed some, and then the blood clots form a scab. Once your cut has scabbed up, you may notice that it shrinks over time, causing some pinching of the skin. It's almost like your body is trying to sew the wound back together. This is also likely to cause some itching to occur, which is why people often pick at a scab.

Scab-pickers are not the lowest form of life there is, but you just know that if someone picks their scabs, they pick their nose too. It only makes sense! Anyway, sometimes a cut is so big or deep that a scab can't repair all the damage that's been done. In those cases, the body forms "connective tissue" to repair the damage. The flesh won't look the same as it was before the injury, and we call what is left a "scar."

Scurvy is a disease that sailors used to get because of a lack of Vitamin C. What happens if you have scurvy? First the victim gets loose teeth, rotten gums, and joint pain. Then scabs stop healing and actually turn back into open wounds. Finally, old scars open up again; it's as if time was going backward! Old healed broken bones break again! Scurvy used to be so common among sailors, one-third of a ship's crew often fell victim to it as late as 1800. If you want to avoid it, suck on an orange.

SNOT, BOOGERS, AND SPITTING DEPARTMENT

You've got a lot of *mucus* in you. The wet mucus in your nose traps nasty things like dust and germs from the air that you are breathing in. But what is this mucus made of? Well, besides the dirt that lands on it, mucus is made of water, a little salt, and a little bit of a sticky protein called *mucin*.

Mucus can dry up after it traps enough dust and dirt, and then it turns into a booger, which needs to be removed. You should know that 70 percent of people admit that they pick their boogers regularly; that means that 30 percent of people *lie about it*! If you see someone picking their nose, call them a "*rhinotillexomaniac*" (ri-no-til-ex-o-MANE-ee-ack). That's fancy talk for a "nose-picker." You probably know one of these types. Heck, you probably *are* one of these types! Ever pick and flick? You know what I'm talking about! It's not so bad that you picked your nose; it's what you do with the booger that's gross.

Out of all the nose-pickers in the world, 3 percent of them pick a winner and *eat it*! That is disgusting. Boogers aren't dead brain cells, so you won't get any smarter by eating them!

Now the fact is that a lot of your snot ends up going down your throat. As a matter of fact, you drink about a quart of snot a day by swallowing it. Don't worry, the acid in your stomach kills any germs that are in your mucus. In addition, your snot can lubricate your throat and help you when you need to spit. This is called "*hawking a loogie.*"

As you probably know, you hawk a loogie by coughing a little bit and bringing up some of that snot in the throat. You then get it in your mouth, and "*Patooie!*" Hawk it! Loogie spitting contests are fairly disgusting, and therefore a lot of fun. Most of these contests revolve around who can spit their loogie (or "lootch") the farthest. The best you can hope for is that someone will fail to get the loogie away from themselves, and it will end up on their shirt. That always cracks me up.

I once had a neighbor who could do very well in these contests simply by firing snot directly out of his nose. He would close one nostril with his finger and blow or snort out the other one. *Wham!* These snot rockets would fly a good distance. My neighbor called them "*Hoboken zephyrs.*"

Here is a nose tip: If you have to blow your nose in front of other people, when you're done, don't look into the tissue as if precious stones fell out of your nose. They didn't. And if you thought it was a booger, it's snot.

YOU SURE KNOW HOW TO PICK A WINNER.

 Spittin' Fish! Archerfish can spit at distances over 3 feet very accurately. They spot bugs on overhanging branches from below the water, come up near the surface, and snap their gill covers shut. Wham!

- Your eyes get dried mucus in them while you sleep. The stuff is sometimes called bed-boogers or eye-snot, but to be accurate, it is "gound."

- People in China spit anywhere they want to. Because of the air pollution in many of the cities, they find it best to clear the soot and gunk in their throat and nose by leaving loogies all over the place.

- Cool Word! "Ambeer" is the spit juice from chewing tobacco. Come on . . .

FUN SNOT FACTS

- For a time, there was a delicious candy on the market called Snot Candy. It came in a big plastic nose. To get the gooey candy out, you had to stick a finger up the container's nostril. Of course, Snot Candy had a mascot: everyone's favorite superhero, Loogie Man!

- There is an Eskimo tribe that has a unique solution to a baby's stuffed nose. The mother sucks the snot out of the baby's nose and then spits it on the ground!

- We all know what diarrhea is, but did you know you can have the same problem from your nose? "Rhinorrhea" (ri-no-REE-uh) is the word used to describe a lot of really runny mucus coming out of your nose.

ZITS

Are you getting a little grossed out yet? After all, I've been writing about the most disgusting things imaginable for a whole chapter! So I'm going to write as little as possible about zits so that you don't blow chunks. Zits are little pus pockets that form on your body. During your teen years, your body starts making hormones called "*androgens*" and suddenly you have much more oil in your skin than before. The excess oil can get trapped in the sweat pores of your skin, forming whiteheads. When dirt gets trapped with the oil, blackheads appear. If these get infected with bacteria, pus is made and *ta-dah*! A zit is born!

I hate to give you bad news, but here it is: boys produce 10 times more of these hormones than girls, so boys are *10 times* more likely than girls to get really bad acne. You know that old poem that says, "*Girls are made of sugar and spice and everything nice*"? Back in the old days, this line was "*Girls are made of sugar and spice and not very much androgen.*"

If you don't have zits already, get used to the idea, because the odds are that you will have at least some. What a rip-off, huh? If it makes you feel any better, eating chocolate does not make your acne any worse.

Dang it—the chapter's over? But I have so much more to say! So if your favorite hobbies are reading, pooping, and barfing, be sure to read my revolting book *The Big Book of Gross Stuff*!

FOLLOW-UP ACTIVITY

Interview a medical doctor for your school newspaper. Tell him that you want to invent your own internal organ and name it after yourself. Explain to the doctor what your organ does. (Hopefully, it is something disgusting.) Ask the doctor if he has any advice for you. Watch him carefully to see if he tries to call a nurse for help getting rid of you.

HALLOWEEN!

October 31 ("All Hallows' Eve")

Why does Halloween exist? To boost the sales of candy companies? To give dentists some extra business during the slow winter months? Let's find out!

A version of Halloween was first celebrated by the *Celts* (kelts), a group of people who once lived in Ireland. The Celts believed in elves, fairies, and supernatural beings. These "wee folk" had many names: *leprechauns, bogies, brownies, knockers,* and *pookas.* And all of these troublemakers came out on the last day of October, which was called *Samhain*! A saying from the old days was, "*On Samhain, there's a bogey in every stile.*" Although this sounds like a painful medical condition, a *stile* is a doorway, and you know what a *bogey* is, so stop picking them! (If you've heard of the "Bogey Man," this is where the name comes from.)

The Celts believed that the spirits of the dead could come back on this Samhain night. These spirits would tell each other dumb jokes (*Spirit One:* What kind of mistakes do ghosts make? *Spirit Two:* Boo-boos!) and frighten the living. Celts also feared that as winter came and the days grew shorter and colder, the sun would be destroyed. To save the sun and honor the forces of darkness, the Celts had a unique ceremony.

WOW! EARTH IS A FUN PLACE! I FIT RIGHT IN!
TRICK OR TREAT

Huge bonfires were lit on hilltops to burn sacrifices, to guide the ghosts of the dead back home, and to scare off any dark spirits in the countryside. Townspeople would sometimes take an ember with them as they walked to their home. The ember would usually be carried in a turnip or gourd. Because people felt nervous about walking home in the dark, they may have carved scary faces in their ember holders so the spirits would not bother them. (So *that's* where jack-o'-lanterns come from!)

You couldn't usually see the leprechauns during the year because of a magic fog called the *fé-fiada,* which made them invisible to ordinary folk. But on the *last* day of October, this fog disappeared, and the spirits could be seen running around the countryside. The Celts hoped to encourage the good fairies and to protect themselves from the pranks and mischief of the evil ones.

Since ghosts and leprechauns were out having fun on this night, some brave humans imitated them. The Celtic people left out treats of food for the souls of the dead and the goblins, and over time, people began dressing like these creatures and also demanding treats. (This was sometimes called "mumming.")

Christianity eventually came to Ireland, and the Samhain holiday was changed to "All Hallows' Eve" or "Halloween." (The word "*hallow*" means holy.) The day *after* Halloween is *"All Hallows' Day"* or *"All Saints' Day,"* a day to remember all the saints. The old Celtic ritual of Samhain was *combined* with this new tradition.

The problem with All Saints' Day is that it is followed by All Souls' Day. On this day, *any* soul could return at midnight and visit their old haunts. Souls without homes to remember them prowled the countryside . . . *look out*! All Souls' Day is known as *Dia de los Muertos* in Mexico. One tradition there is to heap graves with brilliant orange and purple blossoms and white orchids called *Flor de Muerto,* or "Flowers of Death."

Historically, children born on Halloween supposedly had special powers that let them see ghosts and the future. Halloween was also a time when boys liked to play different games. For example, "*Snap Dragon*" was a Halloween game in which raisins were placed in a bowl of brandy. The brandy was then set on fire, and the contestant tried to get the raisins out without getting burned. If you win, you get to eat the raisins! Yahoo!

When the Irish began to move to the United States, they brought many of their beliefs of leprechauns playing pranks on Halloween with them. Soon, boys began to copy the "wee folk" in playing practical jokes on Halloween. To keep kids out of trouble, some adults encouraged children (the real "wee folk") to dress up as the spirits and goblins themselves.

Nowadays, kids carry on the old Halloween customs by showing up at a doorstep and shouting "Trick or treat!" If a treat is not given to them, children may play a *trick* on the resident. I encourage you to put a leprechaun in the bathroom of any house unwilling to give you a treat.

FUN FACTS

Jack-o'-lanterns! Turnips were used in Scotland and Ireland for jack-o'-lanterns, which were originally used for light sources before there were flashlights. Anyway, the Irish legend is that a man named Jack died, but he was too cheap to go to heaven, and too tricky to get into the other place, so he was forced to wander the dark places of the earth, carrying a turnip for a lantern.

As for **pumpkins,** they are not vegetables . . . they're fruits! Pumpkins have been grown in America for more than 5,000 years. They are native to the Western Hemisphere and were completely unknown in Europe before the time of Columbus. Pumpkins were not used for Halloween until the last few hundred years.

Cats! The "druids" were priests of an ancient religion in France and Britain. They thought that cats were sacred, and that they may have once been humans, but, because of the evil deeds they'd done, were changed into cats. (Since cats are usually either very foolish or very evil, or both, there may be something to this.) Of course, you know what happens if a *black cat* crosses your path, but did you know that the same superstition says that if *a light-colored cat* crosses your path, it's good luck? "Here, kitty kitty . . ."

Leprechauns! A leprechaun looks like a small old man about 2 feet tall. Leprechauns dress with a cocked hat and a leather apron, and they like to spend their time making shoes. They are grumpy and unfriendly . . . but they also possess a hidden pot of gold! If caught, the leprechaun must be threatened with violence to tell where his treasure is, but you must keep your eyes on him. If you look away from the leprechaun even for an instant, he vanishes and so does his treasure! If you lose your leprechaun, I suggest a big bowl of Lucky Charms as a consolation prize. Those little colored marshmallow treats can be as good as gold.

FOLLOW-UP ACTIVITY

Research whether there has ever been a haunted house or ghost sighting in your community. Explore and discover if the ghost (or other creature of the night) really exists. If it does, introduce yourself to it and invite the creature over to your house for an ice cream social.

HOLIDAYS!

Every day of the year is special for someone. For example, think of your birthday. That's your *special* day when we celebrate how *unique* you are. (Never mind that 10 million other people have the same birthday as you!) But as William Shakespeare once almost said, "If every day was a holiday, having fun would be as boring as work."

Now here are some other special days that you might not know about.

JANUARY

January is **National Prune Breakfast Month, National Oatmeal Month, It's Okay to Be Different Month,** and **International "Get Over It" Month.**

January 3: J. R. R. Tolkien's Birthday. *The Hobbit* came out in 1937, and it's still one of the best books ever written. (This is also **Humiliation Day.**)

January 7: Rock Day

January 11: International Thank You Day. Hey, do you know when International You're Welcome Day is? Neither do I. Thanks for nothing!

January 14: "It Boils" Day. This day is called "Pongal" in India, which means, "It boils!" The new rice crop is harvested and boiled. *Pongal!*

January 16: Moby Dick Parade. A day to celebrate the 4,000-mile migration of gray whales from Siberia to Baja California. (Also **National Nothing Day!**)

January 20: Penguin Awareness Day

January 23: National Pie Day

January 27: Thomas Crapper Day. Crapper was an Englishman who helped perfect the flushing toilet in the 1800s.

January 28: Bubble Wrap Appreciation Day

January 29: Dead Animal Rights Day

FEBRUARY

February is **Return Shopping Carts to the Supermarket Month, Low Vision Awareness Month, Canned Foods Month,** and **National Snack Food Month.**

February 2: Groundhog Day. I've never understood this holiday. (Please don't explain it to me; I'm happier this way.)

February 3: Bean-Throwing Festival. In Japan, a day to throw beans into the corners of houses to drive out evil spirits. Hanging sardine heads from your doorway also keeps them away.

February 7: Love Your Robot Day

February 9: Toothache Day. And in Brazil, **Underwear Day!**

February 13: Get a Different Name Day.* For anyone who hates his birth name, today he may change his name to whatever he wants!

February 14: Ferris Wheel Day

February 24: Fastelavn! In Denmark on this day, children can poke their parents awake with decorated sticks. Nursery schools have events called "*Slå katten av tønnen*" (knock the cat off the barrel). Children hit a wooden barrel with a stick and try to knock a stuffed cat off the top!

February 27: No Brainer Day

February 28: Public Sleeping Day. (In other words, take a nap in a public place!)

MARCH

March is **National Peanut Month, National Noodle Month, National Umbrella Month,** and **National Frozen Food Month.**

March 1: National Pig Day

March 6: National Procrastination Day (You can celebrate this at a later date if you want.)

March 9: National Brutus Day (a.k.a. **Backstabbers' Day**)

March 10: Middle Name Pride Day

March 15: Dumbstruck Day

March 17: Submarine Day

March 20: Extraterrestrials Abduction Day

March 22: International Goof-Off Day and **International Day of the Seal**

March 26: Teacher's Day. Hey, in the Czech Republic, all the teachers get gifts from their students on this day. Impress your teachers by celebrating this holiday, and see if it affects your grade!

March 28: Something on a Stick Day

APRIL

April is **International Twit Award Month, National Humor Month, National Welding Month,** and **National Twinkie Month.** April also has **Dumb Week** (celebrated in Greece) and **Cussing Day** (this was historically a day to insult sinners who didn't change their ways). The third Thursday of April is **National High Five Day,** a day when people can freely exchange high fives with anybody. (And don't forget **Black Monday,** the first Monday back at school after spring break!)

April 1: In Scotland, they call this **Huntigowk Day.** Okay, it's also **April Fools' Day.** Things got a little bit confused in Europe about 1,500 years ago. Although most cultures used the Roman calendar (the same one we use now), not all kingdoms celebrated the start of the year at the same time.

In France, the New Year celebration ended on April 1. But in 1562, Pope Gregory introduced a new calendar for Europe, and the new year began on January 1. It was hard to communicate with large groups of people back then; there were no computers or phones or even newspapers. There were some people who hadn't heard of or didn't believe in the change in the date of the new year, so they continued to celebrate New Year's Day on April 1. They were fools. Others played tricks on them and called them "April fools." They sent them on "fool's errands" ("Go collect the teeth of a hen!") or tried to make them believe that something false was true ("*The Big Book of Boy Stuff* is no good!"). Anyway, see the "Practical Jokes!" chapter, page 234, for some good material to use on this day.

April 2: National Peanut Butter and Jelly Day

April 4: Tell a Lie Day

April 6: International Pillow Fight Day

April 7: No Housework Day.* If someone suggests you do some housework, quote the philosopher Baruch Spinoza: "Nature abhors a vacuum."

April 12: Big Wind Day. (So feel free to pass a mighty wind!)

April 14: International Moment of Laughter Day

April 15: Festival of the Sardine in Spain

April 17: Cheeseball Day and **Blah Blah Blah Day***

April 18: International Jugglers Day

April 23: Children's Day in Turkey. This is a time for kids to take over the government and get free ice cream and movies—all day!

April 30: National Sense of Smell Day

MAY

May is **National Get Happy Month, National Hamburger Month,** and **National Salsa Month.** Also, **National Digestive Disease Week** is celebrated at the end of this month.

May 4: Kite Day

May 6: No Homework Day.* Let your teachers know!

May 8: Furry Day

May 11: Eat What You Want Day*

May 13: Frog Jumping Day

May 18: Mike the Headless Chicken Day. Mike was a rooster whose head was chopped off in 1945, but who lived a full year and a half after that! Mike's owner was a farmer named Jeb Olsen. He chopped Mike's head off and then watched the bird flap back to the barnyard. Mike hung out with the other chickens and even tried to eat corn off the ground with no head! Jeb learned to feed Mike with an eyedropper right down his neck hole! He would eventually choke on a kernel of corn that got stuck in his throat and die, but not before he became the most famous headless chicken in the world!

May 23: World Turtle Day

May 24: National Escargot Day. Time to eat some snails!

May 25: National Tap Dance Day

JUNE

June is **National Accordion Awareness Month, National Frozen Yogurt Month, Aquarium Month,** and **National Pest Control Month.** The third Saturday in June is **Hollerin' Day.** And this is also the month the world celebrates **International Pickle Week.** (Sweet!)

June 1: Dare Day

June 6: National Yo-Yo Day

June 8: Best Friends Day

June 18: International Panic Day

June 19: World Sauntering Day

June 20: World Juggling Day

June 24: Stalk Like a Ninja Day (Yes!)

June 26: Shrimp Festival Day. A day to celebrate seafood and short people!

June 27: Ferret Awareness Day

JULY

July is **National Baked Bean Month, National Hot Dog Month,** and **Anti-Boredom Month!** The third week of July is the **Nothing Festival** in Telluride, Colorado. Its motto: "Thank you for not participating." The festival's events include sunrises and sunsets as normal. Also, the force of gravity continues to be in effect. (And there's a parade . . . but you can't see it!)

July 1: International Joke Day

July 4: Turtle Independence Day in Hawaii!

July 6: Nothing Day

July 10: Don't Step on a Bee Day*

July 14: Pandemonium Day

July 15: Be a Dork Day.* This is the day to be a dork and be proud. Wear goofy clothing, don't brush your teeth, eat yucky food, and fall off a swing set.

July 23: "Hot Enough for Ya?" Day

July 27: Take Your Houseplants for a Walk Day*

July 31: Mutt's Day

AUGUST

August is **Foot Health Month** and **National Catfish Month.** August also includes **International Clown Week.**

August 2: National Ice Cream Sandwich Day

August 4: National Sisters' Day (Boooo!)

August 6: Wiggle Your Toes Day

August 9: International Noogie-Givers' Day. A day to sneak up on people and give them noogies!

August 10: Lazy Day. (You'll need to save your energy for what's coming up August 15!)

August 13: Blame Someone Else Day

August 15: National Relaxation Day

August 16: National Tell a Joke Day

August 26: Dog Day

August 30: Frankenstein Day

Last Wednesday of August: The Festival of the Tomatoes (Festival de la Tomatina) in Buol, Spain. More than 800,000 tomatoes are used in this colossal tomato fight. The streets run red to celebrate a time when a tomato cart was knocked over in the town decades ago, resulting in an argument and a tomato fight. Go figure!

SEPTEMBER

September is **National Little League Month** and **National Mushroom Month.** It also includes **National Dog Week.** Oh, and the last week of September is **National Eczema Week** in the United Kingdom.

September 2: Beheading Day

September 6: Read a Book Day

September 10: Hot Dog Day

September 12: Destroy All Video Games Day. This is a day to reflect on the influence of video games. (A big video game bonfire usually follows. FIRE!)

September 13: Fortune Cookie Day and **Defy Superstition Day.** So eat a cookie, read your fortune, and then crumple it up and defy it. (Unless the fortune is a really good one!)

September 14: National Cream-Filled Doughnut Day

September 19: Talk Like a Pirate Day. Avast, matey! You scurvy dogs will be swabbin' the poop deck if you don't talk like a pirate today! Ahoy, me hearty! Arrr! (See the "Talk Like a Pirate" special feature, page 261, for tips.)

September 23: Checkers Day

September 25: National Comic Book Day

September 28: Ask a Stupid Question Day. Example: What is the best type of cookie to make a mattress from? (Stupid answer: Fig Newtons are soft, but still provide back support.)

OCTOBER

October is **Sarcastic Month, National Toilet Tank Repair Month, National Pretzel Month,** and most importantly, the **Month of the Hedgehog.** October includes **National Pickled Pepper Week** and **Hug a Vending Machine Week.**

October 4: World Animal Day

October 9: Moldy Cheese Day and **Curious Events Day**

October 12: International Moment of Frustration Scream Day.* Go outside and scream for 30 seconds!

October 13: Skeptics' Day

October 14: Be Bald and Be Free Day*

October 15: National Grouch Day

October 18: No Beard Day

October 21: Babbling Day

October 24: National Bologna Day. *Yes!*

October 25: Punk-for-a-Day Day

October 29: Laugh Suddenly for No Reason a Lot Today Day

October 29: The Feast of the Dead. Once every 12 years, the Iroquois Native Americans held their Feast of the Dead. A huge common grave was dug. All tribe members who had died during the past years were reburied together and honored with prayers. Almost all the wealth of the dead was given away or buried in the earth to give comfort to the dead. The values of the Iroquois hold that any wealth or possessions not needed for survival should be sacrificed to the gods or given to the dead, not kept by the living. The worst sin to these people was for a tribe member to focus on possessions instead of *trying to be the best person they could be.*

NOVEMBER

November is Peanut Butter Lover's Month and International Drum Month. It also includes **National Split Pea Soup Week** and **National Make Up Your Own Week Week!**

November 3: Cliché Day

November 4: Chair Day and **Mischief Night**

November 5: Gunpowder Day

November 6: "Do Tater Tots Ever Grow Up?" Day

November 8: Dunce Day

November 17: Take a Hike Day

November 20: Absurdity Day

November 21: False Confession Day

November 22: Start Your Own Country Day

Thanksgiving is held on the fourth Thursday this month. The tradition started in 1621 with the Puritans in New England. But the Puritans celebrated Thanksgivings (plural!). Anytime that something really good happened ("The pirates are gone!"), it was time to have a festival and give thanks.

So how many Thanksgivings did the Puritans celebrate? Sometimes as many as nine a year! So don't just have Thanksgiving *once* a year. The next time something good happens ("The ninjas are gone!"), break out the gravy!

DECEMBER

December is **Read a New Book Month** and includes **National Hand-Washing Awareness Week!**

December 5: Krampusz Day. He's incredibly ugly. He's seven feet tall and carries a stick. And his name comes from the German word for "claw"—*Krampusz*!

I'm talking about Krampusz, the scariest mascot of the Yuletide season. He sort of looks like a hairy giant with a goat's head. For 800 years, Austrians have dressed up as Krampusz on this day. Then they go around the neighborhood knocking on doors. If children answer, Krampusz rings a cowbell and scares the kids to make them REALLY look forward to the arrival of Saint Nicholas.

In the town of Schladming, there's a huge parade of people dressed as Krampusz and ringing cowbells. What fun! As they say in Austria: "*Krampusz gerne Partei*" ("Krampusz likes to party"). So remember, if you hear cowbells today, don't answer your door!

December 9: Boring Celebrities Day

December 21: National Flashlight Day

December 23: Night of the Radishes

December 26: National Whiner's Day

December 28: Card Playing Day

December 31: Unlucky Day and **You're All Done Day**

FOLLOW-UP ACTIVITY

Discover a lost tribe of primitive people. Impress these primitive people with a laser pointer and maybe some card tricks. After they make you their king, have them celebrate your birthday with a great festival where you get many presents. (Don't let the fact that the presents are mostly rocks and leaves ruin it for you.)

* These holidays were discovered by Thomas and Ruth Roy. More information at www.wellcat.com/holiday.html.

INSULTS!

Marge: Kids can be so cruel.
Bart: We can? Thanks, Mom!
—*The Simpsons*

Part of being a boy is enjoying a good insult. I say "enjoying" because boys know that *when done properly,* one of the best parts of friendship can be insulting or dissing your buddies. It's an excellent day when you can hang out with your buds and get in some good zingers. Hey, if you can't laugh at yourself, make fun of your friends!

Just remember that you should only enjoy insults with friends and relatives who are in a *good mood.* Like practical jokes, they are not to be used on strangers or people you do not get along with.

People in different parts of the world define what insults are differently. For example, making an "O" shape with your finger and thumb (*A-OK!*) is fine in the United States, but it is like flipping someone off in Central America. However, there is one body language insult that is the same everywhere: mooning! If you show someone your butt in *any* part of the world, it is always an insult.

In some cultures, the spoken insult is an art form. Sometimes they are curses, like the classic Arab insult, "*May the fleas of a thousand camels infest your armpits.*" (My version of this is "May the jelly of a thousand doughnuts fill your underwear.") A good Yiddish curse is this one: "*May all your teeth fall out, except one—so that you can get a toothache!*" Some cultures have insults that may seem a little strange to an outsider. In the African country of Ghana, a terrible insult is to tell someone that they stink like a river turtle. In New Guinea, never call someone a *yam thief,* or you will have trouble. My

favorite insult is this one from the Swahili of East Africa: "*I curse you, and my curse is that you be what you already are.*" That's cold!

Unfortunately, most American insults are weak. Insults that use the same words that everyone else uses are BORING. So if you insult someone in a boring way, you're insulting *yourself*. Using a "bad word" (or "profanity") is especially idiotic. I mean, the *Oxford Dictionary of English* states that there are 350 useful one-word insults in English. Sweet! And that means using "bad words" is the sign of a poor vocabulary—and a *weak brain*. It's like advertising the fact that you're a nitwit! "*Hey, look at me! I memorized eight bad words!*"

The best insult is the *clever* insult. For these, you need to use words in a *creative* and *original* way. Some of the best examples of creative insults come from William Shakespeare's time (1564–1616). People back then had big vocabularies and they liked to combine words in unexpected ways. The insult was something that inspired great put-downs!

Let's try some examples. You want to tell your friend that he is ugly. Saying "*You are ugly*" will not exactly impress him. Saying "*You are* very *ugly*" is not much better. What if you said, "*You look like a monkey-faced tomato*"? Or "Wow, your FACE! Was anyone else hurt in the accident?" Or even. "On a scale of 1 to 10 . . . you're ugly." Good!

Now how about this: "*You know who would win in a beauty contest between you and a baboon? Nobody.*" *Wow.* That's pretty great!

LET'S PRACTICE

To a friend you want to call "ugly":

Beginner: "You're ugly."

Intermediate: "You're so ugly, when you were born, they put tinted windows on your hospital room."

Advanced: "Can I borrow your face for a few days while my butt is on vacation?"

To a friend you want to call "chubby":

Beginner: "You are chubby."

Intermediate: "You are a wonderful, all-around person. It just takes a while to walk all around you."

Advanced: "You remind me of a map. A globe, to be exact."

To a friend who just got a haircut:

Beginner: "Your haircut stinks!"

Intermediate: "Did a lawn mower attack you?"

Advanced: "Hey, nice haircut. Was it half-price day at the barber shop?"

To a friend who is short:

Beginner: "How's the weather down there?"

Intermediate: "I've heard of half-pints, but you must be a quarter-pint."

Advanced: "Do you know why you aren't allowed on ships? Because you have to ride in a shrimp boat."

Genius: "I don't trust short people. Their brains are too near their butt."

To a friend you want to call "stupid":

Beginner: "You are stupid!"

Intermediate: "Want to see something stupid? Look in a mirror."

Advanced: "Brains aren't everything. In your case, they're nothing."

Genius: "I don't think you're stupid. But what is MY opinion worth against the thousands of people who disagree with me?"

To a friend who sings with a bad voice:

Beginner: "Your voice stinks."

Intermediate: "You couldn't carry a tune if it had a handle on it."

Advanced: "Your voice could peel scales off a donkey's butt."

To a friend who just insulted you:

Beginner: "Oh yeah?"

Intermediate: "You must be tired of living. Prepare to die."

Advanced: "Now I know this isn't a perfect world, because you are in it."

SPECIAL FEATURE: READY-MADE INSULTS

Combine two of the adjectives from columns **One** and ***Two*** with a noun from column ***Three*** to create an insult you can be proud of! Don't worry—even if you don't know what some of the words mean, they still sound great!

One	*Two*	*Three*
gap-toothed	surly	dipstick
crawling	wretched	monkey
diseased	pusillanimous	numbskull
mangled	rotten	wussy
silly	prune-faced	cheese-eater
dumb	chicken-hearted	fish face
blubbering	foot-licking	chucklehead
infected	blabber-mouthed	fink
impudent	foul	moron
noisy	repulsive	maggot
creepy	cowardly	scoundrel
slack-jawed	greedy	lout
lumpy	poisonous	vermin
mangy	filthy	ape
puking	freakish	dolt
puny	miserable	clod
stinking	bawling	shrimp
low-down	scurvy	blockhead
spongy	grubby	parasite
cheating	cheesy	twerp
slow-witted	fiendish	nincompoop
grinning	greasy	toad
vain	stuttering	nitwit
pimply	baboon-breathed	villain
warped	tiny-brained	tootyface
subnormal	loopy	acorn brain

Here are some other words you may wish to slip into your creatively insulting speech. (All of these are "real" words!)

barkled: Covered with dirt. "*Your zits are so bad, you'd be better off barkled.*"

bluntie (BLUN-tee): Scottish term for a dumb person. "He is not keen or sharp; he's a bluntie!"

bromidrosis (brom-uh-DRO-sis): Stinky sweat. "Good grief, look at those pit stains! And even worse, you have bromidrosis!"

cacafuego (ka-ka-FWAY-go): A person who brags. This word means "*poop-fire*" in Spanish; the person thinks they're so hot, even their poop is on fire!

cepaceous (suh-PAY-shus): Smelling like an onion.

chichiface (CHEE-chee-face): Someone with a bony face.

cockalorum (kok-uh-LOR-um): A little squirt who thinks he's a big shot.

conky: A person with a big nose. "*Holy shnozz-ola! Look at that conky!*"

diamerdis (dye-uh-MURD-is): A person covered in poop.

dunderwhelp: A complete nitwit.

fopdoodle: A chowderhead.

fubsy: An overweight person; a doughboy.

furfuraceous (fur-fur-AY-shus): Covered in dandruff.

gink: A nerd or a nobody.

gleet: The phlegm found in the stomach of a hawk. "*You call this food? It's covered in gleet!*"

gongoozler: A nitwit who stares at things.

gubbertush: Someone with big teeth.

gundygut: A slob, especially when eating.

igly: Really, *really* ugly.

imbulbitate (im-BULB-uh-tate): To poop in one's pants. "*From little Timmy's expression, we knew he had imbulbitated.*"

micrencephalus (my-kren-SEF-uh-lis): A person with a really tiny brain.

mucopurulent (myoo-ko-PURE-yoo-lent): Containing a mix of mucus and pus.

plooky: To be covered in zits. "*Not only are you barkled, you are very plooky too.*"

protohuman: A primitive form of a person, not really human at all.

scombroid: Looking like a fish.

slotterhodge: A sloppy eater.

slubberdegullion (slub-er-de-GULL-yun): A slob.

smatchet: A small, nasty person.

stinkard: Someone who stinks.

verrucose (ver-OO-kose): Covered in warts.

whiffle: A pipsqueak, a twerp.

zowerswopped: Bad tempered.

FOLLOW-UP ACTIVITY

Give someone a nice, sincere compliment.

JOKES!

A researcher from Norway has found that children laugh an average of 400 times a day. That's pretty good! Unfortunately, adults only laugh an average of 15 times a day. That is *pitiful*! Maybe you get all the laughter out of your system when you're a kid. So enjoy your laughs now while you can!

Funny things happen to boys like you all the time. Let's say you want to go out skateboarding with your friends. Your mom or dad gives you permission, but they say, *"Be careful! Don't get hit by a car or crack your head open on the sidewalk. And remember to be polite!"*

That's funny! Of course, you were *planning* on getting hit by a car, cracking your head open, and then being rude to the ambulance driver.

The things that make people laugh come in different categories. Some jokes are gross or sick, and we laugh at them out of surprise. Sometimes if something bad (but not *too* bad) happens to someone, we laugh at the person's bad luck. And sometimes a joke is so *stupid*, it's funny. This chapter has a few examples of all these types of humor.

As you tell these (or any) jokes to other people, watch them carefully. Researchers have found that if a person is *really* laughing, they will close their eyes for a moment. If a person laughs

without closing their eyes, they're *faking* it! Don't worry, though, as many of these jokes are so good, it will be hard to open your eyes and stop laughing as you read them.

 The Funniest Joke in the World! In 263 BC, a Greek comedy writer named Philemon discovered the world's funniest joke. This joke was so funny that Philemon laughed to death after his discovery. (From his notes, we know the joke had to do with a goose and a lawyer.) More recently, a 24-year-old carpenter in the Philippines was told a joke by a friend. The carpenter thought the joke was so funny, he laughed until he cried, collapsed, and then died. (Although I know what the joke was, I cannot tell it to you for your own safety.)

 The Funniest Animal in the World! In 2002, a British study of humor released its findings. Almost two million people from all over the world rated different types of jokes in an attempt to discover the funniest joke in the world. (Some of the jokes in this chapter are from this study.) One of the interesting things they found was that ducks are the funniest type of *animal* used in most different jokes. So, if you are going to tell a joke, try to work a duck into it.

SCHOOL AND STUDIES

Father: From this report card, son, it looks like you studied underwater.
Timmy: What do you mean, Dad?
Father: Well, all of your grades are below "C" level!
Timmy: Good one, Dad.

History teacher: Timmy, name one important thing we have now that we didn't have 12 years ago.
Timmy: Me!

Science teacher: Can anybody define the word "canal" for me?
Prissy girl: A canal is a small stream of water, made by humans.
Timmy: You bet we do. Heck, I make those all the time!

Father: What did you learn about today?
Timmy: Our science teacher told us all about fossils.
Father: Did you learn much?
Timmy: Yeah. Before taking her class, I didn't know what a fossil looked like.

Timmy: Yahoo! Our science teacher said we'd have a test today, rain or shine!
Dan: Yeah, so why are you so happy?
Timmy: It's snowing!

Teacher: Timmy, why are you tardy again?
Timmy: You started class before I got here!

Timmy: Hooray! Today's the last day of school! I'm free! I'm free!
Preschooler: So what? I'm *four.*

FAMILIES

Timmy: My dad says that you can make ice cream out of anything. You can make chili pepper ice cream, avocado ice cream, tomato ice cream, anything!
Noah: Oh yeah? I bet you can't make ice cream out of cow poop.
Timmy: Why not? They're both dairy products!

Father: Hey Timmy, did you notice? I bought a new toilet brush for your bathroom.
Timmy: I noticed, but I still prefer toilet paper.

Timmy's pregnant mother: Timmy, I'm going into labor! Call the hospital!
Timmy (on the phone): Send help! My mom is going to have a baby!
Nurse: Calm down! Is this her first child?
Timmy: No! I am!

Timmy: Dad, please don't make me go to summer camp with my sister. I'll give you 20 bucks if you keep her at home!
Father: Why Timmy, she's your only sister! Think of all the years you've spent with her.
Timmy: You're right. I'll give you 40 dollars, but I'm not going any higher.

Mother: Timmy, how do you get so dirty?
Timmy: Well, I'm a lot closer to the ground than you are.

Timmy: Dad's got holes in his underwear! Dad's got holes in his underwear!
Father: No, I don't!
Timmy: Then how do you get your legs through them?
Father: Good one, Timmy.

Timmy: Dad, can I steer the car down the road?
Father: Timmy, what did I tell you when you asked me the same thing yesterday?
Timmy: You said I could drive the car when I was older.
Father: So?
Timmy: So I'm 24 hours older now.

Mother: Timmy, what did your father say when you threw the baseball through the kitchen window?
Timmy: Do you want me to leave out the bad words?
Mother: Yes, please.
Timmy: He didn't say anything.

DOGS

A girl is eating a hamburger when she notices a dog is watching every move she makes. The girl breaks off a piece of the hamburger and calls the dog over. It politely advances.
"Speak!" the girl commands. "Speak!"
"Under the circumstances," the dog replies, "I hardly know what to say."

A boy is in a movie theater and sees another boy and his dog both watching the movie intently. After the movie, he goes up to the dog owner.
First Boy: I saw your dog watch that whole movie. It's amazing!
Second Boy: I know . . . he hated the book.

A golden retriever and a boxer are in the front yard, barking at cars.
Golden retriever: Ruff, ruff!
Boxer: Bark, bark!
Golden retriever: *Mooo! Mooo!*
Boxer: Hey, what the heck are you doing? Dogs don't say, "Moo."
Golden retriever: I'm studying a foreign language.

First boy: My dog doesn't have a tail.
Second boy: But how do you know when he's happy?
First boy: He stops biting me.

"QUESTION AND ANSWER" JOKES

Q. What's the difference between snot and cauliflower?
A. Kids will eat snot.

Q. How do you catch a unique rabbit?
A. Unique up on him.
Q. How do you catch a tame rabbit?
A. The tame way. Unique up on him.

Q. What did the fish say when he hit a concrete wall?
A. "Dam!"

Q. What's yellow, smells like bananas, and sits at the bottom of a tree?
A. Monkey barf.

Q. What kind of a primate can fly?
A. A hot-air baboon.

Q. What do you get when you cross a turkey with a centipede?
A. Drumsticks for everyone!

Q. What do you call a fish with no eyes?
A. Fsh.

Q. What's red and looks like a bucket?
A. A red bucket.
Q. What's blue and looks like a bucket?
A. A red bucket in disguise.

Q. What's green and has wheels?
A. Grass. I lied about the wheels.

Q. What did the apple say to the banana?
A. Nothing—apples don't talk.

Duck Joke Alert
Q. Why do ducks have webbed feet?
A. To stamp out fires.
Q. Why do elephants have flat feet?
A. To stamp out burning ducks.

A HUMOROUS RECOMMENDED READING LIST

The Yellow River by I. P. Freely

Make a Million Dollars in One Week! by Yu Dum Gai

Whoopee Cushions and You by Mike Easter

Eggs, Toilet Paper, and Your School

Timmy, the Boy Who Was So Bad, His Family Kicked Him Out by B. Goode

The Little Sissy Who Told on His Friends

Why Can't the Fork and the Electrical Outlet Be Friends?

Oreos and Me: A Love Story by Chin Tu Phat

Whining and Crying to Get Your Way

Spots on the Wall by Hu Flung Dung

Places Where Mommy and Daddy Hide Neat Things

The Tiger's Revenge by Claude Nutz

The Curious Cat and the High-Voltage Fence by Kitty Gobybye

STORY JOKES

A sixth-grade boy named Timmy was in charge of taking his little brother to school for the first day of kindergarten. As Timmy got on the school bus, the bus driver stopped Timmy and said, "Timmy, who is *that*?" while pointing to his little brother.

"That's my little brother," said Timmy.

"Just between you and me," the bus driver whispered, "that's the ugliest kid I've ever seen."

Timmy grabbed his little brother's hand and walked back to a seat with an angry expression on his face.

"Hey, Timmy, what's wrong?" asked one of his friends.

"That bus driver just said something really rude and mean to me," said Timmy.

"When we get to school, you should go tell the principal," said his friend.

"Really?" Timmy replied.

"Yeah," said his friend. "You go ahead. I can watch your pet monkey for you."

Jokes!

A burglar watched a house carefully for a couple of days. After making sure that nobody was home, he broke into the house in the middle of the night.

As the burglar stuffed goodies in his bag, he was horrified to hear a deep voice say, "*God is watching you!*"

"Who's there?" the burglar cried, swinging his flashlight around. Then he saw a large parrot in a cage, and the parrot said again, "*God is watching you!*"

"Heehee," the burglar said. "What's your name, birdie?"

"My name is Edmund," the parrot answered.

"Edmund? Who names their parrot *Edmund*?" the burglar asked.

"The same person who names his pit bull *God*," said the parrot.

One morning after waking up on his 10th birthday, Timmy told his mom, "I had a dream that you gave me a BB gun for my birthday. What do you think that dream means?"

"You'll know what it means tonight," Timmy's mom said with an encouraging smile.

That night, after the birthday cake, Timmy's mom came in with a long narrow package and gave it to her son.

Timmy tore the box open. *Finally I get a BB gun,* he thought. But he thought wrong. The box was empty except for a book called *The Meaning of Dreams*.

Two boys are hiking in the deep woods. One boy suddenly stops and takes off his backpack.

The second boy asks, "What's wrong?"

"I just saw a huge bear down the trail watching us," the first boy says as he takes off his hiking boots and starts putting on his running shoes.

The second boy says, "I understand taking off your backpack, but you can't outrun a bear just because you're wearing running shoes."

The first boy responds, "I don't need to outrun the bear. I just need to outrun *you*!"

The world-famous detective Sherlock Holmes and his assistant Dr. Watson decided to go camping. They backpacked into a remote area and pitched their tent. That night, the stars came out, they had a campfire and some conversation, and then they crawled into a thin tent and went to sleep.

Sometime later that night, Holmes woke up Watson.

"Watson, tell me what you can deduce from looking up at the stars," he said.

Watson was puzzled. "Well, there are thousands of stars up there. Assuming that there are enough stars with planets, there is a possibility that some of those planets may have life like we have on planet Earth."

Sherlock Holmes shook his head. "Watson, you chowderhead, somebody stole our tent!"

There was once a boy named Be Quiet, and he had a little brother named Trouble. One day, Trouble got lost and Be Quiet went to the police station.

The police officer asked, "What's your name?"

The boy answered, "Be Quiet."

The police officer frowned, and repeated, "What's your *name*?"

"Be Quiet."

Angry now, the police officer asked, "Are you looking for *trouble*?"

Be Quiet answered, "How did you know?"

Two boys named Bill and Tyrone went hiking. As they walked along, the two boys argued about the best way to treat a snakebite.

"I'm telling you, the best way to treat a snakebite is to cut an "X" into the wound and suck the blood out!" said Bill.

"Whatever," said Tyrone.

Later that afternoon, Bill went off to get firewood. While he was out of Tyrone's sight, he started screaming. Tyrone quickly ran to him.

"What is it?" Tyrone asked.

"I was bit by a rattlesnake!" Bill said, pointing. And sure enough, a big diamondback rattlesnake slithered away even as he pointed at it.

"Tyrone, you know what you have to do! Do you have a pocketknife?" Bill asked.

Tyrone nodded and got his pocketknife out. "Where did you get bit?" he asked.

Bill pointed to his rear end. "Back here," he said.

Tyrone looked at Bill. "I hate to say this, but you're going to die," he said.

Three brothers, named Dante, Buddy, and Tyler, each decided to get their dad a special birthday gift.

Dante said, "Since he likes to golf, I'm going to get a set of golf bags for the old man."

Buddy said, "You know how Dad likes to go bird hunting? I've decided to get him a hunting dog!"

Tyler shook his head. "You know how Dad hates to read but likes being read to? I've decided to buy Dad a parrot. The parrot *can* read; it's specially trained, and if you set a book in front of him, it will read the book out loud. It's an expensive bird, but I think he's worth it."

The other two brothers were amazed!

Later, the father wrote his sons their thank-you notes.

"Dante," he wrote, "I've given up on golf. It's too expensive and the people who play it are idiots. Thanks for the thought, though!"

"Buddy," he wrote, "I've matured in my old age. I now realize that hunting is a cruel sport. Plus, that dog you sent has awful gas. But thanks for the thought!"

His last note went like this: "Dear Tyler: You were always my favorite son. Thank you for the thoughtful gift. That chicken was delicious!"

Two boys named Brian and Jeremy went to the zoo. They went to the primate section and looked into the gorilla cage.

"I wonder if I can get the gorilla to imitate me?" said Brian.

"Fat chance," Jeremy replied.

So Brian made a face at the gorilla. Amazingly, the gorilla made the same face back at Brian! Brian then stuck his thumbs in his ears and waved his fingers around. The gorilla stuck his thumbs in his ears and waved his fingers around. Brian and Jeremy smiled at each other.

Brian stuck his tongue out at the gorilla. *The gorilla went bananas!* It jumped up and down, screamed, pounded his chest, and then burst out of his cage, grabbed Brian, and slammed him onto the sidewalk. The gorilla then went quietly back into his cage.

As medics and zoo workers rushed to the scene, Jeremy asked the gorilla's keeper why the ape had gone so berserk.

"It's because your friend stuck his tongue out at him," the zookeeper said. "In gorilla language, that's like flipping someone off."

When Jeremy visited Brian in the hospital, he told him what the zookeeper had said. Brian didn't care. He wanted revenge on that great big ape.

Brian was eventually released from the hospital. He went home and got a soft rubber hammer that his little brother used as a toy. He also got a real hammer. Brian then went to the zoo and walked right up to the gorilla's cage.

The gorilla looked at Brian. Brian made a face at the gorilla. The gorilla made the same face back. Brian smiled at the gorilla. The gorilla smiled back. Brian threw the real hammer into the cage and held up the toy hammer. The gorilla held up the real hammer. Brian then hit himself in the head with the soft toy hammer.

The gorilla paused and then stuck out his tongue.

A boy went in to the doctor for a follow-up on an earlier exam. The doctor says to him, "I have bad news and really bad news."

"Huh? What's the bad news?" the boy asks.

"You only have 24 hours to live," says the doctor.

Stunned, the boy just sits there. Finally, he asks, "How can the other news be any *worse?*"

"I've been trying to get ahold of you since yesterday," says the doctor.

Two boys named Daniel and Albert were cutting wood in the forest, but they weren't being careful, and Daniel cut off his arm! Albert wrapped Daniel's arm in a plastic bag and took it and Daniel to the hospital. The doctor told Albert, "I can reattach it; just come back in 2 hours." And 2 hours later, the arm was as good as new!

A month later, Daniel and Albert were out cutting wood again, and Daniel cut off his leg! Albert put the leg in a plastic bag and took it and Daniel back to the hospital. The doctor said, "You kids need to be more careful! Come back in 3 hours." Albert came back 3 hours later, and Daniel's leg was as good as new!

A week later, believe it or not, Daniel and Albert were out cutting wood again. Daniel somehow cut his own head off! Albert knew this wasn't good, but he hoped for the best. Albert put Daniel's head in a plastic bag and took it and the rest of Daniel to the hospital. The doctor said, "I can't believe you kids! Well, come back in 4 hours, and I'll see what I can do."

So Albert came back in 4 hours and the doctor said, "I'm sorry, but Daniel didn't make it."

Albert said, "I understand. He did cut his head off after all."

The doctor said, "Actually, the surgery went fine. It's just that he suffocated in that plastic bag!"

Two boys are hiking in the woods. Suddenly, one of them falls to the ground. He doesn't appear to be breathing.

Luckily, the other boy has a cell phone and he calls 911.

"911! 911! My friend is dead! What should I do?" he asks.

"Slow down," the operator says. "Don't worry, okay? Now, let's make sure he's actually dead, okay?"

The operator hears silence, and then a sound like an axe hitting a watermelon. Then the boy's voice comes back on the line.

"Okay, now what?" he asks.

A dog went into a bank to send a telegram. He put a pen in his mouth, and on the form for the telegram's message, he carefully wrote, "*Ruff. Bark. Ruff, ruff. Bark. Ruff.*"

The cashier looked at the form and said, "There are only six words here. You could send another '*Bark*' or '*Ruff*' for the same cost."

"Yeah," the dog answered, "but then the message wouldn't make any sense."

Little Timmy was digging a big hole in his backyard when the next-door neighbor looked over.

"Why are you digging that huge hole?" he asked.

"My ferret died," Little Timmy replied, throwing another shovel full of dirt over his shoulder.

"But why are you making the hole so big?" the neighbor asked.

"Because your dog ate it," Little Timmy replied.

SICK JOKES

Man in grocery store: Your frozen chickens are all too small. Do they get any bigger?
Clerk: No sir, they're dead.

Boy: Dad, I hate my sister.
Dad: Then just finish your vegetables and leave the rest on the plate.

Q. What is big, green, fuzzy, and if it fell out of a tree would kill you?
A. A pool table.

Q. What has four legs and flies?
A. A dead cat.

Boy: Mom, why are we pushing our car over the cliff?
Mom: Be quiet, or you'll wake your father.

Boy One: My cousin died of a bee sting last week.
Boy Two: I'm sorry; was he allergic to bees?
Boy One: No, he was a tightrope walker.

Q. What do you get when you cross a pit bull with a collie?
A. A dog that bites your face off and then runs for help.

Q. Why did the monkey fall out of the tree?
A. It was dead. (*I know this joke is stupid, but it's still funny!*)

WARNING: *This joke is the sickest of all time!*
Q. What is green, lies in a ditch, and is covered in cookie crumbs?
A. A Girl Scout that got hit by a car.

FOLLOW-UP ACTIVITY

Based on the clues provided earlier in the chapter, find out what Philemon's funniest joke of all time was. To avoid dying of laughter, have an antidote to laughter nearby, something that would wipe the smile off of anyone's face. I recommend a picture of your math teacher. (And to learn more about what makes people laugh, check out *Bart's King-Sized Book of Fun*!)

JUGGLING AND YO-YOS!

Every person should have a "trick" they can do; it is almost like having your very own superpower! I think that juggling is a good choice for a trick like this. It is a skill that anyone with two hands can master, but because it takes a little bit of practice, most people can't do it.

So far as we know, juggling has been around as long as there have been people. Ancient civilizations in Egypt, Greece, Mesoamerica, and India had entertainers who could juggle. Throughout history, most jugglers were also people who could sing, dance, mime, and so forth . . . in short, they were interesting people.

Many jugglers had their own specialties. "Power jugglers" worked with cannonballs, anvils, or other heavy objects. Juggling on horseback has long been a favorite; one juggler named Briatori could juggle seven balls from the back of a galloping horse. Another type of juggler was the "salon juggler," a person who juggled different types of objects found in a civilized house: gloves, vases, billiard balls, chain saws, etc. Finally, there have even been *antipodist* jugglers: people who juggle with their feet!

Many people call Enrico Rastelli (1896–1931) the greatest juggler of all time. As a youth in a traveling circus, he often practiced for 12 hours a day until he got a trick right. Many people back then thought it impossible to juggle more than seven balls at once. (This is because there have to be six balls in the air if you are juggling seven!) Enrico proved skeptics wrong by becoming the master of juggling eight balls. (He even juggled 10 balls once, just to prove he could.) Plates are very hard to juggle, but Enrico could juggle eight of these as well. He invented many tricks, and could carry on long conversations while bouncing two soccer balls off his forehead.

As for you, don't worry about becoming the next Enrico Rastelli just yet. This chapter tells you how to juggle three items in a basic rotation. Practice each of the steps before going on to the next step. It takes your muscles a while to build up their "muscle memory," so be patient. Many people can learn how to juggle in a day, but even if you can't, it shouldn't take more than a week if you practice. Practice often, but not for more than 10 minutes at once or you may get burned out. *Stop practicing when you start to get frustrated. Pick up the bags again when you are relaxed.*

What to juggle? There are all sorts of juggling rings, glow-in-the-dark balls, clubs, bowling balls, etc., that you *could* try to juggle with, but small beanbags or actual "juggling" bags are best. I tried learning juggling with tennis balls, but I ended up chasing the balls more than I juggled. This is why most people encourage beginning jugglers to use beanbags. I like to use three hackysacks, but any beanbag or juggling bag works.

Okay, let's start! One good spot to juggle is right next to a bed. That way, when you drop the bags, you don't have to bend as far to pick them up! Or, you can go to a spot where you have a little room to move about. Outdoors is good, but a large room without a lot of furniture works too.

1. Take just *one* beanbag and cradle it in the *palm* of your hand. (Not on your fingertips!) When you juggle, you will do much better if you use your palms. Put your elbows in and extend your arms in front of you at about waist height.

2. Now throw the bag repeatedly from one hand to the other. Try to get the beanbag to go right in front of your eyes with each throw. Try aiming for a spot in front of your head and above where the hand waiting to catch the ball is. Use a nice little arc. As you catch the beanbag, let your hand move down with the beanbag as it falls, then bring your hand up and throw it with a nice rhythm. Your hands should go up and down with the beanbag.

   Keep doing this until it feels natural. You should be able to do this equally well with either hand. When you can do this motion under control (try it with your eyes closed!), you're ready for the next step. Don't move on until you have mastered the one-bag throw or you will get frustrated.

3. Next, take *two* bags. *Whoohoo!* Put one in each hand. Now, remember how you were throwing one bag to the other hand before? You will do that in a moment. The problem is, there is already a bag in the hand you are throwing toward!

What you will do is throw the first bag, wait a moment, then throw the second. **WARNING:** Once you throw that first bag, what you will *want* to do is pass the second bag across to your other hand (the one that just threw the bag). In other words, one bag will go *up* and one will bag go *across* to the hand that threw it. That's not juggling!

Instead, try this: When the *first* bag reaches its peak in front of your eyes and starts going down, throw the *second* bag a little lower than the first bag. Don't panic! Yes, you now have two balls in the air! Just be cool! You throw the first one, wait, and then throw the second one. If your throws are good, the bags will practically land right in your hands. Don't reach up for the bags. Let them come down to your hands. If your throws are bad, go back to the first step and practice your one-bag throws.

Practice this! If you have trouble, try throwing the first bag a little bit higher and the second one a bit lower. Repeat it over and over. Work on a good "throw-throw-catch-catch" rhythm. Once you can do it well, start your *first* throw with the other hand. (You are now juggling two balls!)

I should mention that some people recommend that you begin learning to juggle by putting one hand behind your back and then learning to juggle two bags with one hand. This is a good skill, but it is more difficult than the technique I describe here.

4. Once you have the two-bag throw down, you're ready to do some real juggling. The moment has come! Get the third bag! *Yes!*

   Okay, stand in your position. Put two bags in one hand, and one in the other. (For my example, let's assume that the two bags are in your left hand.) Here is the idea: You will throw a bag from your left hand to your right hand. Just like you normally do, you then throw the ball from your right hand to your left.

   Instead of catching and holding the bags when they land, you will now keep throwing them. The *first* bag you threw is now landing. The *second* bag you threw is about to land in the hand holding the *third* bag. Before it gets there, *throw the third bag*! If you are normal, you will now drop the bags. Pick them up and try again.

   This time, try counting the bags as you go. Count *one, two, three* as the different balls leave your hands. You know that you can get two throws down . . . keep reaching for that third catch! There is usually just one bag in the air, and it is going to switch places with one of the other two. After a while, you will learn to only pay attention to this bag. Once you can catch the third bag, you are juggling. With practice, you will find a good rhythm and three catches will become 300!

Problems: The most common problem is that you will lose your rhythm and start throwing the bags to spots where you have to reach out to catch them. Remember, keep your hands extended in front of your waist and let the bags come to you. It's okay to reach out for a bag, but if you find yourself racing across the room to catch them, go back to juggling by the side of the bed or in front of a wall. This will force you to make good throws to yourself.

The best advice? Relax and let the bags come to you. Keep your hands moving up and down with the bags. Throw the bags to that spot in front of your head and above your hands.

ADVANCED JUGGLING

At some point, you will be able to juggle three bags very well. The question then becomes "*What next?*" One good thing to practice on is juggling while walking around. Or change the items you are juggling. Try the "two bags and an apple" trick. (In this trick, you take a bite out of the apple while it is moving through your hands.) Or juggle cell phones! Some people like to juggle "clubs" and other items that are available from juggling stores.

The most obvious thing to do is to teach a friend how to juggle and then practice passing items between you. If you can both juggle three items, you can do it! Or, try to learn how to juggle four bags! When you are ready for your next juggling challenge, go to your library for a good book on juggling, or check the Internet: there are probably juggling clubs where you live that you don't even know about.

- Looking for a wet juggling challenge? Try "gluggling"! You gluggle by going underwater with lead balls and juggling them!

- The most common injury among professional jugglers is "bruising" according to a *Juggler's World* survey.

- Juggling records do change over time, but right now, the record for juggling with balls is 12 catches with 12 balls! And to think that you complained about three!

- **Q.** What has two heads, looks really stupid, and knows how to juggle?
  A. Sorry, I forgot you don't have two heads. (BOOM! JUGGLING SLAM!)

YO-YOS

Yo-yos are the oldest toy that you'll ever play with. (Dolls are older, but you don't play with them, do you? You play with "action figures!") People in China were playing with yo-yos 3,000 years ago. Yo-yos are fun to goof around with or to take seriously; using them may even be an Olympic sport someday . . . really!

Yo-yos have been popular in the Philippines for hundreds of years. (The word "yo-yo" means "come back" in the native language of the Philippines.) Like the Frisbee, the first yo-yos in the Philippines may have been used as weapons, with strings as long as 20 feet. They were much larger than toy yo-yos are today, and they were thrown around an animal's legs to trip it up.

In the 1920s, a man named Pedro Flores moved from the Philippines to Southern California. He often played with small yo-yos in his new home, and he noticed that people seemed to like this "new invention," so he started a yo-yo company. In 1929, a businessman named Donald Duncan bought this company from Flores for $25,000, which is why you may be familiar with the brand name Duncan Yo-Yos. (Donald Duncan also invented the parking meter. *Hip-hip hurray!*)

Yo-yo popularity has its ups and downs; they have been so popular at times that adults have frowned on them and called yo-yoing "the idiot's pastime." Since the yo-yo has been around for thousands of years, it's a good bet that they'll be around the world for at least another couple of weeks. In that case, maybe you should learn a few tricks.

YO-YO TYPES

If someone asks you if yo-yos are cool, just say, "Yo." Why do you think rappers use the word so much? As you look at all the different kinds of yo-yos, you may wonder which kind you should get. The basic yo-yo model (sometimes called a "fixed axle yo-yo") is usually the best place to start. More expensive models (like the "ball-bearing transaxle") are terrific, but you need to be able to do a few string tricks before you get one. Get any yo-yo you want, but if you spend two bucks, you'll get what you paid for!

Okay, so let's say you've unpacked your yo-yo. Keep the manual! It will give you important tips on restringing and taking the yo-yo apart. As for the yo-yo's string, take the loop that is already tied into the end of the string and push the string through the loop to make a slipknot. Put your finger through that and try a few motions.

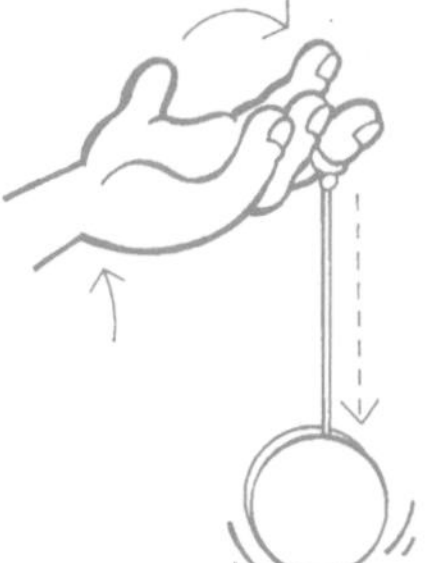

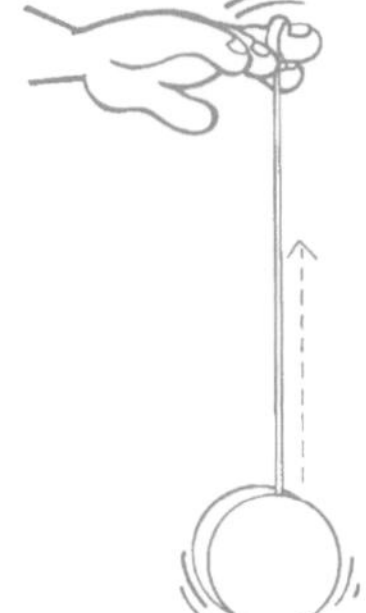

To check and see if the string is too long, take the yo-yo and let it dangle to the ground at the string's full length. Where the string meets your belly button is where you should tie the loop.

The Power Throw! Wind your yo-yo up and get it into starting position as shown in the picture on the left at the bottom of the previous page. Raise your hand up almost to your ear, then quickly throw your hand down in front of you, releasing the yo-yo as you do. Stop your hand around your waist and turn it so that the palm is now facing down. When the yo-yo gets to the bottom of the string, give a slight jerk and catch it on the way up. That's it!

The Hand Jumper! Throw your power throw, but as the yo-yo comes back up, don't catch it! Let the yo-yo jump over your hand and head right back down. If the yo-yo isn't going fast enough to make the jump, keep doing this one until it is!

THE TRICKS

As you practice your tricks, remember not to *reach* for the yo-yo. If you spin and throw it correctly, it will come back to you. Remember that a twisted string is the most common problem for yo-yoers. To untangle your string, hold the yo-yo by the string's loop, let it hang, and watch the yo-yo spin itself back into business. You may get a nasty knot in your string doing a trick. If so, try to use a needle or pin to undo it; if you're having trouble, ask a parent to help. If the string ties itself tightly around the axle, twist or "unscrew" the yo-yo to loosen it.

Sleeper: This is the first trick most people learn. Make a good power throw, but don't jerk the yo-yo back. It will reach the end of its line and start spinning, or "sleeping." If you can get your yo-yo to sleep for 15 seconds, you are pretty awesome. If you can get it to take a nap, you really rule.

Walking the Dog: Get a good sleeper going, and then just lower the yo-yo to the ground, where it will begin rolling away until you jerk it back up. Try the "*Buzz Saw*" version of this, where you Walk the Dog across newspaper. It makes a cool sound! Or do a "*Creeper*": start Walking the Dog. *Let* the yo-yo creep forward and keep lowering your hand to the floor. When you get close to the ground, give a sharp jerk and bring the yo-yo back to your hand. Or, Walk the Dog and let go of the leash altogether to see how fast your yo-yo rolls away!

Forward Pass: Pull your yo-yo hand back as if you were going to bowl. Then snap your hand forward, releasing the yo-yo. It will spring forward and then snap back to your hand.

Most Muscular: Make a muscle with your bicep in a bodybuilder pose. ("*The beach is that-aways!*") Then snap the yo-yo out to the side. It will go out and start to sleep. Swing it sideways across your body and bring it up to your other shoulder, sideways across the front of your body. If it is really humming, it may appear to hang in the air for a moment! As it reaches the other shoulder, tug it back to you.

Inside Loop: Start with a Forward Pass, but don't catch the yo-yo when it comes back. As it returns, use your wrist (not your arm!) to shoot it out in front of you again. With practice, you can do this over and over. Try doing one loop up high, one loop down low, etc.

Around the World: Do this one outside or in a room with high ceilings. Start with a Forward Pass and keep your arm moving up and around (without pulling back) so that the yo-yo sleeps. Go all the way around with your arm trying to keep the yo-yo at the end of its string. When you are ready to pull it in, give it a tug. (Extra credit if the yo-yo goes into orbit around the planet.)

The Butt Stopper: Wise old men of yo-yoing sometimes whisper about this legendary trick. You need to be wearing baggy shorts or pants for this one. Spread your feet a couple of feet apart and do a vicious power throw between your legs, arcing the yo-yo so that it comes up and hits your butt as a Sleeper. Give it a little tug. What may happen is the yo-yo stops dead when it jams the fabric of your shorts into its space. To someone watching from the other side, it looks like butt magic. Try it and see if you can get it to work!

The Cradle Will Rock: Everyone has heard of Rocking the Cradle, so you may as well learn it. Practice this with a "dead" yo-yo hanging from the string before doing it "live." Throw a good Sleeper. Pull the string close to your body and reach down with your off hand to about halfway down the string. Fold the string over this hand (with its palm facing up) right at the base of your fingers. With your yo-yo hand, pinch the string about 5 inches above the yo-yo. Push your free hand forward while bringing your yo-yo hand up. Swing the spinning yo-yo back and forth in the triangular space, then flick the yo-yo out and bring it back to you.

Pop the Clutch: Begin with a strong Sleeper. Next, turn your hand up and start swinging the string to the outside of your arm. Once the string is behind your arm, bring your hand forward so that the string rests on your upper arm, behind your elbow. Reach back with your yo-yo hand and pinch the string above the sleeping yo-yo. Pull the string up and forward a little bit, and then let go. The yo-yo will zip up over your shoulder and start arcing back down. Let it fall all the way down vertically, and then pull it right up. The clutch has been popped!

There are many other tricks to learn, but space doesn't allow me to go into them all. Some are exotic and dangerous, like the Machine Gun, the Falling Gymnast, the Mustache Waxer, the Rattlesnake Bite, and others. If you are interested, I suggest you find out about them by reading a book.

Slang News! The word "yo-yo" can mean "a fool." I always thought that when my dad said to me "You yo-yo," he was saying that I knew how to use one!

The famous French general and emperor Napoleon liked to play with yo-yos! As a matter of fact, yo-yoing was a favorite of French nobility for a long time. During the French Revolution (1787–1799), many nobles yo-yoed as they were taken to the guillotine to have their heads cut off. Now those were dedicated yo-yoers!

- Yo-Yo Criminal! In 1968, a man named Abbie Hoffman was being investigated by a special committee of Congress. (This is very serious business!) Hoffman brought his yo-yo with him to this investigation, and "Walked the Dog" for them. The committee was not amused, and they found Hoffman in contempt.

- I am working on the invention of a "stringless yo-yo." I'll let you know when I'm done.

FOLLOW-UP ACTIVITY

Impress the neighborhood kids by juggling a bowling ball, a running chain saw, and a feather while at the same time doing yo-yo tricks. (This will take a little bit of practice.)

MAGIC!

Is there really such a thing as magic? Yes. If someone *thinks* something is magic, then it is magic! For example, pretend that you'd never seen or heard of electricity. One day, a mysterious woman with a cape shows you a dark room. With a swirl of her cape, a magic word—and the unseen flick of a switch—the room lights up!

"*How did you do that?*" you would ask.

"*Magic!*" she would reply. And guess what? You *would think* it was magic.

Doing magic tricks for an audience is a blast; it's fun to try to fool people! And because there are an unlimited number of magic tricks, it gets you thinking about creative tricks that you can come up with yourself.

One important tool of the magician is *misdirection*. This is what the magician does to get you to look away while they perform the "trick." This is why professional magicians wear cloaks, swing their wands around a lot, and have assistants that don't wear much clothing. It is to distract you!

A good way for *you* to use misdirection is to always have a live grizzly bear with you when you perform. (I'm just making sure you're paying attention.) Actually, a real good way to misdirect people is to say something random, like "Watch closely; at NO time will my head leave my body!" or "If you take a look out that window there, you will notice a giant spider."

Better yet, ask someone a question just as you're getting ready to do your trick. *What* the question is doesn't always matter, just ask it. "What did you have for breakfast today?" "Is your hair naturally that color?" That sort of thing.

Another way to use misdirection is the *emphasis* you use on certain words. Here is a trick question that works almost every time because of *misdirection.* You say the following sentence quickly (but clearly) to your audience: *"I have two normal U.S. coins in my pocket right now. These two coins total 55 cents."*

(In your next sentence, you say the word "one" quietly and really *emphasize* the words in *italics*): "Please keep in mind that one of these coins is *not a nickel*! One of these coins is *not a nickel*! What are the coins?"

People will often be stumped by this question because of your *misdirection.* Your audience focused on the phrase "*not a nickel*" and so they can't figure out how this could be. (The answer to the question is that *one* of the coins is a 50-cent piece and the *other* coin is a nickel. See, *one* of the coins is not a nickel, but one of them is!) That's misdirection for you.

You don't need to worry about having a costume or putting on a big show for magic. Just look at how famous magician David Blaine got his start. He dressed in jeans and a T-shirt and performed tricks for people in the street. Blaine called this "street magic." Street magic is magic that doesn't require an accent, top hats, wizard robes, or even a lot of props.

Here are some tips for *your* street magic: First of all, don't tell your audience exactly what you will be doing; let the trick speak for itself. Also, if you do a good trick, *don't do it again right away*! It is never as impressive the second time. If your audience requests it, just smile and tell them, "Sorry, I used up all the magic for that one."

If you like, come up with your own phrase when you do a trick. David Blaine says "*Look, look!*" a lot. "*Abracadabra,*" "*Presto,*" and "*Allakazam*" have been around for a long time, but there are many other choices. A magician named Ali Bongo liked to say "*Hocus Pocus, Fishbones Chokus.*" If you're using a snake in your trick, try "*Abrada-cobra.*" (That's a joke.) And magician Al Flosso said "*Happis Crappis,*" which is tough to beat.

Most importantly, don't tell how you did *any* magic trick! Remember, the fun part is *thinking* that it's magic. Even though people may be curious as to how the trick worked, when they find out, they are almost always disappointed. If someone asks you, "How did you do that?" you should reply, "Can you keep a secret?" After they say "Yes," tell them, "So can I."

For this chapter's tricks, you don't need any special supplies or amazing abilities. Anyone can do them! They are arranged from easiest to more challenging. Be sure to practice the tricks in front of a mirror before you try to perform them for an audience, or you may have some disappointed customers.

A magician from New York named William Robinson thought his act would be more interesting if he pretended he was Chinese. When he performed, he did so under the name Chung Ling Soo. Robinson would even use a translator when he spoke with reporters to make his persona more real.

The Most Dangerous Trick in the World! No, it's not pulling a bloodthirsty rabbit out of a hat. It is the trick called the "bullet catch." The idea is that someone fires a gun at the magician and then he catches the bullet in his teeth. To date, over a dozen magicians have lost their lives either doing the trick or from complications after the trick has been performed.

FAKE MAGIC

Let's start with some tricks that are incredibly easy. These are all fun because you will pretend that you are going to do a magic trick, and then show your audience just a trick. (What a treat!)

X-RAY VISION

Tell your audience, "I can see through walls." If anyone disagrees, try to make a friendly bet. After you have accomplished this, walk to a window and look out. Ta-dah!

THE BOOMERANGING PENCIL

Pick up a pencil (or any object you can throw). Tell your audience, "I can make this object fly *through* the air, come to a stop, and then reverse its course back to my hand!" Your audience will be suspicious, trying to figure this one out, so add, "I will not *bounce* it off anything or *spin* it in any way."

Let them murmur and be amazed; when you are ready, take the pencil, toss it straight up in the air, and then catch it on the way down. *Magic!* (Actually, *gravity*!)

YOU AREN'T PSYCHIC, YOU'RE PSYCHO

Tell your audience, "I can predict the score of *any* soccer game before it starts with 100 percent accuracy." Let that sink in for a moment, then challenge them. "How do I do it?" Typically, your audience will have a few guesses, and then you can start giving hints.

Tell them, "I can also predict the score of any *hockey* game before it begins with 100 percent accuracy." String them along for a while, adding different sports to the question. Don't let it go too far or someone will figure it out: the answer is that the score of any game *before* it starts is zero to zero!

THE "NO-MAGIC" MAGIC TRICKS

1. This is a card trick in which you never touch the cards at all. Just get out a deck of cards and have your volunteer shuffle it a few times. (More than a few times if it's a new deck.) When he's done he should set the deck face down on the table.

   Ask the volunteer to think of two different cards, like a jack and a seven. (The *suit* of the card doesn't matter.) Once he gives you his two cards (let's say a jack and a seven), you are ready. Wave your hand over the deck, act like a spazz, and say a magic word if you have one.

   Say, *"I think the magic is done. Please check through the deck and look for the jack right next to the seven."*

   Your volunteer now goes through the deck, and the jack IS by the seven! He is amazed! What he didn't know is that the odds of two values in the deck being next to each other are better than 60 *percent*! If it didn't work, just say, "*I* thought *that might happen,*" and try again. (For some reason, this almost always works the first time. If it does, don't push your luck by going for twice in a row!)

2. (You have to be able to shuffle a deck of cards well for this one!) Set up a card deck so that the cards go RED, then BLACK, then RED, etc. Put them back into their container, and later pull them out. Tell your audience that you will shuffle the cards, but you will be able to throw them out in RED and BLACK pairs when you are done!

   Shuffle the cards once, being careful not to let big clumps of one side fall in before the alternating pile is worked in. If you can, check the last two cards at the bottom. If they are a red and black pair you're ready. (If they're not, drop the deck accidentally and forget the trick!) Begin throwing cards face up two at a time onto the table. Put down one pair and then, next to it, put the next pair. It will probably work!

SLOW DOWN THE BEAT

In this trick, you will convince your audience that you have the ability to slow your heart rate down. All you need is a rubber ball. A tennis ball works well, but so does a rolled-up sock. Before the trick, put the ball a little low in your armpit. Now you're ready!

Have a volunteer take your pulse on the arm holding the ball. Make sure that he can feel your pulse beat before you start "slowing your heart down."

Once the volunteer can feel your pulse, start slowly squeezing the ball with your arm. Squeeze *slowly* and *gradually*. Your volunteer shouldn't notice you doing it, and you don't want to change your pulse rate too fast. You see, as you push the ball against your arm, the ball pushes on the big artery that sends blood down to your wrist. This will slow your pulse down!

Once the volunteer freaks out, stop squeezing the ball and pull back your hand. Don't do this trick more for more than 20 seconds or more than once in a day! (Don't worry, it's not dangerous.)

THE EGG GYMNAST

Everyone knows that you can't balance an egg on its end. That darned oval shape causes them to roll every time. Or does it? Christopher Columbus supposedly used this trick once. Here's the simplest way to do it.

To prepare for this trick, get some raw eggs. Take a couple of the eggs in each hand and shake them energetically for 4 minutes or so. (If you have a helper to assist with shaking them, that's good.) Replace them in the carton, remembering which end of the carton they are in. (You may want to practice the steps below beforehand, so you know it works.)

When you're ready for the trick, pull the egg carton out. Invite your audience to try to balance the eggs with your unshaken ones. Then take a shaken egg and VERY carefully set it on its end. Hold it still with your hand for a few moments. It will stand still if you shook it long enough! (It's because you scrambled the yolk while shaking it!)

COIN MAGIC

Tricks with coins are good because you just might make a little money!

THE NICKEL SOMERSAULT

This is a trick that requires no skill at all. Put a nickel between two quarters. (It's a coin sandwich!) Hold this coin sandwich with your thumb and index finger so that the edges of the coins are parallel with the ground. Your other hand should be 5 to 10 inches below the coins to catch them.

Now let go of only the bottom quarter! Both the quarter and nickel will fall. However, even though the nickel was on TOP of the quarter when you let go, it will end up UNDER it. Try it!

MAKING MONEY

For this trick, you will need a handful of coins and a hardcover dictionary. You decide what kind of coin you will use and how many of them will be included. (In this example, there will be eight dimes.)

Before getting your volunteer, you need to secretly slip three of the dimes into the spine of the dictionary. The coins will go into the hole in the binding created when the book is opened.

Now you are ready. Have your volunteer look up a word in the dictionary. "*Earnings*," "*money*," and "*profit*" are all good words to turn to. Pick one of these words and tell your volunteer that if they think about money hard enough, they can make more of it!

Then have the volunteer place the coins in the dictionary's page crease on the page you've turned to. Now it's time for the magic! Close the dictionary, wave your hands, say a magic word, and be dramatic. Then with great intensity, quickly open the dictionary to the page the coins were on and tilt the dictionary up to pour the coins out into the volunteer's hands.

He might be surprised to find that he has made a profit!

DIRTY COPPER

This is the world's easiest disappearing coin trick. To do it, you need a glass jar with a lid and a penny. That's it!

Fill the jar with water and screw on its lid. You're all set to go. Show the penny to your audience so that they know it's real. Then set the penny on the table and, using a little drama, put the jar right over it so that the glass bottom covers the coin. *Happis crappis!* The penny is gone! (Actually, it's still there, but its image is reflecting off of the inside of the jar so you can't see it.)

If you want to be fancy, cover the jar with a cloth napkin as you do the trick to build suspense. After you show the "disappeared" penny, cover it again with the napkin for more magic before removing the jar.

HEADS UP

This is a trick where you will magically know for certain if someone has a coin that is heads or tails. For this trick, you need at least five coins. (It doesn't matter what kind of coins you use.)

First, set the coins on a table. Count how many of the coins have their heads up. Remember that number!

Turn your back to the table. Have the volunteer turn over at least one coin (but not all of them) and say "Artichoke" as he turns over each coin. Every time that you hear "Artichoke," *add one more to your number.*

Now, have him cover one of the coins with his hand. You will be guessing whether that coin is "heads" or "tails."

Turn back around and look at the table. If the number you have in your head is an even number, count how many coins on the table are "heads up." If there is an even number on the table heads up, the coin under your volunteer's hand is a "tails." But if there is an odd number of heads on the table, his coin is a "heads."

If the number you are left with is an *odd* number, when you count the "heads up" coins and there's an odd number of them, his coin is "tails up." And, of course, if there is an even amount of "heads up" coins, his coin will be "heads up."

CARD MAGIC

Card tricks are good to know because the supplies are so easy: one deck of cards! For these tricks, don't let your audience touch the cards or look at them in any way except the way you want them to. Be polite, but firm. Tell the audience you will kill them if they disobey, but say it nicely.

IT'S ALL FOUR YOU

This is the easiest trick of all time! Like many card tricks, in this one a volunteer takes a card from the deck and you magically figure out what the card is.

Before doing the trick, take one of the "four" cards (like the four of diamonds), and place it *fourth* up from the bottom of the deck. Flip it over, so that it faces the other direction from the rest of the cards.

Now you're ready. Have a volunteer select a card anywhere from the pack. (Hold the pack in your hand, so that it is unlikely that they will see the turned four of diamonds at the bottom.)

He should look at it and then put the card on the *top* of the deck. Now cut the deck. Their card is now somewhere in the center of the deck, but your trick is now set up.

Say your magic word, wave your arms, or be dramatic. Now, hand the deck of cards to your volunteer and have them go through the deck until they see a card that is turned around. They'll come to the four of diamonds and say, "That's not my card!"

Act surprised! Then pretend that you remember how the trick went. "Oh yeah, try counting off four more cards from there." They will, and there is their card!

SPECIAL FEATURE: PLAYING CARDS

Here's a piece of card trivia you may not have known: If you add up all the letters in the words "Ace," "Two," "Three," "Four," and so forth, up to "King," you get the number 52. That's how many cards there are in a deck!

Now, there are 52 cards in a deck of cards and there are 365 days in a year. That means that for every card in the deck there is *one week*, because 52 x 7 = 364. What about that *extra* day? It's Joker Day, April Fool's!

A version of playing cards was "invented" in China, but the Chinese cards did not have jokers in the deck. "Joker-less" playing cards were used in Europe in the 1300s, where each card had to be drawn and then painted by hand. (They didn't have printing presses back then.) This meant that each card was a *real* work of art.

In Holland (as the story goes), it was common for the artist of the cards to include one extra card that was a self-portrait. A popular card artist in Holland was Johann Emmanuel Juker (YOO-ker). Juker's cards became so widespread that his style was imitated and the extra card in the deck came to be known as the "Juker" card. It was mispronounced as "JOO-ker" by English speakers, and was finally just called the "joker" card. Since it was called a joker, card-makers naturally put a joker on that card. By the late 1800s in the United States, it was common practice for Mississippi gamblers to have an extra joker card in their decks.

What about the kings? In France, all four kings in a deck were based on a real historic king. The king of spades was King David, the king of diamonds was Julius Caesar, the king of clubs was Alexander the Great, and the king of hearts was King Charlemagne. All of the kings have beards, but only three have mustaches. The one without a mustache is King Charlemagne (or "Charles the Magnificent.")

ROUNDING OFF

Okay, here's another way to find a card that uses an easy strategy. First, you need to know the difference between the "round" cards and the other cards in the deck. The "round" cards are the ones that have a *rounded* number or letter at the top: **2, 6, 8, 9, 10,** and **Q**ueen. (Depending on your deck, the **"3"** may also be a round card.) The "nonround" cards are **4, 5, 7, J**ack, **K**ing, and **A**ce.

Separate the round cards from the others in your deck and you will have two roughly equal piles. You can shuffle these two separate piles if you want. Then place one pile on top of the other carefully, offsetting the top pile slightly so that you know the difference between the piles.

Now you're ready for your audience. You need two volunteers. Hand each of them half of the deck and step away from them. They can shuffle their piles if they want. You want each of them to pick a card from their pile and hand it to the other person. That person will then "bury" the card in their pile. They can still shuffle their pile if they want.

When they're done, take one of their piles and quickly look through it for the card that doesn't belong. It will be easy for you to spot the cards they chose; there is only one round card in the nonround pile, and vice versa for the other pile! Set the card aside without showing it. Now do the same thing with the other pile. When you have both cards, dramatically lift them up! *Wow!*

Variation: Before doing the trick, separate the deck in four piles in this order: ace, two, three (and so forth), up to king. Then combine the four piles. (Don't shuffle!) Now, for the trick, have someone pick a card. Have them memorize it and put it back anywhere in the deck. You can close your eyes while they put it back in. Then look through the deck (but don't spread it out so they can see) and find the card that is out of order . . . *their card*!

THE BOTTOM FEEDER TRICK

This is one of the classic ways to find a card. Here's how to do it. Shuffle the deck once or many times, or let a volunteer shuffle it. Then have your volunteer pick a card from the deck. Don't worry about what card this is.

You need to know what the BOTTOM card on the deck is. You can do this by slyly peeking at the bottom card as you pick up the deck. Another way is to pick up the deck and turn your back to the person who has picked the card, saying, "*I want to make sure I don't see your card.*" While your back is turned, glance at the bottom card of the pile. ***Don't forget this card!*** (For an example, let's say the bottom card was the ace of spades.)

You then turn around again and have the person put their card on the top of the deck. Then "cut" the deck yourself. (This means you remove the top part of the deck and set it *next to* the *bottom* part. You then *pick up the bottom* and put it on the *top*.) Make sure to do this yourself, but in plain sight of everyone. By cutting the deck like this, do you see what happened?

The ace of spades *was* on the bottom. Now, after cutting the deck, it is right on *top* of the card the person picked! All you have to do is take the deck and start turning the cards over in front of the person. A *bad* magician will race through the deck until they get to the ace of spades. He then turns the next card over and says, "Ah ha! This is your card!" *No fun.*

The good magician will make it seem like magic! This means some creativity is in order. For example, you could tell your volunteer that every time a person touches a card, it gets a little heavier. As you turn the cards over, you pretend to weigh them with your hand. When you come to the card after the ace of spades, you *almost* go past it, but then you hold it in your hand and say, "This seems a little heavy. Is this your card?" Much more impressive!

Other ways to do the same trick: *pretend you are scanning for the person's fingerprints on each card, or pretend you can spot the person's card by watching their reaction to each card.*

DOWN IS UP

This is a trick where your volunteer picks a card and then puts it back in the deck. You will put the deck behind your back for a moment, and when you bring it back around, the person's card is magically the only card that is turned over in the deck!

All you have to do for this trick is turn over the bottom card in the pile before you begin. Hold the deck in your hand and then have the volunteer pick their card from the deck and memorize it. (Don't let them see that the card on the bottom of the deck is turned over.)

Now, you need to turn the deck over so that the bottom, upside-down card is on the top of the deck. Try turning your back to the volunteer, saying, "*I want to make sure I don't see your card.*" While your back is turned, turn the deck over.

Turn back around with the deck upside down. Have the volunteer put the card into the pack, but don't let them *take* the deck of cards and don't let them spread the cards. They have now put their card in upside down.

Now put the deck behind your back and say a magic word. While you say it, *turn over the top card of the deck. Now ALL cards in the deck are facing the same way.* Bring the deck around and start to spread the cards out on a table. Spread the cards facedown on the table. Feel free to make it dramatic with magic words or pauses. No matter how you do it, your volunteer's card will be faceup!

I READ YOUR MIND

For this trick, you will tell a person what card they were thinking of. Here's how you do it. If you ask a man to think of a card, most men will think of the ace of spades, and then the seven of spades. Most women will think of the queen of hearts, and then the seven of hearts.

Take these four cards out of a deck of cards and put them in your pockets. (If you have *more* than four pockets, also pull out the four of spades and the four of hearts. Remember which card is in which pocket!

Hold up the deck. Ask your person to quickly think of a card. Now, you can do this trick a couple of ways. If you are feeling sure of yourself, just pull out one of the cards in your pocket. If it's not the card, no big deal. Or, you can ask them to name the card. If they name any of the cards in your pockets, just reach in your pocket and pull it out!

If they didn't pick any of these cards, just smile and say, "That's nice!" Then run away.

21-CARD SALUTE

This amazing yet easy trick is also sometimes called the "21 Card Trick." *Even more amazingly, it works every time!*

Start with 21 cards from your deck and a volunteer. With these 21 cards, you will deal three columns of seven cards each. *Deal from left to right, one card to each column as you go.*

When the columns are complete, ask the volunteer to pick a card without telling you what it is. *He needs to remember this card.* After he has done this, straighten each column into a pile, so that you have three piles of cards.

Ask the person which pile the card they picked is in. Whichever pile they point to, pick it up and set it *on* another pile. The third pile then goes *on top of* the other two, for one pile of cards. (Just to be clear, the pile in the middle has the card your volunteer selected.)

Now, do the same thing again. Make three columns again, dealing left to right. Ask the person to find their card, then straighten up the piles. Whichever pile the volunteer points to should be picked up and set on another pile. The other pile goes on top of it, just like the first time.

Now deal out your three columns again, and stop. Ask the person what column their card is in. Whichever column they point to, you now know their card. *Their card is the **fourth** card down from the top of that column!* (*This is **always** true!*)

A rookie magician will point to the fourth card and say, "*This is your card.*" They will be right, but that's not much fun. A good magician will do something more creative. Here is one good way to end the trick. Organize the columns into piles one last time. (The pile with the "magic" card is picked up and set on another pile, with the other pile on top.) *The "magic" card is now the 11th card down from the top of the pile.*

Pick up the pile and spell out a magic, 10-letter phrase like "*mumbo jumbo*" or "*stinky poop.*" With each letter you spell, throw down a card. When you are done, the next card you turn over will be the magic card!

TRICKY MAGIC

The following tricks require the assistance of another person.

THE RESTAURANT TRICK

This trick is incredible! Use it when you are going to any restaurant with a group of three or more people. One of these people will need to secretly work with you.

You Need: pen or pencil
1 piece of paper or index card for each person eating
(a small pad of paper would be perfect)

The idea of this trick is simple: you will magically figure out what each person in your group is ordering without them knowing it!

To do this trick, you need to know one thing BEFORE you sit down at your table. *You need to secretly have your secret assistant tell you what he is going to order.*

Once you know this, you announce to your group that you will try to figure out what *everyone* is going to order. You will be asking them some questions about themselves to help give you the magic insight to do the trick.

Pull out your paper and pencil, holding them so that nobody can see what you are writing. You can start with anyone, but *not* the person who is your helper. Ask the first person a couple of questions about food; make them general. "Do you like meat? What is your favorite meal?" That sort of thing. Ask the person if he has decided what he is going to order. (*Wait until he has decided!*)

When they have decided, write down the name and meal choice of your secret assistant on your piece of paper. Then fold it in half and set it near you. Don't let anyone grab it or look at it. See, they think you just made your guess for the person you were interviewing, but you didn't.

Now ask your first person (let's call him Leroy) what it was that they ordered; it's safe now, and you would like to confirm your guess. Leroy tells you he ordered the Spamburger. Just nod and smile. Then turn to the next person. Ask them some questions. (As you know, the questions don't matter!) When you are ready to make your "guess," write down the name and menu item of your first volunteer! In this example, you would write down, "*Leroy: Spamburger.*"

Fold the paper and set it down. Ask the person to confirm what she decided to order. She tells you. You nod and smile and go on to the next person. Keep using the same method. When you come to yourself, write down your name and selection. You're ready!

If you want to be cocky, call the waiter over and say that you're ready to order. Then pick up the pieces of paper, say the person's name and their choice, and watch the amazed expressions form!

NOTE: Make sure to give your secret assistant a tip for helping out!

MIND READING

This is another secret assistant trick. Your audience can be two people or many, but remember that you need a secret assistant that you have talked with beforehand. Offer to show the audience a mind-reading performance. You will leave the room and a volunteer will touch any item in the room. You will then come back in and be able to identify the object.

Here's how to do this: when you come back in to the room, ask for a second person to help by pointing at different items in the room. Remember: you must pick your secret assistant for this job!

Tell your secret assistant to start silently pointing at different, random items in the room. Ask him to avoid looking at you or talking to you while he does so. *What nobody else knows is that* ***right before*** *your assistant points to the secret object, he will first point to something that is* ***black!***

Once you see your assistant point to something black, you know the next item is your "secret" item. When that item is pointed out, frown a little, but let your assistant continue. Then slowly walk to the secret item, touch it, and look at your first volunteer.

"*I sense that this is the item you picked. Is that right?*" Of course it is, and they will be amazed!

Variation: You can make up all sorts of tricks with this tactic. For example, seat a group of people at a table. Make sure that your secret assistant sits next to you. Take a deck of cards and have anybody or everybody shuffle the deck.

Now, leave the room. From the other room, have someone pick a card from the deck and show it to everyone in the room so they all know the card. Have them put the card randomly back in the deck.

Come back in the room, pick up the deck, and put it on top of your head. (*Careful! Don't drop it!*) Tell the group that you will pick a card off the deck, hold it over your head, and be able to identify the card simply by reading their minds. (You can even do this with your eyes closed.) The reason you can do this is because your secret assistant is going to nudge your foot with his when the card comes up! As long as you're not seated at a glass table, it should work fine.

 Want to learn more cool magic tricks? Take a look at *The Pocket Guide to Magic*!

FOLLOW-UP ACTIVITY

As a part of your magic act, mock Harry Potter as a fraud and a fake. If Harry Potter magically appears, deny everything and offer him some freshly made Kool-Aid.

MAKING FACES! MAKING SOUNDS!

MAKING FACES

Tarzan was not only the king of the jungle, he was also the king of making faces. See, in the books about Tarzan by Edgar Rice Burroughs, Tarzan could "make" almost any kind of face that you can imagine. I don't mean that he wore makeup and masks. I mean that Tarzan could sneer with either nostril, raise one eyebrow and then another, and wiggle his ears, his scalp, and even pieces of skin on his face. This is because Tarzan was raised with the apes, and apes use their faces a lot to communicate with each other.

Your face has muscles that can be used to make cool expressions too, *if* you exercise them. The muscles of your face are probably weak because you don't use them very much. You rely on words to communicate. But facial expressions can be even better than words. If you practice, you can get your face muscles to move around much more than they do now. You just need to give yourself a face workout! If you don't want to live with a bunch of apes to learn how to do this, read this chapter. (If you already *do* live with a bunch of apes, you may skip this section.)

Why make faces? Well, making faces is a good way to get people (especially little kids) to laugh. Also, by making faces, you are also making history. You see, history is full of examples of people who were professional facemakers, or people who made faces for a living. These were the gifted men and women with the magical ability to twist their faces around into a variety of contortions, grimaces, and expressions.

Jim Carrey is one of the great facemakers of modern times. He has practiced changing his face so many ways, he can look like a different person altogether. There have also been other famous performers with this talent. More than a hundred years ago, a Japanese man named Mirimoto was a "facial artist" who could cover his nose with his mouth! Mirimoto didn't use his fingers or any object to do this. He just reached his lips up and *voilà*! Other Japanese performers have used chopsticks and string to push up their nostrils, pull their ears in, or stretch out the skin on their faces.

Have a facemaking contest with your friends. Why not? In *The Hunchback of Notre Dame,* the hunchback Quasimodo enters a contest like this at the Feast of Fools. He wins the competition simply by putting his face through a hole in the wall and NOT making a face. (Quasimodo wasn't very attractive.) In 1768, a facemaking contest in England (with the motto "The Ugliest Grinner Shall Be the Winner") was won by a man who was later disqualified because it was found that he had vinegar in his mouth to help him make a face. *Cheater!*

LET'S START WITH THE BASICS

Eyes: Open your eyes as wide as possible—both together, and one at a time. Squeeze them tight, or stretch the skin below them down to look scary.

Crossing the eyes: This is an old favorite, but you have to be careful not to do it very often. It causes a strain on the eye muscles that just ain't good.

Wrinkling the nose: The basic "sneer" or look of disgust is when you wrinkle up your nose, as if you just smelled something bad.

Opening the nostrils: When you open (or "dilate") your nostrils, open them as wide as you can. Extra credit to anyone who can dilate one nostril at a time!

Grinning: Make the biggest grin you can! Try it *with* and *without* showing the teeth. How many different ways can you smile? Now try a variety of leers, smirks, and smiles.

Contorting the lips: See how many different ways you can squeeze and stretch your lips. Press them together at one side of your mouth and open them up at the other end. Now try to make your whole mouth move side to side! Squeeze them together in the middle! Stick your lower lip out as far as you can!

Sticking out the tongue: Like grimacing, there are many different ways to stick out your tongue. Shove the whole thing out at once, make it flat or round, or try to curl it. Most people can curl their tongue upwards at the sides . . . but only one person in 1,000,000 can curl their tongue *downwards*!

Puffing the cheeks: Puff out your cheeks to look like a chipmunk. Remember, there are many ways to puff out your cheeks. You can include your lips in the "puff" or not; you can also just do one side of your face or the other. Or just suck your cheeks in to look weird!

Grimacing: This is a classic. Squeeze ALL of your facial muscles at the same time to create a leering look of anger.

Squishing the face: Try to squeeze your face into the tiniest expression possible.

INTERMEDIATE FACEMAKING

When you are ready, start doing combinations of some of the faces above. Be creative! One of my favorites is puffing out my cheeks, and then opening my eyes and nostrils as far as possible!

Experiment with pushing your face up against a glass window; you probably won't be able to see what it looks like, but the people on the other side will!

Try sneering with only one nostril at a time. Switch sides so that you can do both!

Use your fingers or other props to help you make a face. Everyone knows how to pull the sides of the mouth down to create an unhappy face. Try other stuff. For example, push up the end of your nose to look like a pig! Push your ears out from behind to look dorky! Tape your eyebrows up so that you look surprised!

Practice the *ultimate expressions* of looking totally shocked, frightened, angry, happy, sad, hungry, greedy, and so forth.

ADVANCED FACEMAKING

Moving one eyebrow: There's only one way to do it and that's by practicing. Try to move only one eyebrow at a time!

Moving one side only: Try smiling with one side of your face and looking sad or angry with the other side.

Wiggling the ears: The muscles to move your ears are there. You just have to try using them!

Flipping your eyelids inside out: This is somewhat controversial, because it is somewhat painful, and there are those who say it is bad for you. It is gross to look at and it is painful. Try it!

Showing the whites of your eyes: Some people can roll their eyes down so far that you can only see the white part! This is always creepy, and it is also a strain on your eyes. It's a good trick to use if someone is trying to take your picture and you don't want to have "red eye"!

Turning your face inside out: Painful but dramatic!

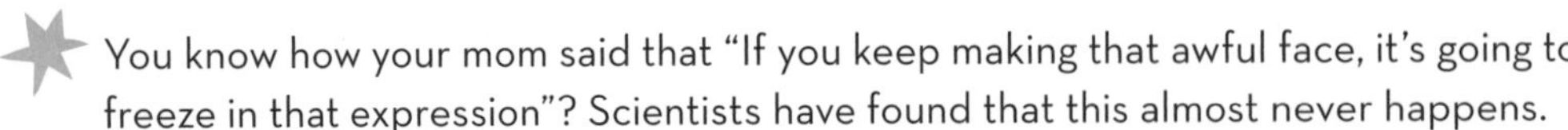

- You know how your mom said that "If you keep making that awful face, it's going to freeze in that expression"? Scientists have found that this almost never happens.

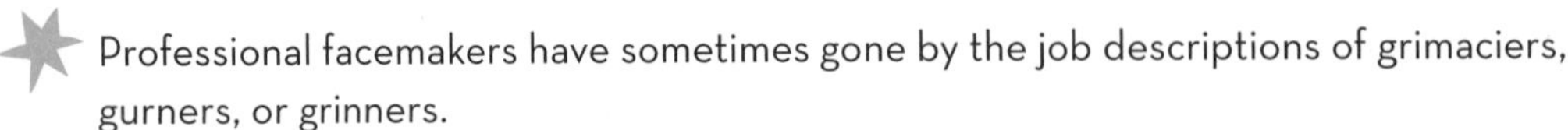

- Professional facemakers have sometimes gone by the job descriptions of grimaciers, gurners, or grinners.
- Make a bet with someone that you can stick out your tongue and touch your nose. Whether the person takes the bet or not, stick out your tongue and then reach up with your finger and touch your nose. Ta-dah!

MAKING SOUNDS

Sounds are more important than you might think. Heck, without them, you wouldn't be able to hear anything. (My, that is funny!) Here's how to make some cool sounds.

PART I: ARMPIT BOMBS

Being able to make a farting or bombing sound is very important to your career as a boy. The time may come when you are called to make this sound: if you cannot, you are ruined. This section of the book will show you how to make some basic sounds.

I will assume that you already know how to make the sound known as a "Bronx cheer" or a "raspberry." This is when you stick out your tongue, put your lips firmly on the tongue, and blow. *Pwpwpwpwpw!* (It works even better if you put your thumb on your nose and waggle your fingers back and forth while you do this.)

There are other, more impressive ways to make this sound.

Beginner: Makes an Okay "Pwpwpwpwpw!" Sound

This works with dry hands, and sometimes even a little better if you get your hands a little wet or oily. (Water or lotion works fine.) Cup your hands together by pretending you were going to clap or applaud for someone. Not the sissy way, but almost as if you were going to shake your own hand.

Wrap your fingers around the back of the opposite hand and squeeze the base of your palms (near the thumbs) together quickly. Then release and do it again. Practice with different positions to get different tones. *Pwpwpwpwpw!*

Intermediate: Makes a Decent "Pwpwpwpwpw!" Sound

Again, you may want to have a slightly moist hand for this. You will also need access to your armpit. Take your hand and cup it, then stick it under the armpit on the other side of your body.

Take the arm that is over the cupped palm and bend it at the elbow. Now bring that arm down so that it "squishes" the cupped hand under the armpit. Pump the arm up and down, as if you were doing a one-armed chicken imitation. Change the position of the cupped hand to get different sounds. *Pwpwpwpwpw!*

Advanced: Makes Such a Great "Pwpwpwpwpw!" Sound, You Can Play Songs

For the advanced training, you will need a drinking straw. It will work best if it is one of those drinking straws that has a bendy part in it.

Turn your head toward the armpit you are going to use. Put the end of the straw about halfway into the middle of your armpit, and the other half into your mouth.

Push your arm down, lightly "squishing" the straw's end. Now blow into the straw! You will quickly notice that changes in location and pressure alter the tone of your *"Pwpwpwpwpw!"* sound. Where the straw is, how tight your armpit is, and how hard you blow will all change the sound you get. If you practice, you will find that you can play songs!

Danger: Make sure you only blow through the straw. Do not breathe in through the straw! You would be breathing in your own armpit air, which can be deadly. Do not switch the ends of the straw around, as that would be gross. And never trade straws with anyone else!

Super Advanced: For Experts Only—The Armpit Bagpipes

Use the straw method described above, but instead of using one straw, use two or three! Even tougher (but great sounding!) is putting two or more straws in BOTH armpits at the same time and then blowing them!

"Pwpwpwpwpw!"

PART II: MOUTH POPS

Being able to make the sound of a cork coming out of a bottle is a must. (Don't ask me why, it just is.)

Beginner: Makes a Nice, Echoing Plop Sound

1. Breathe through your nose.
2. Pull your tongue as far to the back of your mouth as you can.
3. Push your lips forward and make an "O" shape with them.
4. Flick your finger into the side of your cheek. If you flick your cheek repeatedly, it will sound like a glass filling up with liquid. You will notice that you can change the sound of your "Plop!" by opening or closing your mouth or making strange faces. Do so as much as possible.

Intermediate: Makes a Good "Cork-Out-of-the-Bottle" Sound

1. Wash your hands.
2. Stick your index finger (that's your first one!) into your mouth. Your palm should face away from you, and the finger should poke the inside of your cheek, but be outside of your teeth.
3. Close your lips around your finger. Keep your finger stiff. Fill up your cheeks with as much air as you can!
4. Now POP that finger right out of your mouth by bringing your knuckle in toward your mouth and sliding your finger out. POP!

Advanced: Makes a Great "Cork-Out-of-the-Bottle" Sound!

1. Buy a bottle with a cork in it.
2. Pull the cork out.

PART III: HOW TO WHISTLE LOUDLY

I am assuming that you are able to do the usual "pursed lips" whistle. But can you do the "piercing, get everybody's attention" whistle that you have to put your fingers in your mouth for? If not, read on. (And remember, you will have to *practice* and *experiment* to get this right.)

1. Wash your hands. Your fingers will soon be in your mouth.
2. To do this whistle, your lips will be tight and tucked in, and they have to cover your teeth.
3. Keep your tongue flat as you bring it right to the edge of your bottom lip.
4. Get ready to shove some fingers in your mouth. You have two choices, and I will explain both. Just don't use your toes for this. It could result in instant death!

Method A

Try using your thumb and the index finger (first finger) on one hand. (You could also use one finger from each hand.) Put these fingers into the edges of your mouth and push out so that your lips stretch. Remember your tongue? Bring the tip so that it just about touches the bottom of your mouth just behind your teeth. You want air coming out of your mouth to get aimed at that spot of your mouth.

Blow gently. As you do this, try to adjust your fingers and mouth to find the perfect position. Eventually, you will find the spot. At first, you will have nothing, then a low whistle, and then something that could wake up a sleeping buffalo!

Method B

Put your two pinkie fingers into the edges of your mouth. Let the fingertips touch inside your mouth so that they form a wide "V" shape. Shove the tip of your "V" under the tip of your tongue and roll the tongue tip up and over. Your upper lip should now be touching the first knuckle of your pinkies.

Don't let the tongue tip touch the roof of your mouth. If you looked in the mirror, you would see a triangle between your pinkies and your lower lip. You want to blow air over your tongue and into that space. It won't work right away, so experiment and try different angles and lip or tongue positions. You can do it! It's easier than juggling or playing poker, so if you can do those things, you can do this!

PART IV: BABY SOUNDS

The time will come when you will be losing an argument. (Just make sure this doesn't happen when you are arguing with your brother!) The other person will be right, and you will be *wrong*. Whatever you do, don't admit defeat in this situation. Instead, when all seems lost, make *baby sounds*! It will confuse your enemy, and people will think you are funny or insane, or both!

1. Stick out your lower lip.
2. With a finger, flip down on your lower lip repeatedly and make an "*Uhhh*" sound in your throat.
3. Combined with the lip flip, your "Uhhh" sound will become an "*Uhwubbawubbawubba*" sound. Change your "*Uhhh*" throat sound up or down, louder and softer, for cool variations. Watch your enemy run away in fear!

FOLLOW-UP ACTIVITY

When walking in the halls of your school, make different "random" faces at your friends as you see them. If they smile and wave, puff out your cheeks and sneer. If they nod, grimace as if you're in pain and bug your eyes out. Enjoy their reactions.

MAN FOOD FOR MANHOOD!

"Guy" foods are where it's at. If it has salt, grease, and/or sugar, it's got to be good, right? Or, if you can take some food, shove it on a stick, and stick it into a fire, that's good eating. Some people say, "*You are what you eat.*" Does that make you a *jerk* if you eat beef jerky? What about chicken? Are you calling me a chicken? Maybe it means that if you eat healthy foods, you'll *be* healthy.

Real men (like the Iron Chef) know there are a lot of good reasons for knowing your way around a kitchen. The kitchen is a big science lab where you can conduct creative experiments. You get to dig your hands into the ingredients and make a mess! Of course, you have to clean it up too, but never mind that now! Who knows what will happen when you combine Spam with Tabasco sauce until you try it? It could be delicious!

Food that you make yourself magically becomes extra tasty. Anyone who has ever caught a trout, fried it up in a skillet, and eaten it knows what I'm talking about. Because you put the effort into it, the meal tastes that much better. Once you start cooking, you begin appreciating different types of foods than you did before. A traditional Japanese belief is that your life is extended more than two months for every new type of food you try. So live long! Eat different foods!

Other people will appreciate your efforts too. I'll let you in on a very important secret: *girls are impressed by boys who can cook.* That may not mean much to you now, but trust me, in a few years, if you can cook a romantic meal, it'll be *pure gold.*

Almost everyone has *one* recipe or thing that they can make well. Ask some of the people you know what their favorite recipe is; you might learn something *and* get something good to eat at the same time! Anyway, here are some fun and weird recipes that you might want to try making someday. I'll assume that you will be in a kitchen where you have access to an oven, measuring cups and spoons, and so forth. Follow the rules below (someday you'll thank me for all these rules) and have at it. The easiest recipes come first, and then they get a little more complicated.

BEFORE WORKING IN THE KITCHEN

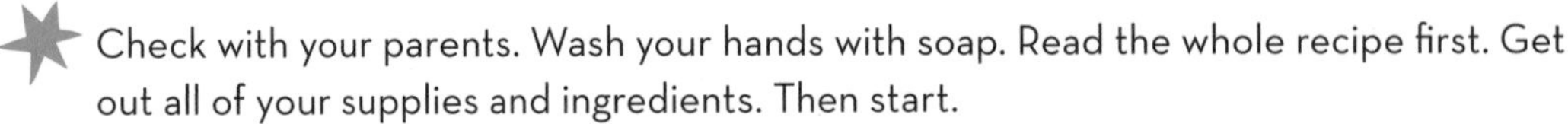

- Check with your parents. Wash your hands with soap. Read the whole recipe first. Get out all of your supplies and ingredients. Then start.

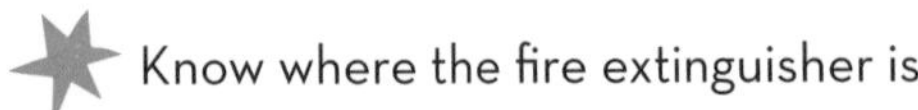

- Know where the fire extinguisher is.

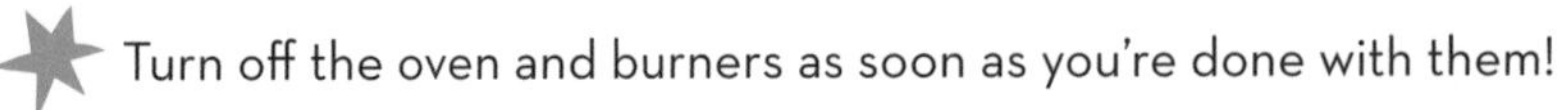

- Turn off the oven and burners as soon as you're done with them!
- Poison Cheese! Poison can show up in unexpected places. Did you know that the plant called "Poison hemlock" has poison in it? Who'd have guessed? But seriously, many natural things (tomato leaves, mistletoe, and even bananas and potatoes) contain very small doses of poisonous substances. For example, there is a chemical called "tyramine" that is found in different cheeses. Tyramine can raise a person's pulse rate and cause nightmares if eaten before bedtime.

SIMPLE BASICS

CINNAMON TOAST

Are you kidding me? This is the best! When I was growing up, I probably had this once a day.

You Need: a toaster
bread
butter
cinnamon sugar (use a 5 to 1 ratio of sugar to cinnamon to make this)

1. Toast the bread.
2. Butter it right when it comes out of the toaster so the butter melts.
3. Sprinkle cinnamon sugar on the top.

4. Now here's the hard part: try not to eat it in one bite!

For advanced cooks only: Try this complex recipe! Instead of regular bread, use raisin bread. Or, use applesauce instead of butter.

You Are Eating Mars and Murries! M&M's are named after the founders of the candy company that made them, Forrest Mars and Bruce Murrie. Forrest also invented the Milky Way bar and the Snickers bar. The M&M's candy was invented in 1941, but the letter "m" was not put on the candy itself until 1950. (Bonus Trivia: The rapper Marshall Mathers has the initials "M" and "M"—so his showbiz name is *Eminem*.)

HARD-BOILED EGGS

Great for sandwiches or just right out of the shell!

You Need: eggs
a pot with a lid
water

1. Put the eggs in the pot first. Then put enough water in the pot to cover the eggs with 1 inch of water. Put the lid on the pot, and get that water boiling! Once it is boiling, turn the heat *off*. Now start timing it. If you'd like a soft egg, leave the lid on for 3 minutes, then go to the next paragraph. If you like it soft with no goo at all, go for 5 minutes. If you want it hard-boiled, leave the lid on for 15 minutes.

2. Then I like to put the whole pan into the sink and run cold tap water onto the eggs for a few minutes. When the eggs are cold, start peeling the shell at the fat end of the egg. When you're done, put a little mayonnaise, salt, and pepper on them and power 'em down! Don't eat it too fast though; because they're so tasty, hard-boiled eggs are one of the most choked-upon foods there is.

By the way, if you're ever in doubt as to whether an egg is hard-boiled, just spin it. If it doesn't spin fast and evenly, it's not hard-boiled!

RAISIN HELL

Any punk can buy them . . . but do you have what it takes to make them?

You Need: seedless grapes
a windowsill with sunshine

Follow these directions closely or *disaster* will result!

1. Take the grapes. Wash them. Pull out those annoying little stems.
2. Now put the grapes on a windowsill that gets sunlight. Leave them there for a couple of weeks. They will magically turn into raisins! For full Hakuna Matata credit, try soaking them in water for 3 hours. They turn back into grapes!

(I was just kidding about the "disaster" that could happen.)

GRILLED CHEESE, PLEASE

You could put melted cheese in a bowl of motor oil and I would eat it. This old standby tastes even better than that!

You Need: bread
cheddar cheese
sliced tomato (optional)
butter
a griddle or pan
a spatula
napkins

1. Okay, this is an oldie but a goody. Lay out your bread and slice your cheese.
2. If you have any tomato slices, put them on the bread with the cheese slices.
3. Then close the sandwiches and spread butter on the outside of both pieces of bread. This will help the sandwich not stick to the pan, plus it's tasty.
4. Have the flame under the pan on medium and, using a spatula, put the sandwich on it. Put a lid over the pan to melt the cheese quicker. As soon as the cheese starts to melt, flip it over. I flip my grilled cheese sandwiches many times, but I also like my bread to be a little blackened.
5. Once it's cooked to perfection, use the spatula to put it on a plate and let it cool. It will be one greasy, tasty sandwich so use your napkins!

 Yes, We Have No Bananas! Hostess Twinkies have been around since 1926 and were originally filled with banana filling. There was a shortage of bananas during World War II (1939–1945), so Twinkies were switched to vanilla filling; they have never been changed back.

PEANUT BUTTER AND JELLY SUSHI

Don't worry, there's no raw fish in this, but it is a great variation of an old favorite!

You Need: bread of your choice
a cutting board
a rolling pin
peanut butter
jelly

1. Put the bread you will be using on the cutting board and cut off its crust.
2. Then take the rolling pin and roll it back and forth over the bread until it's completely squished.
3. Spread the peanut butter and jelly on the bread, leaving some room at the edges.
4. Using your fingers, peel the bread up along one edge of the cutting board. Then start rolling it on itself, as if it were a carpet or Ho Ho. Keep it tight!
5. When you have your sushi-style sandwiches rolled up, take a knife and cut them into bite-size pieces. Mmmm, baby!

 Great Inventors! "Mr. Peanut" was created by a 13-year-old named Antonio Gentile in 1916. He drew the character for a contest held by Planters, and won its grand prize: $5! And in 1905, an 11-year-old boy named Frank Epperson left his drink (with a stirring stick in it) outside one winter night. The drink froze, and when Frank came out the next day, the stick made an excellent handle to carry the frozen treat around with. Eighteen years later, Frank Epperson started selling his frozen treats as "Epsicles." Frank's own children asked him to change the name to "Popsicle," and so he did. He went on to also come up with the Fudgsicle, Creamsicle, and Dreamsicle. Hurray!

SOLAR-POWERED MARSHMALLOWS

Harness the ultraviolet rays of the mighty sun!

You need: a large bowl
aluminum foil
some clay or Play-Doh
a toothpick
marshmallows
the sun

1. Take the bowl and line the inside of it with foil, with the shinier side facing out. Smooth it down as much as possible.

2. Take a good little blob of clay and set it in the middle of the bowl. Stick a toothpick into the clay so the toothpick is standing up. Now stick a marshmallow on the toothpick.

3. Put the bowl someplace where it catches the direct rays of the sun. Prepare to be amazed! The energy of the sun is all-powerful!

A man named Michel Lotito lives in France,
And though it sounds whack, he eats underpants.
His nickname these days is "Mr. Eat Everything"
Even as a boy, glass and metal he was nibbling.
Michel has since made himself a decent career
Eating bikes, computers, coffins (even planes) without fear!
His stomach lining's thicker than yours, so's his head,
So don't try to be like him or you might end up dead!

INTERMEDIATE ABILITY

GODZILLA'S QUESADILLAS (KAY-SA-DEE-YUHS)

I wouldn't put this recipe in here if I didn't think it was one of the tastiest and easiest-to-prepare foods that there is!

You Need: corn or flour tortillas (I much prefer corn for this recipe)
refried beans (optional)
cheese (cheddar, mozzarella, or Monterey Jack work well), sliced
salsa or hot sauce
1 tomato, thinly sliced (optional)
a skillet, pan, or griddle, with lid if possible
nonstick cooking spray

1. I prepare the quesadillas first by laying out the tortillas on a counter. If I am going to use refried beans, I smear those on the tortillas next. Then I put the cheese on. I use thin slices of cheese and lay them down; you can grate it if you prefer, but that just takes longer. Finally I put on the hot sauce and/or the tomatoes.
2. After I have the insides ready to go, I lay another tortilla on top of it and it's ready to cook.
3. As for my cooking surface, it doesn't need to be that hot; a burner on medium is fine. Spray your cooking surface with nonstick spray. Carefully place the quesadilla on the pan; if you can put a lid over it, that's the best. It will melt the cheese a little faster, which will make it easier to flip the quesadilla without the food falling out. (Melted cheese is a good glue!)
4. After the cheese has melted a little, carefully flip the quesadilla over. If anything is going to go wrong, it will here! Keep flipping and browning until it looks good enough to eat.

WARNING: A. Microwaves don't work well for this recipe.
B. Don't burn your mouth powering this one down!

VOYAGE TO THE BOTTOM OF THE SEA

This may seem like a simple recipe, but for some unfathomable reason, it is deeply delicious!

You Need: 1 to 6 boxes of blue Jell-O
any clear glass casserole dish; clean aquariums and fish bowls also work
Skittles, M&M's, or any colorful candy
gummi fish or worms

1. Make the Jell-O according to its instructions.

2. Cover the bottom of your glass container with your candy. This is your ocean floor!

3. As the Jell-O is just beginning to firm up, carefully pour it into your container.

4. Then add your gummi creatures at various depths of the sea. Put it into the refrigerator until it's true Jell-O, and then voyage with your spoon to the bottom of the sea!

If you ever add fruit to your Jell-O, here's what you need to know. Fruits that sink in Jell-O are grapes and any canned fruits with heavy syrup, like fruit cocktail, peaches, and pineapple. Fruits that float include canned fruits in light syrup, as well as apples, bananas, orange sections, sliced pears, and strawberries.

How to Make Jell-O: Boil the skins and bones of pigs and cows. This releases a protein called "collagen." Boil, filter, and reboil this until you get a powder. Add fruit flavoring. What do you have? Jell-O!

SPAMBURGERS

Spam rocks! It was named in 1936 by the famous Kenneth Daigneau. He had entered a contest to name the new canned meat from Hormel. "Spam" is a contraction of "spiced" and "ham." (Weird, since there isn't much spice or ham in it.) Spam is mostly made from pork shoulder meat, homey!

You Need:
1 (12-ounce) can Spam luncheon meat
a frying pan
4 slices of pepper Jack cheese
lettuce
1 tomato, sliced
1 onion, sliced
4 hamburger buns
ketchup

1. Cut the Spam into 4 thick slices.

2. Fry the Spam in frying pan or skillet until it is lightly browned.

3. Place Spam, cheese, lettuce, tomato, and onion on bottom halves of buns. Spread ketchup on top halves of buns and place on Spamburger.

4. Eat. Smack lips a lot and roll eyes to indicate enjoyment.

Ketchup (also spelled "catsup") is used all over the world in different ways. In Canada they have ketchup-flavored potato chips, and in Thailand they use the ketchup as potato chip dip. In Spain and India they put it on eggs, and in Sweden and Denmark they pour ketchup on pasta. The Japanese put ketchup on rice! In some eastern European countries they pour it on pizza. Me? I put it on macaroni and cheese.

SPECIAL FEATURE: HOT DOGS

Wieners, frankfurters, franks, sausages . . . people have been trying to figure out exactly who invented them for years. But what about the hot dog? Many people agree that a hero named Anton Feuchtwanger (anton FOIK-twang-er) of Bavaria brought his seasoned sausages to the Louisiana Exposition of 1904. The problem he faced was that his customers had to eat their franks with their hands, which was not convenient. Anton tried giving them white gloves to protect their hands, but this was very messy, and people sometimes walked off with the gloves.

Like all great heroes, Anton did not give up. Instead, he asked a baker to make some long buns to hold the franks . . . and there it was: *a hot dog*! Three cheers for Anton Feuchtwanger!

FRUIT LOG

Everybody likes to chew on logs. The bark is especially delightful. The beauty of eating logs is that it is easy on your body because it doesn't have to convert food into a log, like it usually does!

You Need:
2 cups of dried, chopped apples
2 cups of dried, chopped apricots
½ cup instant dried milk
any big bowl
2 teaspoons cinnamon
4 tablespoons honey
4 tablespoons light corn syrup
4 tablespoons frozen orange juice concentrate (or any flavor you like), thawed out and liquidy
1 cup chopped nuts
½ cup powdered sugar
a cookie sheet that you can make your log on
an oven

1. Wash your hands.
2. Now mix the fruits and milk together in the bowl with your hands.
3. Then add everything else except the chopped nuts and powdered sugar.
4. Mix it up well! Mix it some more! Is it mixed yet?
5. Once it is, grab a handful and start molding it on the cookie sheet into a log.
6. Remember when you used to make snakes out of clay in kindergarten? Do that with the mixture and make your snake about 1 ½ inches across. Once you have your snake/logs done, roll them in the nuts, and then in the powdered sugar. (You may want to transfer your logs to a new sheet now.)
7. You're almost done. Turn the oven on to 140 degrees Fahrenheit. Put the cookie sheet into the oven and leave the oven door open just a little.

Call Your Dentist Today! Would you ever take a glass of carbonated water and mix 12 spoonfuls of sugar into it? Seems like a lot, huh? Well, if you drink a 16-ounce soda, you get carbonated water with more than 12 teaspoonfuls of sugar and some artificial flavoring. Delicious! Just leave your teeth by the bottle, since they'll be falling out soon anyway.

ADVANCED

FRIED WORMS

Yeah, this is what it sounds like! You've seen enough reality TV to know that it can be done. What's the matter, you chicken? I dare you to make this recipe! I double-dog dare you! No, I'm not kidding: this is pretty tasty (I've heard).

You Need: mealworms or earthworms
a colander
paper towels or wax paper on a plate
olive oil
a frying pan
breadcrumbs

Mealworms are eaten in many countries. Thailand, for example, is one of them. Anyway, what you want to do is get some *live* mealworms. Check your yellow pages, or go to a big pet shop; they usually have them there. (If you're using earthworms for this recipe, just start digging for them yourself.)

1. To prepare your worms, just put them into a colander and rinse them off. Make sure that you get all the gunk off of them; you just want to eat the worm, right?

2. Lay the worms out on some paper towels (to dry them out) or wax paper. They may be squirming a bit, so shove them into the fridge to chill them out.

3. While the worms are chilling, pour enough olive oil into the frying pan to cover the bottom.

4. Break up a couple of pieces of bread into breadcrumbs and you're almost ready. Get the frying pan hot and get the worms out of the fridge. They should be "knocked out" enough at this point that they won't feel you roll them in the bread crumbs and then put them into the frying pan.

5. You want to stir-fry the worms in the oil until they are crispy, then get them out of the pan, let them cool, and enjoy! Like I said, worms *are* good, if you're man enough to try them!

JERKY BOYS

It's hard to beat good beef jerky. It's a tasty, manly snack, perfect for camping or between meals. You can even add it to stews and soups. There are dozens of types of beef jerky that you can buy; some are terrific, but some of them seem like pieces of shoe leather that you could break a tooth on. Making your own jerky guarantees that you have good quality. You don't need a smokehouse; just follow this recipe, and get jerkified!

You need: beefsteak
a sharp knife
wire or good string
a good-sized pot of water
salt
a stove
a platter or large dish
other seasonings that you like, such as soy sauce, Worcestershire sauce, steak sauce, onion powder, garlic powder, etc.
pepper
cloth or paper towels
a cookie tray
an oven
a room or garage where you can dry the meat

You can make jerky out of high-quality beefsteak or a cheaper cut of flank steak. I would recommend buying one of each and preparing them the same way to see if you can taste the difference later.

1. Cut your steak lengthwise into strips that are about 1/8 to 1/4 inch thick. Some people like to take a sharp knife and cut off strips in a spiral direction around the steak until they reach the center. This makes the jerky more tender. After you have your strips ready, thread wire or string through your meat strips. Don't make your string too long, as the strips will be dipped into the pot of water.

2. In the meantime, get your water boiling in the pot. (Use 1/8 cup of salt for every 1/8 gallon of water.) When the water is ready, dip your meat strips into the boiling water for about 10 seconds, or until the red color disappears.

3. Put the paper towels on the platter. Now, keep the strips on the wire or string and arrange them over the paper towels. Feel free to use any of your seasonings on the meat, but make sure to get your seasonings on both sides of the strips and to use plenty of pepper!

4. Now you just need to dry the strips. I usually unstring them and put them on a cookie tray.

5. Then I stick the jerky in the oven at 150 degrees Fahrenheit for 12 to 14 hours. A good way to test whether the jerky is done is to break it open and see if the strip is dry all the way through.

You can also dry the jerky in the air. Make sure that there are no flies in the space the jerky will dry in, and then let it hang on its wire for 3 to 4 days. Be sure that the jerky is dry and leathery when you break it.

As I said, experiment with your meat quality, seasonings, and drying techniques, and you are guaranteed to have a nutritious, lightweight snack that will last for months, even years!

Foiled Again

The only camping recipe you'll ever need.

You Need: 1/4 pound hamburger meat
1 potato, thinly sliced
1 carrot, thinly sliced
1 onion, cut into wedges
ketchup
salt, pepper, tasty seasoning
foil
a campfire

1. The ingredients listed above are just a suggestion. Feel free to add corn and other vegetables. Anyway, get a large piece of foil and put all of your ingredients into it. That's right, all of them!

2. Then fold up the foil carefully around the pile, crimping and folding the edges as you go so that there is a tight seal over and around the whole mess. Wrap it again in foil if you don't think the juice will stay in it.

3. Then carefully put the foil container on the coals of your campfire (not in the flames themselves!) Try letting it cook for 10 minutes on one side and 10 minutes on the other. I'd leave it in for about 30 minutes total, but this isn't an exact science.

Pull the package out with a couple of sticks and open it carefully to let the heat escape. It's going to smell darned good and taste even better, but don't burn your fingers or your tongue.

Do I Feel a Draft in Here? If you are average, about 5 percent of the food you eat in your life will be eaten in front of the refrigerator with its door open! Also, in 6 out of 10 houses, at least one person drinks milk right out of the carton. So if you're not putting your lips on the carton at home . . . who is? ("Mommy? Is that you?")

BEER

What the heck were you thinking? This is ROOT beer, young man!

You Need:
- measuring cups and spoons
- 1 teaspoon dry yeast
- 8 ½ cups warm water
- a bowl
- 2 cups sugar
- 5 teaspoons root beer extract (look in the spice aisle of your supermarket)
- a gallon jug with lid

Root beer is an American invention. Early colonists were looking for *anything* to flavor their beers with and they began experimenting with plant roots to make their drinks. *You* don't have to dig up anything for this recipe though.

1. Sometime before noon, mix yeast with ½ cup of warm water in a bowl.
2. Then pour this mix, the sugar, and root beer extract into your jug. Put in 8 more cups of warm water, and shake it good and hard!
3. Once it looks like it's mixed up, let the jug sit in a sunny window spot for the rest of the day. When it gets dark, put the jug in the refrigerator, and enjoy your own root beer the next day!

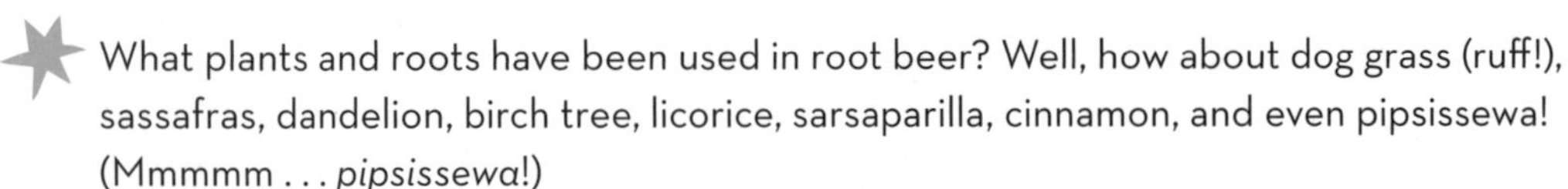

What plants and roots have been used in root beer? Well, how about dog grass (ruff!), sassafras, dandelion, birch tree, licorice, sarsaparilla, cinnamon, and even pipsissewa! (Mmmmm . . . *pipsissewa*!)

SPECIAL FEATURE: BRAIN FREEZE

Bam! You've just been hit between the eyes! There is a blinding pain in your head, and as you moan, it turns into a severe throbbing. What happened? Were you hit in the head by a baseball? Nope, it's just brain freeze. During a good brain freeze, your forehead temperature can fall by two degrees.

Brain freeze (or "ice cream headache") is probably caused by a sharp drop in temperature at the roof of your mouth. This drop is caused by you shoving too much ice cream (or frozen yogurt, or anything frosty) into your mouth all at once. Some people think that if they swallow the cold item, it will make the headache worse, so they hold it in their mouth. *That's* what makes the headache worse!

Another problem with brain freeze is that it takes a while for the cold to really affect your brain. The headache may not come for a full minute after you've eaten the cold item. The brain freeze will pass in a few moments if you're lucky, though.

Luckily, with hard work, scientists have discovered an amazing cure for ice cream headaches. Eat slower!

CRAPOLA COOKIES

These are great for a practical joke or a conversation starter (or ender!). Although they look suspiciously like someone's stool sample, they are pretty good!

You Need:
½ cup white sugar
4 teaspoons cocoa
½ cup butter or margarine
a pan
1 cup flour
½ teaspoon vanilla
½ cup brown sugar
1 egg
1 cup rolled oats
a mixing bowl
green food coloring (or any colors of your choice!)
peanuts and/or flaky wheat or fiber cereal (optional)
a cookie tray

1. Put the white sugar, cocoa, and butter or margarine into the pan and let them melt, mix, and simmer, stirring occasionally.
2. Mix the flour, vanilla, brown sugar, and egg energetically in the mixing bowl.
3. When you have them well mixed, add the melted mix from the pan and stir it well.
4. A crucial step is the addition of the food coloring(s). Add the amount of color you want to make it look realistic!
5. Add the oats and mix in. (If you want, add peanuts or fiber cereal and mix that in too.)
6. Now you're ready to start your fun factory for crapola. Roll the dough into tootsie rolls. They can be huge Sasquatch-sized turds, or big human-sized ones, or even small terrier-sized ones. Shape them to your taste (blech!) and put them on the cookie sheet.
7. Bake them for 10 to 15 minutes at 350 degrees Fahrenheit, or until you think they look just right.

Serving suggestion: Set one on a piece of toilet paper or a single plastic newspaper bag to make it look more realistic. Offer it to a guest; when they decline to eat it, shrug your shoulders and shove it in your mouth!

Oreo Chocolate Sandwich Cookies have been around since 1912. At just under 2 inches across, an Oreo is just the right size for stuffing into your mouth. Some psychologists say that you can judge a person's maturity by how they eat an Oreo. If they pull the cookie apart and eat the cream filling first, they are immature. If they eat the cookie all at once, they are mature. (Of course, it's more fun to be immature!)

When Oreos were introduced, Nabisco also put out their Mother Goose Cookies. You could eat Cinderella, Goldilocks, and all your favorite nursery rhyme characters. But the idea of eating humans wasn't a big hit, and these cookies didn't sell. Go figure!

PRACTICAL JOKES!

Practical jokes are a lot of fun, but you must use good judgment when playing them on someone. It is important to play practical jokes only on people who are your friends or family. If you play a joke on someone you do not know well, it is not a joke at all. Stepping into an elevator full of strangers and saying, "*P.U.!*" or putting sugar in the saltshaker is not a nice trick to pull on someone you don't know. Therefore, play these tricks on friends and relatives as often as possible.

The best way to test a practical joke to see if it is appropriate is to *imagine that the practical joke was played on you.* Would you think it was funny? *If the answer to that question is "No," then do not play the joke on someone else.* The best joke is the one where everyone laughs, especially the person upon whom the joke is played.

There are a *few* jokes you can play on strangers. For example, a boy once went to a tanning salon and poured a little pile of ashes on one of the tanning beds. He then put an extra set of clothes next to the tanning bed and left. That's a good one!

When done properly, practical jokes can show affection for the person the joke is played upon. The joke says, "*Look, I cared about you enough to play this joke on you. I thought so highly of you, I thought you would like it!*"

When you play the joke, make sure that the joke is not on you. For example, my brother Erik once put lotion on a doorknob so that it would be too slippery to open. This is a good trick. Unfortunately for Erik, the door was shut at the time, and he couldn't get out of the room! (Erik was stranded for days.) Here is another example. You might tell a friend that school has been canceled for the day. After your friend then takes a day off at home, you can rush to his house after school and shout, "*Guess what? We had school after all!*" In this case, your "tricked" friend might just smile mysteriously and say, "Darn."

The following idea may be the best joke of all time. Rent a parrot from a pet shop. Teach the parrot to say, "*I will destroy you*" and then return it to the store . . . the people at the pet shop will be so amused! (Wait; can you rent a parrot?) Prank calls with fake names can be worth a chuckle, if the fake names are good enough. Bea O'Problem, Hugh Jass, and Ollie Tabooger make the cut, but don't call the zoo and ask to speak to Guy Rilla, Mr. Lyon, or Al E. Gator. Trust me, they've heard those jokes a thousand times before.

The first recorded prank call was in 1884, when a joker in Rhode Island called an undertaker to come pick up a dead body. But when the undertaker got to the house, the "corpse" was very much alive!

April Fool's is a great time to play a practical joke. Try to find someone young or foolish (or both) and get him to run an errand for you. Important jobs include getting a tube of elbow grease, finding a left-handed screwdriver, or catching a wild snipe. Just remember that for a practical joke to work, you have to keep a straight face. That means you do not start smiling or laughing until *after* the practical joke is over. The good practical joker needs to be a little bit of an actor and storyteller. You have to be able to play along!

Some of the following practical jokes are old classics, some are ones that I have played in my time, and some are courtesy of professional pranksters like Penn & Teller. They are *all* funny!

Practical Jokes Can Pay! In the late 1990s, two high school students from Virginia wanted to play a practical joke on their teacher. They experimented with a slime that accidentally turned out to be an edible plastic. The two students ended up with $100,000 from a medical technology company that makes melt-in-the-mouth capsules.

President George Bush Sr. loved to use joy buzzers to break the ice at get-togethers with other bigwigs.

OLDIES BUT GOODIES

If you want some basic gags, take a trip to your local novelty shop or magic store. Joy buzzers, stink bombs, dribble glasses, and whoopee cushions are all pure gold. They may be corny, but they still get a laugh. In case you haven't already heard of or tried the following practical jokes, these are ones that you should have memorized back in first grade.

Take a small Post-it note or piece of paper and stick it under someone's computer mouse. The paper should cover the sensor on the bottom of the mouse. When they go to use the mouse, it won't do anything! Extra credit for writing a message on the note like "Got you!" or "I win. You lose."

Food coloring is in all grocery stores. It's cheap and nontoxic, and it doesn't change the flavor of the food it's in. Buy any bright color of food coloring and add it to the milk carton. (This only works if it is in a cardboard container so nobody can see inside before they pour.) Be there when someone pours out the bright green milk onto their cereal. Their screams will make you laugh!

- Float a suspiciously dark candy bar in a pool. Then scream and try to get away from it! Then run home and short-sheet somebody's bed. (If you don't know how to do this, you want to tuck the sheet of the bed in so far, it only extends a couple of feet from the end of the bed. Put the blanket over it normally.)

- If you have one of those sink hoses with a hand nozzle on it in your kitchen, wrap a rubber band around the nozzle's handle so it is "on." When someone turns on the water, they get a nice shower.

- If you are a good athlete, wait for your team's most important game of the season. Then show up on crutches! Everyone will completely freak out, which will really help their concentration when it's game time.

FOLDING FOOL

This is an excellent challenge for someone who thinks they can do it all!

You Need: a piece of paper

Find a cocky victim, er, volunteer for this simple trick. Tell them it is a test of the person's ability to meet a challenge.

Hand them a piece of paper and challenge them to fold it *exactly* and *perfectly* in half. Once they have done it, have them take the paper and fold it *exactly* and *perfectly* in half again.

Then have them do it again and again. They may be puzzled, and they will certainly get more challenged as you go. If the person can make it to the seventh fold of the paper, congratulate them on a job well done. (Many people give up before this!)

But to pass the test, they must fold the paper in half *eight* times. What the person doesn't know is that it is *impossible* to fold any piece of paper eight times . . . it doesn't matter how big or small or thick or thin the paper is. It can't be done!

Watching them wrestle around with the little chunk of folded paper should be good for a laugh!

Beware: The little piece of paper your friend is wrestling with turns into an excellent device to throw at someone after about six folds!

THE HEADLESS PUNK

You're going to lose your head doing this trick. (That is a stupid joke.)

You Need: a button-down shirt
people who can play along

This trick works at the dinner table at home or in a restaurant. To do it, you need to wear a button-down shirt with no shirt on under it. (This trick also works best with short people. Yeah, I'm talking to you, squirt.)

You're at the table with your family. One of them gets up to go to the restroom. (Let's say it's your mom.) You quickly unbutton your shirt down about four buttons and move your collar behind your neck. You then rebutton the collar so that it is buttoned behind your head.

Now put your head under the table. (Don't bang it on the edge!) Reach your hands up and grab your fork like you're waiting for your food. Have your dinner companions fix your collar so that it is nice and round, as if your head and neck were still sticking through it.

Now, tell the group at the table to start chatting and acting perfectly normal. When your mom comes back, she'll have quite a surprise!

DAD'S GORILLA ARMS

A good joke to play on any hairy adult who you can trust not to attack you afterwards!

You Need: a rubber band
running shoes

If you know of someone who is hairy, this may be a good joke to try. Take your rubber band and hold one end of it. Turn the other end over and over, until the rubber band is completely twisted around many times.

Approach the hairy victim. (They need to have some body hair exposed. The forearms are a likely spot, but legs can work too.) Ask the person an innocent question like, "Do you like to unravel problems?"

Whatever their answer is, then set the rubber band firmly onto their arm, with enough force to keep it in place, but not so much that it doesn't unravel. (You should practice a couple of times before trying the "real" thing.)

The rubber band should partly unravel in their hair, creating a mildly painful problem for them to remove! (If you are *really* successful, they may need to cut it off with scissors.) The laughter will be deafening!

FAST MONEY

A good trick to play on anyone who thinks they have fast reflexes.

You Need: a crisp, new bill of any amount of money

This is a very easy trick. Just challenge someone to catch a bill that you will release. Most people think they can catch the bill . . . and most people are wrong!

Make sure that your bill is fresh, and then fold it lightly lengthwise. Drop it a couple of times and tell your victim that they can have the bill if they catch it properly. (If they can't, maybe they should pay you!)

Have the person make a fist and hold it in front of them. He then needs to stick out his thumb and index finger. (The index finger is the finger closest to the thumb.) He must catch the bill as it falls by pinching it between these two fingers.

Make sure your fingers are dry and hold the bill halfway between the person's thumb and finger. Tell the person that he cannot drop his hand down in the air to catch the bill; his arm *must* remain motionless. Then release the bill.

He will not be able to catch the bill, but he will want to try again! Go ahead and do it, but now as you hold the bill between his fingers, talk a little bit to throw him off guard and then release the bill. It is almost impossible for someone to do so, because the bill falls beyond their grasp in one-fifth of a second. Most people just can't react that fast!

SPECIAL BONUS MONEY TRICK

Take a bill of any amount. Fold two lines across the face of the person on the bill. These two folds should each go through the person's eyes, running up and down their face across the short part of the bill.

When you're done, there should be two "valley" folds running across the face. Now hold the bill up to your face. Tilt it toward you. *The face is smiling!* Tilt it away from you. *The face is frowning!* Do it over and over until the face talks to you! Then put the bill down and go see a doctor.

HE WET HIS PA-ANTS

A classic!

You Need: a glass of water
a dollar bill
a funnel

NOTE: Have the glass of water nearby, but not in an obvious spot. If you can hide it, do so. You don't want anyone to notice the glass of water.

There are many ways to try to get someone to wet their pants. I think that we have all heard of (or tried) putting a sleeping person's hand in a bowl of warm water. That trick doesn't actually work that often. This one does.

You might want to use a couple of the "innocent" tricks in this book to make your volunteer relax. As long as he's not suspicious, and you are acting normally, he will probably agree to cooperate. (If he doesn't agree to do the trick, try him again some other time. Don't try to *force* him into doing it, or it won't work.)

If you can, do this trick in an area where a little water spill won't matter. Hand your friend the dollar and the funnel. Make sure that the glass of water is somewhere nearby. Tell him that if he does the trick correctly, he can keep the dollar. (You're not lying; it will be worth a dollar if the trick works!)

Keep acting innocent. Tell your volunteer that this is a test of balance and coordination. First, he needs to put the funnel down the front of his shorts or pants. (Just so that the spout goes into the waistband.) So far, so good. Then he needs to tilt his head back. He should then place the dollar bill across his forehead and hold his arms out to his sides. (If he asks, tell him that in a moment he will try to drop the bill into the funnel.)

The rest is easy. His eyes are up and his arms are up. Quickly grab your glass of water. *Pour it down the funnel.* Do this fast! Now run away! Do this fast too! It might help the trick to run away yelling, "*He wet his pa-ants! He wet his pa-ants!*" On the other hand, this might make you laugh so hard that your friend actually catches you.

MAKING WATER DISAPPEAR

This activity can ONLY be done in the kitchen or other uncarpeted area!

You Need: a broom or mop
a stepladder
a large plastic bowl (preferably one with a "dimple" in the bottom)

Set the stepladder in the middle of the floor. Then pour water into the plastic bowl until it's about two-thirds full. Grab your broom and the bowl and move to the stepladder.

Carefully climb the stepladder until you can reach up and press the bowl against the kitchen ceiling. When you can, take the end of the broomstick and push it up on the center of the bowl. As you push with the stick, you can let go with your hand. Then carefully step down the stepladder so that you're standing on the floor with the bowl held against the ceiling above your head.

Now call a "volunteer" into the kitchen. Tell him to hurry—you have an awesome magic trick to show him. As the person comes in, quickly say, "Okay, hold this stick! I'm going to make this bowl disappear!" He may be confused, so just act excited like what's going to happen is the coolest thing ever . . . but he needs to come hold the stick!

Once you're sure the person is holding the stick with enough pressure to hold the bowl up, step back, grab the stepladder, and run out of the kitchen. Your volunteer will most likely be thinking, "Hey, this isn't right." If so, he might let go of the stick . . . and the bowl will come down!

If the person DOESN'T let go of the stick, see how long he'll hold onto it. But however long it takes, sooner or later, that bowl of water WILL come down!

THE OLD PLASTIC CUP TRICK

This is one of the few jokes you can play on strangers!

You Need: a plastic or waxed cardboard cup
a fairly strong magnet
a car

This is an easy trick. The next time you are going to be driven somewhere, attach a big, empty plastic cup to the top of your car with a powerful magnet at the bottom of the cup. Then drive off. As long as you're not going highway speeds, it should stay up there just fine.

People will frantically try to wave to you to point out the cup you "forgot" on the car. Wave back and smile! Fun for the whole family!

Variation: You need a clear plastic cup for this one, and you need to wear a long-sleeved shirt of any kind. Put the plastic cup well up in your armpit, away from the front of your body. (You don't want anyone to notice it.) Tell someone your neck is out of whack. Reach up with the hand on the non-cup side and place it palm-down on top of your head. With your other hand, grasp your chin. Now pretend to twist your head, and at the same time, *crush the cup against your body.*

The awful crack will frighten everyone!

WOLF JAW

Want to scare someone? This is the trick!

You Need: just you

You need to be seated next to someone for this trick. It helps if they are relaxed. It also helps if you can act.

Rub your jaw on the side your friend is on as if you were in pain. Mumble something about your jaw.

"Your tooth hurts?" your friend will ask.

Tell him that you have a medical condition known as "Wolf Jaw." It is not contagious, but it is very painful. Continue rubbing your jaw. Your friend will probably want to know more about it; even if he doesn't, tell him to feel the part of your jaw that you've been rubbing.

Now here's the trick: as they reach out to touch your jaw, wait until they're almost touching you, and then turn and snarl and snap back and bark while showing all of your teeth! (The more dramatic you make this part of the joke, the better it works.)

Your friend will freak out and pull back, horrified, and you will laugh yourself silly.

STRAW MAN

This is a good trick for when you're in a fast food restaurant.

You Need: a person who orders a different soda than you

Go to a restaurant with at least one victim. Let him order first and pay attention to what he gets. Assuming that he orders soda, order a different colored soda for your meal. (For example, if he gets a cola, you get lemonade, or if he gets a clear soda, you get root beer.) Try to be in charge of getting and carrying the drinks, and make a stop away from the table to get straws while he gets seated.

Put the straws all the way into the drinks and hold your finger over the end of each one. Keeping your finger over the end, pull the straws back out of the cups. Now switch each straw into the other cup, keeping your finger over the end until you feel it touch bottom.

Now bring the cups to your friend. Pretend to drink a little out of your cup (but don't!) and look concerned. "That's the wrong soda!" you say angrily. Put your finger over the end of the straw again and lift it out. "Look! I didn't want fruit punch (or whatever)!" you say, letting the soda flow out of the straw onto a napkin by releasing your finger from the end. If your friend still hasn't taken a sip of his, check his the same way. "It's the wrong soda again!" you insist. At some point, the two of you will actually drink, though, which is when it gets really confusing . . . because they are the right drinks after all!

LET'S GET READY TO GET STICKY

A good joke to play outside. Definitely outside!

You Need: 1 or 2 cans of soda

If you shake a can of soda, it will explode all over, right? *Wrong!* It will only explode all over if you open it *immediately*. If the soda is cold and you wait 25 to 30 seconds after you finish shaking to open it, the can will almost certainly *not* explode. Really.

Here's the joke. Take two cans of soda. Have your friend shake *one* of the cans. Have him really shake it hard! There should be no doubt that this can will blow! When he has shaken it enough, have him give you the can. Be careful to show him that you are not trying to switch this can with the unshaken can.

Now you need to kill about 30 seconds, so pretend that you are magically getting the shaken can to calm down. Wave your hands around and say some magic words. ("*Chudley!*") If you pick up the can, be careful not to shake it anymore. After enough time has passed, just open the can. Your friend will probably be suspicious, so he will be a few steps back. It doesn't matter. The can will not blow up. (If you don't trust me, try it yourself.)

Good trick so far, right? Well now your friend will be amazed and he will creep back in closer to you. Now take the other, unshaken can. Squeeze it a bit and then open it a little, and as you're opening it, squeeze more! This can will explode all over your friend! (That's what soda cans do when you squeeze them as you're opening them.)

You were outside when you did this, right?

VOODOO PEANUT BUTTER

A good joke to play on a friend visiting your house!

You need: chunky peanut butter
a diaper

This is a simple trick with a big payoff! Take a knife and smear a big dollop of the peanut butter into the "payload" area of the diaper. It looks pretty realistic, doesn't it?

Now put the diaper somewhere where you will "discover" it later with your friend. (For this example, it will be in the refrigerator.)

When your friend comes over, do not lead him directly to the peanut butter. This will seem too suspicious. Instead, goof off for a while and then ask your friend if he would like a snack. Even if he doesn't, go into the kitchen and open the refrigerator. There is the polluted diaper.

Now you will need a story about *why* the diaper is in the refrigerator. If there is a baby in your house, tell your friend that your mom is saving a "stool" (poop) sample for a doctor's test. If there is no baby in your house, tell him that you were babysitting a neighbor kid and he went dookie in his diapers. You didn't want to stink up the garbage, so you put it in the fridge. Before your friend can think about how stupid this is, have the following dialogue:

You (dramatically): Look at the load this kid left! It still stinks, too!
Your friend: Yech, gross!
You: Hand me that spoon will you? I want to try an experiment. ***(You get a spoon, gingerly dig into the peanut butter, and scoop some out. You then stick the spoon into your mouth!)***
Your friend: AAAAAAGHHH!!
You: It'z not dat bad!

Your friend's expression should have you laughing for weeks!

EATING DIRT VARIATION

When you were little, you ate dirt if someone didn't watch you. Now you can pretend to eat it WHILE someone watches you!

You need: Oreos
a clean flowerpot
newspaper
gummi worms (optional)

This is similar to the "Voodoo Peanut Butter" trick, but not quite as gross. Again, you need a friend to come over to your house. You should walk into the house with him. But *before* you left the house, you set up the following scene:

You took some Oreos, ate the creme out of the middle, and saved the chocolate wafers. When you had at least six cookies demolished, you put some newspaper down on the kitchen table. You put the clean flowerpot on the newspaper.

Then you got the Oreo wafers and crushed them into the flowerpot. This is going to be your fake "potting soil." Bury a gummi worm or two in the black cookie crumbs if you want to be creative.

So now you walk into the kitchen with your friend. "Looks like my mom was doing some gardening in here," you say. You look at the flowerpot, sniff the air, lift some of the dirt out of it, and stick it in your mouth.

"*Dirt tastes good,*" you mumble. You get another handful and grab one of the worms for effect. Wiggling the worm and the dirt, you stick the whole thing in your mouth. With your tongue, coat your teeth with the black Oreo crumbs. Now smile at your friend; be sure to show your teeth!

THE EXPLODING EYE

A really incredible gross-out; practice to make sure you do it right!

You Need: 1 of those small tubs of dairy creamers from a restaurant

For this trick, your eye will explode, which will be fairly revolting. You can do this trick anywhere, but it really should be at a meal, and you'll need to have a napkin handy.

Take the creamer container and tug a bit at its lid. You don't want to open it, but you do want the lid ready to give way as soon as you give it a squeeze.

Once you're seated at the table, hold your hand like a tube by making an "O" shape with your thumb and index finger. *Put the creamer container in this "O" with the lid facing away from you.* Keep the rest of your fingers curled and closed.

When you think you can get everyone's attention, start scratching with your other hand at the eye that you will "pop." Come up with your own reason why you are scratching; there is a rash, or your eye feels infected, whatever. When you're ready, bring up your "hand-tube" with the creamer container in it.

Rub your eye socket lightly with this hand, holding the tube down so nobody can see the creamer. You may want to moan in pain, or say, "*My eye! My eye!*" When you're ready, squeeze the container hard with your hand. White "juice" will run out! Your eye has exploded! Pull your hand away from the eye, and keep the eyelid closed so that nobody can see the eyeball is still there!

Then just enjoy the horrified screaming.

Sadly, we're out of space here. But you can learn more terrific practical jokes in my lousy book *The Pocket Guide to Mischief*!

FOLLOW-UP ACTIVITY

Play every joke in this chapter on just one person. Then ask the victim with an expression of great sorrow and sincerity, "*I get the feeling that you don't really trust me.*" Take notes on their reaction.

RHETORICAL QUESTIONS!

A "rhetorical question" is a question that doesn't necessarily need an answer. If you ask your friend, "*How's it going?*" and he just smiles and nods, you probably don't chase him down and say, "*I asked you a question, mister!*"

Wise people have selected the following rhetorical questions as the greatest of all time. Enjoy them, and remember: *they don't need answers.*

If a cat jumps into a garbage can, does it become kitty litter?

If corn oil comes from corn, where does baby oil come from?

Is it true that cannibals don't eat clowns because they taste funny?

When you choke a Smurf, what color does it turn?

Does water sink or float?

Do fish ever get thirsty?

How could the Wizard be "of Oz" and live in Oz?

If you melt dry ice, can you swim in it without getting wet?

How do they fit all that hot air into blow-dryers? Why don't they ever run out?

If M&M's melt in your mouth and not in your hand, what about your underarm?

How come Mickey Mouse is taller than his dog Pluto?

Rhetorical Questions!

Why do all the fingers have names (thumb, index, middle, ring, little), but the toes don't? ("Little piggy" doesn't count!)

If you jogged backward, would you gain weight?

If one synchronized swimmer drowns, do the rest have to drown too?

If the #2 pencil is so popular, why is it still #2?

If you try to fail and succeed, which have you done?

Why do people sing "Take Me Out to the Ballgame" at baseball games when they're *already* at a ballgame?

Why are there flotation devices under plane seats instead of parachutes?

If 7-Eleven is open 24 hours a day, every day of the year, why is there a lock on the door?

If a cow laughed really hard, would milk come out her nose?

If you were in a car going the speed of light, and then turned on the headlights, what would happen?

Why do we *park* on driveways and *drive* on parkways?

Why do they report power outages on the TV?

When it rains, why don't sheep shrink?

If the cops arrest a mime, do they tell him he has the right to remain silent?

Can vegetarians eat animal crackers?

Can chubby people go skinny-dipping?

Why do our noses run and our feet smell?

How is it that a building burns up as it burns down?

Why are there no eggs in eggplant? Why is there no ham in hamburger? Why aren't there apples or pine in pineapple?

Why does *quick*sand work slowly?

Why are boxing rings square?

If a vegetarian eats vegetables, what does a humanitarian eat?

Why does your alarm clock go *off* by going *on*?

Why is it that when the stars are *out*, they are *visible*, but when the lights are *out*, they are *invisible*?

After eating, do amphibians need to wait an hour before getting *out* of the water?

Why do you press harder on a remote control when you know the battery is dead?

Why are they called *apartments*, when they're all stuck together?

Why do we wash bath towels? Aren't we clean when we use them?

Is it good if a vacuum really sucks?

How do you know if you're out of invisible ink?

Why is it called "after dark" when it really is "after light"?

What does cheese say if someone takes its picture?

Do you think that trick-or-treaters wearing sheets aren't going as ghosts but as mattresses?

If a mime swears, does his mother wash his hands with soap?

RIDDLES!

Riddle me this: What is more fun than figuring out cool riddles? The answer: Nothing. Some of these riddles are moldy oldies that every boy should know, but *all* of them are excellent. So put on your thinking cap, Sherlock Homeboy, and enjoy!

In ancient Rome, the Saturnalia celebration was a huge party that went on for days. (The Twelve Days of Christmas would later take its place.) Riddle contests took place at that time; if you lost, you had to drink salt water combined with wine. This made you throw up. *Whoo-hoo!*

1. John wrote the name of a certain U.S. state on a sheet of paper in all capital letters. He then turned his page upside down and looked at it in a mirror. It read exactly as he had written it. What is the name of the state that he wrote? (Hint: The state doesn't start with a consonant.)

2. The 22nd and 24th presidents of the United States had the same mother and father but weren't brothers. How?

3. If a doctor gave you three pills and told you to take one every half hour, how long before you would be out of pills?

4. You find yourself in a bit of a pickle. You are trapped in a house that has a roomful of hungry crocodiles, a room filled with angry gorillas, and a room full of lions that haven't eaten in a year. Which room is safest for you to enter?

5. I have holes in my top and bottom, my left and right, and in the middle. Even with all of those holes, I still hold water. What am I?

6. Try to name three days that come right after one another without using the words Monday, Tuesday, Wednesday, Thursday, Friday, Saturday, or Sunday.

7. If a butcher is 6 feet tall, wears size 9 shoes, and has black hair, what does he weigh?

8. Look at the dollar bill. How many heads are there on both sides?

9. I'm light as a feather, yet the strongest man can't hold me for much more than a minute. What am I?

10. A young man and his elderly father are seriously injured in a rock climbing accident. By the time the two get to the hospital, the father is dead. An old surgeon is at the emergency room, and when the doctor sees the injured young man, the old doctor cries out, "That's my son!" The nurse replies, "But doctor, the boy was with his father at the time of the accident." How is this possible?

11. I can turn out the lights and get into bed before the room is dark. The light switch and bed are 12 feet apart. How is this possible?

12. There are 10 white socks and 10 black socks in a drawer. How many socks must you take out (one at a time) before you are sure of having a matching pair?

13. A canoe carries only 200 pounds. How can a mother, weighing 200 pounds, and her two sons, each weighing 100 pounds, use the canoe to cross a lake?

14. In a certain season, this is a common occurrence. A man leaves home, turns left three times, and comes back home to see two masked men. Who are they? (Hint: It's not Halloween!)

15. There is a strange island in the South Pacific called Haircut Island. The law on this island states that you cannot cut your own hair and you must get your hair cut once a week. There are no mirrors and only two barbers on Haircut Island. These two barbers are identical twins. One barber can't cut hair very well, but his brother rules. The locals refuse to tell you which of the barbers is the good haircutter. You need a haircut really badly! How do you know which barber to pick for a good haircut?

16. This is a two-part question: How many players take the field for a baseball team? How many outs in each inning?

17. Two boys have the same biological mother and father. They were born on the same day, in the same year, they look exactly alike, yet they are not twins. They are not conjoined twins and not clones, but they ARE brothers! How is this possible?

18. A sports car traveled at high speed for nearly 5 miles with a flat tire, but the driver was unaware of this. How is this possible?

19. Here is a pattern of numbers: 8 5 4 9 1 7 6 3 2 What's the next number? Why?

20. A man builds a house with four sides. Strangely, each side faces north. A bird goes by the house. What kind of bird is it?

21. While on safari in central Africa, Professor vanderSommen woke up and got dressed. He felt something move in the back pocket of his shorts. He reached back to see what it was. It had a head and a tail but no legs. The professor seemed unworried, and went about his chores, even after feeling the thing move in his pocket! Why?

22. I only exist where there is light.
But if light is on me, I take flight.
What am I?

23. A lonely woman decided to get a pet to keep her company. She visited the local pet shop and looked around.

"What about a parrot?" the pet shop owner asked.

The woman thought this was a good idea, but as she noticed a large green parrot, she asked, "Does this parrot talk?"

"This parrot will repeat every word it hears. I guarantee it," replied the shopkeeper. So the woman bought the parrot.

Three weeks later, the woman still couldn't get the parrot to say a word. She took it back to the store to get a refund, but the shopkeeper wouldn't accept it back. He said his guarantee still held, though. The shopkeeper spoke the truth; how is this possible?

24. I wave and wave at you,
Though I never say goodbye.
It's cool for you to be with me,
Especially when I say "Hi."
What am I?

25. A donkey is tied to a 20-foot rope. A pile of alfalfa is 30 feet away. Somehow, the donkey is able to eat the alfalfa, even though the rope does not break or stretch in any way. How is this possible?

26. A woman announced that she could walk on water for 10 minutes. She said she would do it on a nearby river. A large group of people went out to watch her. They all saw her actually do it! (The river was not dry.) How was this possible?

27. An old, starving wolf came upon a flock of sheep fenced in behind a tall metal fence. This fence was too high to jump over and he couldn't dig under it. The bars of the fence

were close together, but because the wolf was so thin, he could just squeeze through the bars. The problem was that if he ate any of the sheep on the other side of the fence, he wouldn't be able to squeeze back through the fence. The sheep farmer might then come and shoot him!

Puzzled, the wolf sat there. A little sheep said, "Mr. Wolf, I know how to solve your problem!" The other sheep quickly told the lamb to keep his mouth shut! What would the lamb have said?

28. How high would you have to count before you would use the letter "A" in the spelling of a number?

29. A young boy who played on his school's soccer team made the following comment: "Four days ago, my school's soccer team won a game 4 to 1, but none of the boys on the team scored any goals. Also, the other team didn't score against itself accidentally." How is this possible?

30. In a town in ancient Atlantis, they had a law that said *all* men must shave every day. The barber in the town shaved all the men's faces, but nobody shaved the barber's face. The barber was a healthy, normal, 40-year-old person. Why wasn't the barber breaking the law?

31. Tim went to the movies with his only sister's husband's mother-in-law's only daughter-in-law. So who did he go to the movies with?

32. A man carrying three croquet balls comes to a bridge. The bridge has a sign that says, "*Bridge can only hold 200 pounds.*" The man stops and thinks. He knows that he weighs 195 pounds. Each of the croquet balls he is carrying weighs two pounds each. Assuming that this man is very well coordinated, how can he cross the bridge without having it collapse underneath him?

33. What gets wetter and wetter the more it dries?

34. A man stands in front of a painting of a relative. The man says, "Brothers and sisters, I have none. But this man's father is my father's son." (In other words, "I am an only child, but the father of this person is my father's son.) Who's the picture of?

35. In heavy fog on a highway, there was a serious road crash that involved two trucks and six cars. All the vehicles were severely damaged. Police and emergency workers found both of the truck drivers and took them to the hospital. Strangely, no drivers from any of the cars could be found at the scene of the accident. Even more strangely, the police didn't seem to care! Why not?

36. You throw away the outside and cook the inside.
Then you eat the outside and throw away the inside.
What did you eat?

37. What is at the beginning of eternity, the end of time, the beginning of every end, and the end of every place?

38. What is the one crime that everyone tries to prevent if they see it about to be committed, but if the crime is committed, the person is not punished?

39. I have a bow and exactly 60 arrows. If I shoot one arrow at a tree at *exactly* noon, and then shoot another arrow every minute after that, what time will it be when I run out of arrows?

40. My friend calls me up and says, "I've invented a liquid that dissolves everything it touches. Do you want to invest in my discovery?"

I say, "Maybe, let me examine it."

"Okay, I'll bring a liter over right now," he replies.

"Never mind, I'm not interested anymore," I tell him. Why did I lose interest?

41. A man drives his truck under an overpass, and he comes to a screeching halt. The overpass was just a little lower than the truck, and now the truck is wedged in so tightly that it can't go backward or forward. What's the easiest way to get the truck out?

42. Is it legal for a man to marry his widow's sister?

43. Is it cheaper to take one friend to the movies twice or two friends to the movies once, if you are paying for the tickets?

44. Professor vanderSommen's head lay on the desk surrounded by a pool of blood. On the floor to his right lay a handgun. There were powder burns on the right side of the professor's head, showing that he had been shot at close range. The professor's right hand still held the pen that wrote his suicide note, which was coated in blood. The police recorded the time of death as 2:00 a.m. Suddenly, the professor's best friend, Count Feely, burst into the room.

"He killed himself!" the count cries. Then he sees the bloody note. "Why would he want to kill himself?" he asks. You don't care about the note, because you know it was murder. How do you know?

45. What five-letter word becomes shorter when you add two letters to it?

46. Look at the following pattern:

AEFHIKLMNTVWXY
———————————
BCDGJOPQRSU

Does the letter "Z" belong on the top row or on the bottom? Why?

47. If three dogs can catch three cats in three minutes, how many dogs would it take to catch 100 cats in 100 minutes?

48. While exploring the Amazon rainforest, Professor vanderSommen was seized by hostile natives. These natives told the professor that they were going to kill him unless he could solve his way out of the following problem.

The professor had a choice of how they would kill him. Here's how it worked: The professor had to say something. It could be any sentence that wasn't a question. If the professor made a *false* statement, he would be hit with a wet noodle till dead. If he made a *true* statement, he would be forced to drink prune juice till dead.

What is the only statement that Professor vanderSommen can make that will save his life?

49. There is only *one* place where the U.S. flag is flying *all* day and *all* night. It is *never* taken down. It is never flown at half-mast. Where is it?

50. What do turtles have that no one else can have?

51. One person can *hold* one. Two people can *share* one. But with three people, it disappears entirely. What is it?

52. Imagine you're in a plane that's on fire and diving straight for earth. How can you survive a horrible fiery death?

53. This belongs to you. Even so, without borrowing, stealing, or buying it, your friends use it way more than you do. What is it?

54. What's the difference between a toilet and a chair?

55. What is the greatest book ever written?

ANSWERS!

1. *O H I O.*
2. *President Grover Cleveland was our only president who served two different terms at two different times (1885–1889, 1893–1897). Benjamin Harrison was the "in-between" president.*
3. *1 hour.*
4. *Go in with the lions. If they haven't eaten in a year, they're dead.*
5. *A sponge.*
6. *Yesterday, today, and tomorrow.*
7. *Meat.*
8. *15: one George Washington head, one eagle head, and 13 arrowheads.*
9. *A breath.*
10. *The doctor is the boy's mother.*
11. *I go to bed during the day.*
12. *Three.*
13. *The two sons go first. One son brings back the canoe and the mother rows over. Then the other son returns for his brother.*
14. *An umpire and a catcher.*
15. *You pick the barber with the bad haircut. The bad barber has been cutting his hair, which means he is the good haircutter!*
16. *Nine and six.*
17. *They are two-thirds of a group of triplets.*
18. *The flat tire was the spare tire.*
19. *The next number is "0." This is a listing of the numbers in alphabetical order.* **E***ight,* **F***ive,* **F***our,* **N***ine,* **O***ne,* **S***even,* **S***ix,* **T***hree,* **T***wo,* **Z***ero.*
20. *A penguin. The only place this house could exist is at the South Pole.*

21. *It's a coin.*

22. *A shadow.*

23. *The parrot was deaf.*

24. *A fan.*

25. *The rope isn't tied to anything.*

26. *The river was frozen.*

27. *"Squeeze through the fence, kill one of us, tear us to pieces, and then take the pieces through to the other side of the fence. Then you can eat in peace!"*

28. *A thousand.*

29. *Girls scored the goals.*

30. *She was a woman.*

31. *His wife.*

32. *He juggles the balls; that way, one of the balls is always in the air! If you don't know how to juggle, see the "Juggling and Yo-Yos!" chapter, page 186. It's time to learn!*

33. *A towel.*

34. *His own son!*

35. *One of the trucks was carrying a load of cars.*

36. *An ear of corn.*

37. *The letter "E."*

38. *Suicide.*

39. *12:59.*

40. *If it dissolves everything, he can't bring it over. It must be a fake!*

41. *Let some air out of the tires and drive it on through.*

42. *It is both illegal and impossible, since the man would have to be dead to have a widow.*

43. *It's cheaper to take two friends once. Otherwise, you'd end up paying for four people instead of three!*

44. *If the professor has the pen in his right hand, that means he shot himself in the head and then wrote his suicide note. Since this is not possible, it must be murder!*

45. *Short.*

46. *The letter "Z" belongs on the top row because it is made of straight lines, unlike the letters on the bottom, which all have a curve somewhere in them.*

47. *Since the three dogs are already averaging one cat a minute, you just need three!*

48. *He must say, "You will kill me with a wet noodle." If the natives then kill him with a wet noodle, that would make his statement TRUE, which means they should have made him drink prune juice. If they make him drink prune juice, this makes his statement FALSE, which means they should have hit him with a wet noodle!*

49. *The Moon.*

50. *Baby turtles.*

51. *A secret.*

52. *Stop imagining.*

53. *Your name.*

54. *If you don't know, you're never coming to my house!*

55. *You're holding it in your hands!*

SLANG!

One special category of words is "slang" words. These are the casual, colorful words that we like to use, like "cool," as in "*The Big Book of Boy Stuff* is very cool." And there's all sorts of different slang that you can use to make your words more interesting. Instead of throwing away something, you can "chuck" it or "deep-six" it. Instead of jokingly threatening to beat up your friend, tell him that you will "drop him like a bag of dirt." If he gives you any back talk, tell him, "You write the check, and I'll cash it." (Nobody knows what this means, but it sounds great!)

Different countries have different slang. For example, they sure know how to speak colorfully in Australia. Here are just a few of their slang terms for "nerd" in the land Down Under: *boofhead, dag, dill, dipstick, droob, duffer, drongo,* and *nong.*

One great source of slang is money. Money is something that everyone likes, and most people just call it "money" or "cash." But there are other great slang terms for money: *scratch, mazuma, bling-bling, shekels, dinero, greenbacks, loot, bank, cha-ching, moolah, sawbucks,* or *clams.* I also like to use vegetables: *cabbage, kale, lettuce, etc.*

There are other ways to name money. Each type of paper money in the United States has a different important American on it—and they're always dead. (That's why bills are sometimes called "dead presidents"!) So all you have to do is memorize the bill by who is on it. George Washington is on the one-dollar bill, so instead of calling a dollar a "dollar," call it a "George." You can also call it a buck or a single. (Yawn.) Ooh, why not call it a "dead George"? Nice.

The five-dollar bill has Abraham Lincoln, so it's an "*Abe*." It's also sometimes called a *five-spot* or a *fiver*. Likewise, the $10 and the $20 bills can be called *ten-spots* and *twenty-spots*. I like to call the $50 bill a "*fitty*."

The $100 bill has Benjamin Franklin on it. (He was the author of *Fart Proudly!*) It's also called a "*C-note*" and a "*bill.*" The U.S. Mint does not print any larger bills than that, although they used to. The biggest bill *ever* printed was the $100,000 bill. In slang, we call that "*a lot of money.*"

SPECIAL FEATURE: PIG LATIN

Maybe you have heard someone speaking in Pig Latin before and didn't know what it was. It is an easy way to speak in a "secret" code!

Here's how it works: Any word that starts with a vowel ("A," "E," "I," "O," "U") gets a "—way" stuck onto the end of the word. (Example: "Owl" becomes "*Owl-way.*") Words that start with a consonant (the 21 letters that aren't vowels) have their beginning moved to the end of the word, with "—ay" added on. It is not that hard! (Translated into Pig Latin, this becomes "*It-way is-way ot-nay at-thay ard-hay!*")

Let's try some other phrases:

"You smell like monkey cheese" becomes "*Ou-yay ell-smay ike-lay onkey-may eese-chay!*"

"Your voice could peel scales off a donkey's butt" becomes "*Or-yay oice-vay ould-cay eel-pay ales-scay off-way a-way onkey's-day utt-bay!*"

See how great it is? Whoohoo! ("*Oohoo-way!*")

 The Buck Stops Here . . . and STAYS Here! When it comes to having the heaviest money in the world, the people of the Yap Islands in the Pacific Ocean take the piggy bank. There, the people use stones that can be 12 feet across and weigh more than 500 pounds! "Hey Timmy, can I borrow . . . oh, never mind."

 When the Greenback Breaks, the Bling-Bling Will Fall! Speaking of heavy money, take a crisp dollar bill. Fold it twice lengthwise so it looks like a "W" from the end. Rest each end of the bill on a support such as two drinking glasses. Now start putting change in the folds. You should be able to get at least two dollars in quarters on it. Keep going!

FOLLOW-UP ACTIVITY

Learn a foreign language. Start with the slang and "bad words" and take it from there.

EXTRA SPECIAL FEATURE: TALK LIKE A PIRATE

Being able to talk like a pirate is a valuable skill that may save your life someday. For example, let's say you were kidnapped by pirates, and they were making you walk the plank in your pajamas. You could turn to them and bellow, *"Avast, ye scurvy, chicken-livered landlubbers. If ye send me to Davey Jones' locker in these here pajamas, I'll come back and keelhaul the lot of ye!"* The bloodthirsty pirates will be so impressed, they will make you the honorary captain of the ship!

One good way to learn how to talk like a pirate is to see pirate movies, even the ones rated "Arrr!" Another way is to read the list on the next page.

 **Now That's One Tough Pirate.** Blackbeard (his real name was Edward Teach) was a real pirate who once shot one of his sailors without any warning. His only explanation was that if he did not kill one of his men every now and then, they would forget who he was. Blackbeard was attacked by pirate hunters in 1718. Supposedly, the corsair shouted, *"Damnation seize my soul if I give any quarter or take any from you!"* He later died of 20 cutlass wounds and five gunshot wounds. After his death, his head was cut off, and then both head and body were thrown overboard. According to legend, Blackbeard's headless body then swam several times around the ship before sinking.

ahoy: "Hey! Hello! Yo-yo-yo!"

avast: "Pay attention!" or "Knock it off!" or "What the heck are you doing?"

arrr: Good all-purpose word that can show anger, disgust, or happiness.

bilge: "Baloney!" The *bilges* are the lowest parts of the ship that fill with *bilgewater.* They stink.

blimey: "Wow!" or "Good grief!" or "Holy Toledo!"

booty: Treasure or riches. If you take a bag of treasure and shake it, you are "shaking your booty."

buccaneer: A pirate from the Caribbean.

bucko: Friend. "Me bucko" is the same as "my friend."

corsair: A nice word for "pirate."

crikey: A good curse to use. "By crikey, I told ye lubbers to get me a fig newton!"

cutlass: A pirate's sword. It has a curved blade.

Davey Jones' locker: The bottom of the sea.

deadlights: Eyes.

Dead men tell no tales: A good thing to say when you're not taking prisoners. Pirates flying a red flag would kill everyone aboard any ship they fought; this was a favorite saying of theirs.

doubloon: A gold coin. Doubloons are worth more than "pieces of eight."

piece of eight: A silver coin.

gangway: "Get out of my way!" As in "Gangway, I've got to get to the poop deck!"

grog: Usually this was watered-down rum.

(*anything*) ho: The word "ho" means "I see it!" The word is used for spotting ships ("*Sail ho!*"), land ("*Land ho!*"), and even tools ("*Shovels ho!*").

Jolly Roger: The pirates' skull-and-crossbones flag. Why is Roger so jolly? Because he's about to rob you!

keelhaul: This was a nasty punishment. A person was tied to a rope and dragged underneath the ship. Since the sides of the ship were covered with barnacles, this would lead to nasty cuts and near-drowning.

lad: Call anyone your age or younger this.

landlubber or lubber: A person who doesn't know the sea; they "lub" the land.

Long John Silver: One of the most famous fictional pirates, he is a one-legged character with a parrot in the book *Treasure Island* by Robert Louis Stevenson.

maroon: Leaving a victim in a deserted area.

me: "My."

me hearties: Good way to address a large group of people.

matey: A friend. "*I do not hatey me matey.*"

poop deck: Not a place to bust a grumpy. This is the high deck at the back end of a ship.

quarter: Mercy. As in, "Show me some quarter, me hearties. I really need 25 cents."

scurvy: This is both a disease and an insult. *Mean captain:* Why are ye movin' so slow, you scurvy dog? *Sailor:* Beg your pardon, Cap'n, but I actually do have scurvy. *Mean captain:* Oh. Sorry about that. *Sailor:* Ruff!

shiver me timbers: This means that you are so surprised, your timbers are shivering. The *timbers* of a ship are the lumber that the ship is made of. If they shiver, it means that you just ran into a reef, or a cannonball hit you, or the ship is just cold.

sink me: See "blimey."

smartly: Fast or quickly. "Step smartly there, ye miserable swabs!"

swab: A worthless sailor who is only good for swabbing the deck.

swag: Booty or riches.

walk the plank: Forcing a blindfolded victim to walk along a board that extends over the ship's side. Then they drown. It apparently never was used by pirates, but that shouldn't stop us from using the cool expression!

weigh anchor: To haul the anchor up and get ready to haul your butt somewhere else.

yo-ho-ho: This is a good all-around expression to use when singing about dead men's chests and bottles of rum.

AHOY, ME BUCKO. ARRRRRRR!
HE SAID... HELLO, MY FRIEND. IT IS NICE TO SEE YOU!

STORYTELLING!

There is an ancient belief called Zoroastrianism. (Try saying that fast!) In this belief, it was considered a *sin* to be a *boring person*. Unfortunately, many people today are very boring. They have *been* entertained all their lives, but they have never learned how to *be* entertaining. These people definitely never learned how to tell a story! Good storytelling is live performance. So it's the classic "you had to be there" experience. Also, storytelling can save your life! Did you know that dozens of children were crushed to death by falling television sets in the last few years? And many more choked to death on their cell phones! So not only is storytelling a very valuable skill, but it can prevent tragedy as well!

Where can you find stories to tell?

From a *storyteller*. If you think you don't know a storyteller, you're wrong; *we are all storytellers,* whether we realize it or not.

What are the basics of how to tell a story?

Although *anytime* is a good time to tell a story, the best times are late at night, especially when you're out camping. This way the storyteller won't be interrupted. Also, all the hot air that the storyteller gives off can help keep people warm on a cold night.

If you are getting ready to tell your story, be *confident*. If you are not naturally confident, *pretend* you're confident. It works just as well. In other words, *just fake it*!

Relax, breathe, and speak loudly. Tell the story in your own words. Feel free to let the story come out a little differently each time you tell it. Sometimes by experimenting and letting your imagination work, you can come up with a better version of a story. The important thing is *not* that the story is true. The important thing is that the story is *interesting*!

If you forget part of the story, pause while still looking into the audience's eyes. They'll just think it's a *dramatic pause*, but you're actually trying to remember your spot in the story. Your secret weapon is this: nobody but you knows what you are going to say, so there are no mistakes unless you say something like, "*Oops, I messed up.*" In storytelling, admitting to a mistake is a mistake!

Use facial expressions and pauses (also known as "timing"). Often a pause and a lifted eyebrow can accomplish more than words.

Try to relax and enjoy yourself—people aren't judging you if they are enjoying your story. If you have fun with it, so will they!

What kind of stories should you tell? You could tell a story about yourself. Stories about accidents, getting sick at school, fireworks, practical jokes that backfired, and so forth, are always interesting. Or you could tell a story that happened to someone in your family! Finally, there are many myths, legends, folktales, scary stories, and urban legends to choose from. You can take any story that already exists and *change* it! Here are some stories you can use; some are true and some are false, but they are ALL good!

FLYING BLUBBER

In 1970, a 45-foot dead whale washed up onto a popular Oregon beach. The whale had been dead for a while. It *stank*! The smell was so awful, state officials decided to take care of the eight tons of rotting meat by blowing it up with dynamite. Seagulls would then eat the small pieces of meat that the whale was blown into.

Dynamite is a pretty strong explosive. Workers put 1,000 pounds of dynamite next to the rotting whale. Then they detonated it. *Boom!* A huge chunk of the whale did blow up. Big pieces of the whale soared far into the sky!

A local news crew captured the blast on video. A man named Tom Mahoney describes this video as "the most wonderful event in the history of the universe." First, you see the explosion. Then you can hear spectators saying, "*Wow*" and "*Yippee!*" But the pieces of whale did not go toward the ocean. They went toward the spectators up on the dunes! The pieces of rotten whale blubber started falling down on them. *"Aaaah!" "Run away!"*

A big piece of blubber flew a quarter mile over the spectators and crushed the top of someone's car. "My insurance company is never going to believe this," said the car's owner.

What about the seagulls who were supposed to eat the whale chunks? They were so frightened by the blast, they all flew away, and didn't come back for some time.

Okay. So what about the whale? Well, they just buried it with a bulldozer, like they should have in the first place.

(This story is *true*.)

FIDO! IT'S FOR YOU

My older sister, Gretchen, and her husband, Dan, are dog lovers. They owned two boxers and a hyperactive German shepherd. These dogs were very active; if the phone rang, they ran around the house barking like crazy, and if someone came to the door, they went berserk. Gretchen was usually in charge of walking these three nutcakes two to three times a day.

However, she once had to leave town for business, so she told Dan over dinner that *he* was in charge of exercising the dogs.

"How am I going to do that?" he asked. "I'm at work all day!"

"You have to figure out a strategy," Gretchen responded.

Just then, the phone rang, and the dogs began running around the house and barking just like they always did. They continued barking and leaping until Dan answered the phone.

Dan got an idea.

After Gretchen left for her interview in the Bay Area, Dan unplugged the answering machine in the morning. He then left for work. At noon, he called his house and let the phone ring. He let the phone ring 60 TIMES. Then he hung up, knowing that the dogs had gotten plenty of exercise.

At 2 p.m., he did the same thing again. Then, that night, he went home and walked the dogs for real.

Dan was proud of his plan, and then he told me about it. What Dan did not know was that I had a spare key to his house. (Gretchen had given it to me.)

The next day, I let myself into the house at 11:30 a.m. The phone began to ring half an hour later. The dogs went nuts, barking and running around. I let the phone ring once and then I picked it up and held it to one of the boxer's faces. He barked loudly! After letting him bark for a while, I hung the phone up and got out of there.

Knowing that Gretchen was still gone, I swung by Dan's house again that day after his work. He seemed very distracted. I asked how the dogs were.

"Fine, fine," he answered.

"Are they getting their exercise?" I asked.

"Yeah, yeah," Dan responded.

"That was a smart plan you came up with. But your dogs are smart too. Have you ever taught them to 'speak'?" I asked.

Dan looked at me, looked away, and then looked at me again. "Why, yes . . ." he said.

(This story is *false;* feel free to change it around and put yourself in it!)

DR PEPPER LOSES PUNCTUATION

Have you ever wondered what that flavor is in Dr Pepper? It's prune juice! Here's the story of this soft drink.

Supposedly, in the late 1800s, a man named Wade Morrison fell in love with a doctor's daughter. The doctor's name was Charles Pepper, and he disapproved of his daughter marrying Wade Morrison. Now, Wade owned a soda fountain, and one of his workers had come up with a new flavor that his customers seemed to like. At first he called the drink a "Waco," but his customers knew about his failed romance with Dr. Pepper's daughter. They persuaded Morrison to name the drink "Dr Pepper" to butter up the man who could let Morrison marry the girl of his dreams! Sadly, it didn't work.

Another interesting thing about Dr Pepper is that there is no period after the "Dr" like there should be. Some advertising genius thought the drink would sell better without it, so they took out the period. The idea didn't work. Period.

(This story is *true.*)

GO TO HECK

A husband and wife living in Seattle, Washington, were going on a vacation to Mexico. Unexpectedly, the man's wife was called away on business at the last second, so he had to travel alone. His wife was going to meet him down in Mexico in a couple of days.

When the man reached the hotel in Mexico, he sent his wife an e-mail message to tell her that he had arrived. But he got the e-mail address wrong, and accidentally sent it to an old woman living in Indiana whose husband had just passed away.

When the old woman opened her e-mail, she read this message, screamed, and fainted.

Here is the message:

Dear honey,
I just got in. Everything here is prepared for your arrival tomorrow.
Your loving husband.
P.S. It sure is HOT down here!

(This story is *false*.)

PEE GREEN AT THE URINAL

One day in a kindergarten class, a teacher named Ms. Seth was teaching the children about colors. Ms. Seth asked the class if anyone knew what happened when blue and yellow were mixed together.

A kid named Roscoe yelled out, "Green!"

Ms. Seth was surprised. Roscoe rarely spoke, but here he had shouted out the correct answer. "That's right, Roscoe. How did you know?"

Roscoe answered, "My mommy puts this blue stuff into the potty. When I pee into it, it turns green."

(This story could be *true*!)

THE STRANGEST MARATHON EVER

Felix Carvajal was a postman from Cuba who wanted to run the marathon in the 1904 Olympics. (Keep in mind that the marathon is over 26 miles long!) To pay for his trip to

St. Louis (where the Olympics would be held), Felix quit his job and gathered donations. Once Felix got to New Orleans, he lost all his money to a street gambler, and had to walk and hitchhike 700 miles north to get to the games.

The day of his event, Felix showed up with the other 39 runners in pants and a long-sleeved shirt. (Summer temperatures in St. Louis are over 90 degrees!) There was only one water station, located near the halfway point of the race. The race wasn't well organized; one runner was chased through a cornfield by a mean dog and ended up running a mile out of his way!

Felix enjoyed himself. He ran along (sometimes backwards), talking with bystanders. For lunch, he detoured into an apple orchard. Big mistake. If you have ever eaten too many apples, you know what I mean.

Meanwhile, two Americans were doing strange things. The first runner, Fred Lorz, ran for 9 miles, then jumped in a car for the next 12 miles. When the car broke down, Lorz jumped out and ran the rest of the marathon. He entered the Olympic stadium with his arms up and the crowd went crazy! Lorz had his picture taken, and then race officials realized what happened—he was a *cheater*! Lorz was then banned from running in marathons for one whole year. Wow!

Out of the rest of the field, a man named Thomas J. Hicks was in first place. He started getting tired as he got closer to the finish line, so his trainers had him stop and drink brandy and egg white mixed with strychnine. Mildly poisoned, very tired, and drunk, he staggered into the stadium and was practically carried across the finish line. He won the gold medal.

What about Felix? I think he had what it took to beat Hicks, but between the stomach cramps and diarrhea, he came in fourth. The moral of the story: *beware the green apple trots because they don't help you run any faster.*

(This story is *true*.)

THREE IDIOTS AND A GOPHER

In 1995, a boy at Carroll Fowler Elementary School in California caught a gopher on the playground. Not sure what to do with it, he brought it to the school's three janitors. They decided to kill it. (Jerks!) They sprayed the gopher with three cans of the freezing cleaner that they used to remove dried gum with. The gopher was still fine.

While the men decided what to do next, one of them lit a cigarette. Bad move. The freezing solvent they had been spraying was flammable! The explosion that occurred next sent all three men to the hospital, and hurt over a dozen kids. (Most of them were just running away from the explosion and tripped.)

The gopher was later found unharmed. He was set free.

(This story is *true*.)

THE THEATER OF THE MIND

Nothing can top the creative powers of your own imagination! Back in the day, people didn't have anything for entertainment but themselves. One thing they did was tell stories. Then came the age of radio in the twentieth century, where people could listen to a radio drama and re-create the action in their own minds.

You Need: a script
at least one friend
a cell phone, computer, or other sound recording device

Using things that we call "words," create a story with dialogue and sound effects. You might want to have a narrator explain the initial action and setting, and then the actors can start your drama.

It's easy to write the dialogue. Don't worry about the quotation marks, just put the person's name and any stage directions in parentheses after it. If there are any directions for the actor, put them in parentheses. Then just write what the character says.

Example:

Narrator: The crowd advanced upon Charlie with wet noodles in their hands.
Charlie (screaming, afraid): Wait! I know who it is! I know who the monster is! It's . . . it's one of you!

For your story, there needs to be some CONFLICT. Maybe you can think of an interesting character first, and then put him or her into a weird situation. Here are some character ideas: *lovesick alien, magical cowboy, careless princess, really stupid fairy, a lost ghost, etc.*

Keep in mind that ***if you don't describe it, the audience can't see it.*** That means that your characters need to describe what they see.

Sound effects are a great part of any radio drama. And there are many ways to make cool sounds. For example, if you need a gunshot, it's unsafe to actually shoot a gun in front of a microphone. (Rats!) So just drop a heavy book on the floor. *Bang!* For a fire, wrinkle some plastic wrap. For thunder, wiggle a cookie sheet. For breaking glass, throw a chair through a window. Also, silverware shaken in a drawer can sound pretty good. If you don't feel like writing your own script, there are plenty of scripts out there to pick from. One fun thing to do is to take a *Mad* magazine and use the movie parody feature as your script. That'll work!

Whatever script you use, practice your scene once before recording it. When recording, hit your pause button if you run into trouble. Experiment with different voices and accents. It's a blast! You'll laugh so hard on the playback, your face will hurt.

Don't have more than about six characters in your play, or it will be pretty confusing for your listeners.

SPECIAL FEATURE: FAIRY TALES YOU THOUGHT YOU KNEW

Most people don't know that in the original version of *Little Red Riding Hood,* the wolf eats the grandmother and *then* eats Little Red Riding Hood. The End. It was written by Charles Perrault (1628–1703), who also wrote the original stories of *Sleeping Beauty* and *Cinderella*. He also invented Mother Goose!

Many fairy tales were once pretty gruesome before weak-minded adults changed them around. In the original version of *Goldilocks and the Three Bears,* the intruder to the bears' home is an angry old woman, not a cute little girl. She is so mean, the bears end up impaling her on a church steeple. That's got to hurt!

Here's another one: *Snow White and the Seven Dwarfs* was written in 1812 by two brothers named Grimm. At the end of their version of the story, the evil queen has to put on iron slippers that are heated red hot. She goes crazy from the pain and dances herself to death. *Shake it, mama!*

The Wizard of Ag! A famous storyteller once made up a tale about a magical land for his young sons and their friends. Right in the middle of the story, a little girl named Tweety Robbins interrupted him.

"What is this land called?" Tweety asked.

The famous storyteller was stuck. He couldn't think of a name! Later, he tried to write down the story, and still couldn't come up with a name for his magic land. The storyteller stared at the filing cabinet drawers that were by his desk. They were arranged alphabetically, with one drawer holding files "A-G." The next drawer was "H-N." The last one was "O-Z."

That's it! "OZ!" The Land of Oz! And that's how author L. Frank Baum came up with the name for his first Oz book, *The Wizard of Oz.*

TONGUE TWISTERS RULE!

Even though everyone knows what a "word" is, NOT everyone can say words correctly. If you put certain words that sound similar together, you get a **tongue twister:** *Words that can twist your tongue into a knot.*

For example, here are four words. Say all of the words quickly several times in a row.

> *Willy's real rear wheel*

It's not as easy as it looks, is it? A lot of the following tongue twisters don't make much sense, but they sound pretty neat. Challenge your tongue with them! Then challenge your friends' tongues with them! (On the other hand, never mind that; it sounds kind of gross.)

Buy a box of biscuits, a box of mixed biscuits, and a big biscuit mixer.

I wish to wash my wicked wristwatch.

Rubber baby buggy bumpers.

To begin to toboggan first, buy a toboggan.
But do not buy too big a toboggan!
Too big a toboggan is too big a toboggan to buy to begin to toboggan.

Silly sheep weep and sleep.

A Tudor who tooted the flute
tried to tutor two tooters to toot.
Said the two to the tutor,
"Is it harder to toot or
to tutor two tooters to toot?"

Larry Hurley, a burly squirrel
hurler, hurled a furry squirrel through
a curly grill.

She had shoulder surgery.

Give me the gift of a grip top sock: a drip-drape, ship-shape, tip-top sock.

The crow flew over the river with a lump of raw liver.

An elephant was asphyxiated in the asphalt.

There was a minimum of cinnamon in the aluminum pan.

Preshrunk silk shirts.

A lump of red leather.

Good blood, bad blood, good blood, bad blood, good blood, bad blood.

Mr. See owned a saw and Mr. Soar owned a seesaw. Mr. See's saw sawed Soar's seesaw before Soar saw See!

Blake's black bike's back-brake bracket broke.

Sam Smith's fish-sauce shop seldom sells shellfish.

Richard's wretched ratchet wrench.

Buckets of bug blood, buckets of bug blood, buckets of bug blood.

In 2013, a researcher named Dr. Stefanie Shattuck-Hufnagel claimed that she had found the ultimate tongue twister. She said, "If anyone can say this phrase 10 times quickly, they get a prize." So are you ready? Here it is!

> *Pad kid poured curd pulled cold.*

FOLLOW-UP ACTIVITY

Research the life of language scientist Sven Norderodestromfahrer. Learn the ultimate tongue twister that he spent his life discovering. (This twister was so effective, people who used it had to go to the emergency room for severe mouth cramps.) Now use this phrase on your enemies. What the heck, use it on your friends too!

VIDEO GAMES!

It takes very little imagination to play many video and computer games. These games are created by little people sitting in little cubicles inside of big office buildings. Their goal is to rob you of your time and your money. If the little people CAN get you addicted to a joystick, they WILL. And once you are the slave of the game screen, they are happy!

If you want to play a video game sometime, go ahead! But if you are losing all track of time and have little interest in the world outside, then you are OVERDOING it. Don't become a brain-washed troll in a dark room. Don't make the little people happy. Do something with your life!

FOLLOW-UP ACTIVITY

Borrow as many video and computer games as you can from your friends. Destroy them. If your friends ask you what happened, tell them that you did it for their own good.

WEAPONS!

Throughout history, weapons have mostly been used for war and violence. That's bad. Still, there are some good uses for weapons, like hunting, competitions, and self-defense.

Boys (and men) are interested in the weapons that are used for fighting. We hate the need for these deadly gadgets, but we are fascinated by them. Heck, the high point of every James Bond film is when 007 gets his high-tech weapons. Secret agents in real life have also been given some pretty strange devices. Allied secret agents during World War II (1939–1945) who were dropped behind enemy lines sometimes carried special handkerchiefs with them. If the agent urinated on the handkerchief, a map of the territory they were in appeared!

These agents also had guns and knives hidden in unusual places. Belt buckles, gloves, mechanical pencils, and even tobacco pipes could conceal small guns. Some had a knife that was inside of a pencil. Agents were even known to carry small crossbows with them. Amazing! Speaking of *bows*, maybe we should get this chapter started with some . . .

ARCHERY (THAT'S BOWS AND ARROWS TO YOU)

A bow is basically just a spring with string that shoots a little spear (called the arrow). What gives a bow power is that its wood is curved in one direction, but then it is strung in the opposite way. (Look at the letter "C." Now imagine stringing its ends and *puulliinngg* it the other way. It would look like a "D.")

The wood used for a bow should be strong and flexible. Good sources for this wood are ash, hickory, elm, hazel, and yew. As for the bowstrings, they have been made from animal tendons, rawhide, hemp, and, of course, string.

You may hear someone say that a bow "weighs" 60 pounds. That doesn't mean that it's that *heavy;* it means that the archer needs to *pull* with 60 pounds of force to get the bowstring back. (This concept is also sometimes called "pull.") The heavier a bow weighs, the more force it shoots arrows with. The English used to use really long bows; one of them was 6 feet, 7 inches high and "weighed" 110 pounds! Longbow archers were so strong, they could kill someone with a shot from 200 yards away. Longbowmen could also shoot 10 arrows in the air; the 10th arrow was shot up before the first one came down!

There are lots of archery supplies available at sporting goods stores and online. You may want to get (or make) a simple bow and then buy a few target arrows to see if you enjoy archery. Be sure to also get yourself an archer's glove and a bracer. These protect your fingers and forearm from the bowstring. There are also compound bows out there. Compound bows are designed so that you can shoot with great force, but because they have pulleys, you don't have to be able to pull as hard as you would with a simple bow. (Some people call this cheating.)

To shoot with a bow: If you're right-handed, turn so that the outside of your left shoulder lines up with the target. Hold your bow at the full length of your left arm (if you're right-handed) and notch the arrow. When you notch an arrow, don't pinch the string with your fingers. Use the "two-fingered draw." Aim from about 4 inches under your right eye; if you try to sight along the arrow itself, you'll go way too high. The farther away your target is, the higher you have to aim to make up for gravity. A bale of straw is a great target; just make sure there is nothing behind it or to the sides that could get hit!

 The English longbow was so powerful, it was known to pin a knight to his horse by going through one of the knight's legs, the horse, and the knight's other leg! (That's almost as good as the time I shot an arrow through a balloon.)

 The Most Dangerous Frog in the World! There is a frog in Central and South America about the size of your thumb. Like other amphibians, its skin gives off a toxin that discourages predators. But the golden poison arrow frog (*Phyllobates terribilis*) has a toxin so deadly that if you dip your arrowhead in it once, you'll kill anything that gets scratched with it!

BLOW GUNS AND PEASHOOTERS

The idea of the blowgun is totally simple. If you put a small missile inside of a slightly larger pipe and then blow, your missile will come out the other end. The longer the pipe is, the more accurate your shot will be. How hard you blow and how aerodynamic your missile is will also affect your shot. This applies whether you are using a drinking straw with a spitwad or a piece of PVC pipe and a blowdart!

To make a blowgun: Get a drinking straw or hollowed-out pen. You can blow anything through it that will fit. Blow! Do NOT inhale!

What about peashooters? They are about the same size as blowguns, but you don't have to blow into them. They can really fire away, and the beauty of it is, you don't have to use peas for ammunition. Dried white beans, wood matches, spitwads, and even large, dry boogers (blech!) can be shot out of them.

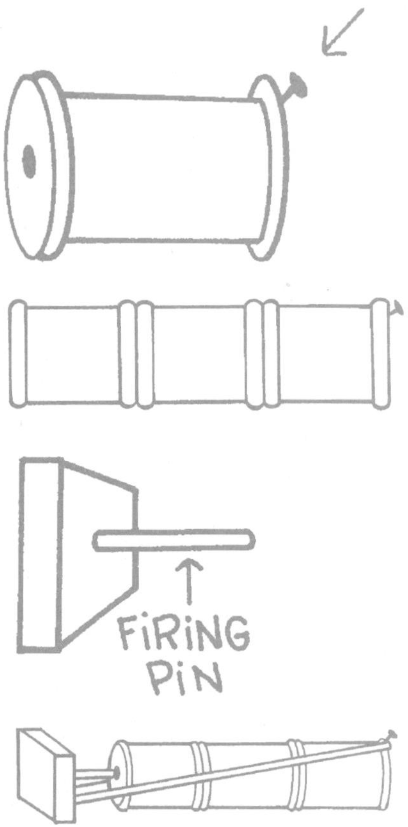

To make a peashooter: It is super-easy to make. Take an empty spool of thread. If it is wooden, stick a small nail deep into the end of it. If it's plastic, Super Glue a nail or small peg to the end. This will be the end of your barrel. Now take two other empty spools of thread; scrape any paper off the ends of them, and then glue them together. Make sure you line them up properly so that it's a smooth line when you look down the "barrel."

To make your firing pin, you need a small stick or dowel that will fit in the barrel formed by your spools. Then take a small square of cardboard or wood, fit your firing pin into it, then glue it in place. This will prevent your firing pin from shooting out the spools along with your ammunition.

Get a good rubber band and wrap one end around the nail and the other around your firing pin block. Put your

ammo in, pull your pin back, and release. *Wham!* It really fires hard, doesn't it? Experiment with different rubber bands and ammunition.

 Liechtenstein is a small country between Austria and Switzerland. It used to have the world's smallest army. There was only one soldier. He served his country until his death at age 95. Since then, Liechtenstein no longer has had an army.

BB GUNS

"*You'll shoot your eye out! You'll shoot your eye out!*" Anyone who has seen the movie *A Christmas Story* knows the classic parent argument against BB guns: you'll shoot your eye out. My brother once shot me in the butt with his BB gun, so I can tell you something: you *could* put someone's eye out with a BB. Dang, that hurt! But (and this is a big BUTT), if you are careful, BB guns can also be a lot of fun.

The first rule of any gun, whether it's a BB gun, paintball gun, or bazooka, is to assume that it is loaded. Handle the gun as if a BB (or paintball, or bullet) could come out of its barrel at any time. Because of this, you will never aim a gun at anything except your target. In addition, always keep your gun unloaded until the time when you are ready to shoot. When you are done shooting, you will completely unload the gun but still treat it as if it were loaded.

BB gun basics: Before loading your BB gun, make sure the safety is on. Don't cock your gun and leave it cocked, or "dry fire" your BB gun. It isn't good for it! And I know you're not stupid, but only load a gun with its proper ammunition.

Okay, you're ready to shoot. But wait! Don't shoot yet! What if you miss? What is BEHIND or NEAR your target? Is it something that shouldn't be hit by a BB, like a glass window or your history teacher? If you are shooting with someone, you need to know where they are. BB careful!

BB guns fall under the category of air rifles. Air guns don't use gunpowder. Can you guess what they use instead? *Air!* That's right, the BB gun is basically just a fancier version of the blowgun. Some BB guns have cylinders that store air inside of them. Others have a "pump-action" that builds up air pressure. Many BB guns simply have a spring inside of them that is pulled back when the gun is cocked and released when the trigger is pulled. The spring then leaps forward and pushes the air behind the BB in the barrel, forcing it forward.

There are air guns (usually pellet guns) that have a pump on them. These types of air guns are more dangerous because the explosion of air can be made extremely strong. The Consumer Product Safety Commission has found that there are about four deaths a year in the United States from pellet and "high velocity" (powerful) BB guns. They recommend that nobody under the age of 16 should use these guns.

Probably the most famous BB gun was the Daisy Red Ryder model, which came out in 1940. Named for a comic strip cowboy, Red Ryder had a Native American sidekick named Little Beaver. He had a cork gun named after him. It shot a cork. What a rip-off!

In England in the 1800s, many people used air rifles disguised as walking sticks or canes for self-defense weapons.

BOLAS

Bolas have been used since ancient times in places as far apart as Australia and Argentina. A bola is basically just a cord with weights attached to it. The bola may have two weights or eight, but the more weights there are, the harder it is to throw. Bolas have usually been used as a way to tangle up an animal's legs to prevent it from running away. This comes in handy when you are hunting wild prey or trying to stop Little Timmy from running off with your hat.

Try making one. For this, you will need some strong thread or heavy fishing line. You will also need three weights for your bola; although these weights can be almost anything, I suggest soft, solid rubber balls, since they are less likely to break something when you are practicing your throws.

Okay, so you're using soft, solid rubber balls for weights. Push a needle with your line attached through one of the balls. Once the line is on the other side, staple, glue, and/or tie it in place so that it can't pull back out of the ball. Now measure about 4 feet of the line from the other side of the ball and attach another ball the same way to that end.

Now take the third ball. Attach a 2-foot line to it and then tie the end of that line to the middle of the 4-foot line. Your bola is ready for action! Take it outside. Grab the third ball and whirl the other two around your head so that they don't get tangled. Practice on a small tree or Little Timmy; you will soon be the bola expert!

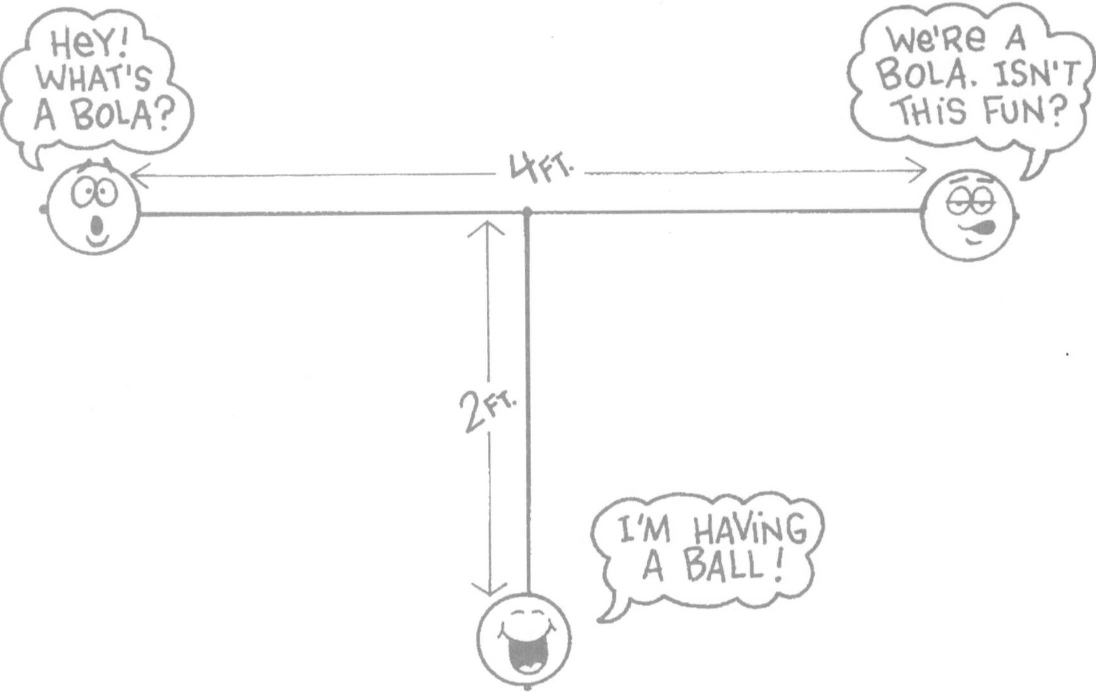

BOOMERANGS

Yep, boomerangs were originally weapons. However, the boomerangs we use today are used for fun, not death. You already know that boomerangs come from Australia. But do you know how they were invented? Native Australians, called "Aborigines" (aah-bo-RIDGE-in-eez), used a throwing stick called a "kylie" to hunt. If you missed your throw, the kylie didn't come back! At some point, an aborigine boy picked up a stick to use for a kylie and threw it through the air. The boy then turned his back on it while his friends watched in amazement. It circled around and then came back and clocked him in the back of the head! Boy, that must have been funny!

How to throw: If you have a boomerang and are ready to throw, make sure you're outside! The less windy it is, the better your throws will be. Keep away from water, trees, little kids, windows . . . you get the idea. If you make a bad throw, yell "Fore!" or "Duck!"

Okay, you're ready. Hold the boomerang vertically. Grab the boomerang wing tip in a tight grip with the curved side facing you. (One side of a boomerang is flat, and one side isn't.) Throw it like a baseball; when you finish your throw, your arm should come down beside your leg. Throw your boomerang at a slight upward angle, almost straight ahead. Snap the boomerang out of your hand when you throw it, because if the boomerang doesn't spin, it doesn't return.

Don't expect it to come right back to your hand on the first throw! Practice the basics described here and you'll figure it out.

At some point, your boomerang will come right back to you. This is when you should panic! Scream "*Look out!*" and run away. This will provide anyone watching with a good laugh. After you're done messing around, try again. Keep your face out of its way! When the boomerang returns, catch it with two hands. If you don't know where it is, turn your back and clasp your hands on the back of your head. That way it won't break your face.

MAKING YOUR OWN BOOMERANGS

1. **Classroom Sneaky Size:** Okay, you're in class and you're sort of paying attention, but you need something to distract you. Get a 3 x 5 inch card, or any piece of paper made with card stock. Trace a boomerang shape onto it; make it about 2 inches long. Next, cut it out. Slightly bend up the right-hand side tip. Gently hold the boomerang against a book, and tilt the book up a bit. Now flick it; it should come back! Experiment with different shapes!

2. **Classroom Not-So-Sneaky Size:** Try using any thin cardboard for this, like a manila folder or cardboard box. Just like above, trace a boomerang shape onto it, but make it 4 to 5 inches long. Bend each of the wings up somewhat. Hold it like a real boomerang (see earlier instructions), and throw by pinching it with your thumb and throwing it like a dart.

3. **Paint Stick/Ruler Boomerangs (Outside Only):** This is very easy. Take two paint stirring sticks or rulers (wood or plastic), and use Super Glue or rubber bands to stick them together at the halfway point to form an X. Bend each wing slightly up; don't break them! Throw like a regular boomerang. If it spins but doesn't return, try bending the wings more.

Q: What do you call a boomerang that doesn't work?

A: A stick.

The all-time longest boomerang throw was 24 hours. See, a man named Bob Reid went to Antarctica and threw a boomerang *around* the South Pole. Since it went through all the time zones in one toss, that was a whole day of boomeranging!

PAINTBALL

Paintball got its start in 1981. Although it requires a lot of specialized equipment, it's still very popular. After all, paintball is really fun and really intense! Of course, the key to winning at paintball is not to be hit *by* the paintball. These small balls are made of gelatin with a drop of colored liquid inside. Although they can be messy, paintballs are biodegradable, meaning they break down naturally.

A paintball gun is an air gun, just like BB guns. It uses compressed gas cartridges to fire the paintballs. These balls should never be moving more than 300 feet a second. At that speed, they will hurt (and even bruise) when they hit someone, but that's it. However, they could easily put out your eye, so players use headgear to protect themselves.

More than any other game, paintball is like war, though with a difference: there are referees to make sure nobody cheats! As you probably know, in paintball games, two teams literally fight it out. Paintballers often play a version of "capture the flag." Any player who gets shot is "dead" and must lie down or leave the field. Games can be as short as 10 minutes or they can go on for hours and hours.

I've played paintball before, and it is very exciting and exhausting! There is nothing as exhilarating as knocking an opponent out with a good shot—or as disappointing as getting shot yourself! But whatever version of paintball is being played, the keys to victory are teamwork, skill, bravery, and luck. (Being sneaky and treacherous can also help.)

Germ Warfare? Modern countries have outlawed "germ warfare" (using diseases as a weapon), but it has been around for a long time, even before people knew what germs were. During the Middle Ages, dead and rotting animal carcasses were sometimes shot by catapult into towns under siege. The animal would land, explode, and release unhealthy germs into the surrounding air.

SLINGSHOTS

A slingshot can be a handheld weapon or something much bigger. Maybe you've seen a catapult before; a catapult is just a big slingshot that can throw giant rocks! (For detailed plans on how to make an impressive catapult, see the book *Backyard Ballistics* by William Gurstelle.)

If you want a store-bought slingshot or wrist rocket, go buy one. It is also very easy to make your own mini-slingshot out of a big paper clip and a rubber band, but I'll assume that you can do that.

But back in the *old* days, when a boy used a sling, it was just as deadly as a wrist rocket, and it required a bit of skill. That *sling* was a long strap of leather (usually) with a pouch in the middle. One end of the sling had a loop for your finger, and the other end was straight.

The idea of using it is simple. Wrap the loop around your finger. Put a rock or marble in the pouch. Take the other end of the sling and clench it between your thumb and forefinger. Twirl it over your head. Aim at an object and let go of the end of the sling! At first, the rock you throw may end up just about anywhere, so practice this in a park. After you improve, you may get quite accurate. Maybe you could clock that Goliath kid who's been bothering you!

 Do NOT Get in a Rock Fight with These Guys! An ancient Spanish tribe called the Baleares used slings that threw stones weighing over a pound. The velocity of the rocks could smash through armor.

 More Fun with Rocks! Everyone knows that if you have a smooth, oval stone, some flat water, and a good sidearm throw, you can do some serious rock skipping. What you may not know is that you can also skip stones on sand. If you're at the beach, go to the wet sand that is near the water. Throw a stone at the sand as if it were water. It won't skip as far as it would on water, but it'll skip!

WATER BALLOONS

Water balloons are the weapon of choice for most boys. They combine the risk of a hand grenade with the joy of getting someone wet!

Whether you're in a water balloon duel or a water balloon toss, here are some basic tips:

Filling the balloon: You don't want to fill the balloon too much if you can help it. More water equals more pressure . . . which equals you being wet!

Throwing the balloon: If you are in a water balloon toss, then you want to make a nice, smooth, underhand throw with a high arc. Your hand should start way behind you and end up over your head after your release!

If you are in a water balloon war, all bets are off! You don't have time to think about how you throw it, but if you do, remember not to make any sudden throwing movements, or it will just burst on you!

Catching the balloon: The key to making a successful catch is not to offer the balloon any resistance. Meet the balloon with both of your hands in front of you, and then let your hands travel with the balloon; don't try to stop it, just slow it down. Go with it! This is how to win the balloon toss, and how to turn the tables on your opponent in the water balloon war! Nothing is more impressive than catching your opponent's balloon, whipping it around, and throwing it back at him.

Escaping the balloon: Three words—duck and dodge! If your opponent is faster than you, run away as fast as you can. When you can hear your opponent's footsteps getting near, drop to the ground! He may just miss you with the balloon, or he might trip over you and fall on his own balloon!

General strategy: In any war, you want the high ground. It is easier to defend yourself and harder for someone else to attack you. If you are higher than your water balloon opponent (say, on a hill or picnic bench), you can see where they are and you have gravity on your side when you throw down on them. And remember, if you want to be the ultimate water balloon gladiator, see "Water Balloon Jousting" in the "Outdoor Games!" chapter, page 117.

WATER BALLOON DUEL

One of the best games to play with water balloons is Water Balloon Duel. You and your friend each get a filled balloon and stand back to back. Then you loudly count to three; with each number called, you both take a step. After you get to three, you both turn and duel! You can throw your balloon, or run away, or run toward your opponent and try to get him right in the face . . . but once your balloon is gone, go into evasive maneuvers!

Duel variation: Try the same duel with Silly String!

BONUS WATER BALLOON INFORMATION

Water balloon volleyball: Get a bunch of balloons ready to go (don't fill them up too much) and string up a volleyball net. Play volleyball with them! Points are awarded if one side bursts the balloon, whether it hits someone or not!

Fun water balloon trick: You know how a magnifying glass can focus the sun's rays into a hot point? Well, balloons can only stand this kind of heat for an *instant* before they blow. Think of creative ways you can use this laser device to create mischief.

Back in the 1800s, the "War of Pork and Beans" was nearly fought between New Brunswick (Canada) and Maine (United States) over a territory dispute. There were no injuries, but there was plenty of gas.

FOLLOW-UP ACTIVITY

Throughout history, there have been a number of catapults and ballistae that shot "arrows" that were bigger than spears! Make your own ballista and use it for target practice! And to learn about more sneaky weapons and gadgets, turn to *The Big Book of Spy Stuff*. (Sure, it's written in invisible ink, but you'll figure it out!)

FAMOUS LAST WORDS!

This is the end of the book, so let's come to a close with the last words of some interesting people!

"They couldn't hit an elephant at this distance. Urk!" *Civil War General John Sedgwick (1813–1864) during the Civil War, on how enemy riflemen couldn't hit him.*

"Oh, what a nice dog! Can I pet it?" *Leroy Skaggs* (1990–2019).

"Go away, I'm all right." *H. G. Wells* (1866–1946).

"Precious, precious, precious! My Precious! Oh, my Precious!" *Gollum.*

"I don't care if you ARE a bunch of pirates, you're still dressed funny!" *Tyrone Fauntelroy* (1685–1731).

"Never felt better." *Douglas Fairbanks Sr.* (1883–1939).

"Either this wallpaper goes or I do." *Oscar Wilde* (1854–1900).

"Die, my dear doctor? That's the last thing I shall do." *Viscount Palmerston* (1784–1865).

"Only one man ever understood me. And he really didn't understand me." *Georg Hegel* (1770–1831).

"I don't feel good." *Luther Burbank* (1849–1926).

Nurse: Is anything bothering you?
Buddy Rich (1917–1987): Yes! Country music!

"Go on, get out! Last words are for fools who haven't said enough!" *Karl Marx* (1818–1883).

FOLLOW-UP ACTIVITY

Act like you are dying. Say something clever in a dramatic way. Then pretend to die. (**NOTE:** Be careful not to *actually* die, as this would make the activity less fun.)

ACKNOWLEDGMENTS

Many people contributed to this book in one misguided way or another. Those who were particularly helpful were Dallas Wassink; Troy Taylor; Peter Ford; Mary Groh; Andrew and Aaron Judd; Erik King; Simon Wintle; my dad; Richard Feely; Linda Holt; Dr. Matthew Grow; Lt. Col. Melinda Grow; Kathleen, Shannon, and Luke Twomey; Kristin Heintz; Michelle Herrmann; Sarah Enbody; Kris, Oliver, and Michael Ivan King; Michael Lepene; Kelby Smith; Tanner Johnson; Gretchen and Dan Ryan; Mary Falkenstein; Jenny Ball; Andrew Simon; Kay Moore; Deb and Marcus Triest; Jim Murai; Sean Fronczak; Peter King; Mary Wiley; Genevieve Smith; Anita Phillips; Jakob Lovato; Jen Blair; the wonderful staff at the Multnomah County Library; and all members of the Kodiak and Sasquatch Teams at Cedar Park Middle School. Many thanks!

A note of appreciation also goes to Brody vanderSommen, both for his "useful" ideas and for his excellent website designs. Check out his skills at www.bartking.net.

Finally, to my wife Lynn, all my love and thanks.

RECOMMENDED READING!

A good book can entertain you *and* enrich your life and imagination! (You might even learn something from it!) I didn't used to like to read, but once I found the right book, I was hooked. Finding the right book for YOU may take a little bit of experimenting, but once you find an author you like, read everything you can by them!

The books below come with *high recommendations* from boys—so take them for a spin!

NONFICTION!

"I read a lot of books."

—*Jeremy Glick (a high school student) talking about how he got a perfect score on his college entrance tests.*

Barton, Chris. *Can I See Your I.D.? True Stories of False Identities*, 2011. True crime, fraud, and adventure: 10 stories of mind-blowing masquerades.

Becklake, Sue. *The Visual Dictionary of the Universe*, 1993.

Bragg, Georgia. *How They Croaked: The Awful Ends of the Awfully Famous*, 2012.

Brooke, Michael. *The Concrete Wave: The History of Skateboarding*, 1999.

Byam, Michele. *Arms & Armor*, 1988.

Cassidy, John, and B. C. Rimbeaux. *Juggling for the Complete Klutz*, 1988.

Cordingly, David, and John Falconer. *Pirates: Fact & Fiction*, 1992.

Deem, James M. *Bodies from the Ice: Melting Glaciers and the Recovery of the Past*, 2008. As glaciers melt, once-frozen bodies are thawing out. Awesome! (Not the glaciers melting part, though.)

The DK Science Encyclopedia, 1998.

Eisenberg, Linda. *Magic and Perception: The Art and Science of Fooling the Senses*, 1996.

Ellis, Chris. *The Complete Book of Radio Controlled Models*, 1999.

Elsaeed, Rasha, and Chris Oxlade, editors. *150 Great Science Experiments*, 2001.

Ficarra, John, and Nick Megline, editors. *The Mad Gross Book*, 2001.

Guinness World Records (most recent edition!).

Gurstelle, William. *Backyard Ballistics: Build Potato Cannons, Paper Match Rockets, Cincinnati Fire Kites, Tennis Ball Mortars, and More Dynamite Devices*, 2001; 2nd edition, 2012.

——. *The Art of the Catapult: Build Greek Ballistae, Roman Onagers, English Trebuchets, and More Ancient Artillery*, 2004.

——. *The Practical Pyromaniac: Build Fire Tornadoes, One-Candlepower Engines, Great Balls of Fire, and More Incendiary Devices*, 2011.

Harding, David, editor. *Weapons: An International Encyclopedia from 5000 BC to 2000 AD*, 1990.

Hawk, Tony. *Tony Hawk: Professional Skateboarder*, 2002.

Hoose, Phillip. *Moonbird: A Year on the Wind with the Great Survivor B95*, 2012. This is the story of a robin-sized shorebird that's flown more than the distance to the Moon . . . and halfway back!

How Things Work Encyclopedia, 2009.

Janeczko, Paul B. *Top Secret: A Handbook of Codes, Ciphers, and Secret Writing*, 2006.

Johnson, Rebecca L. *Zombie Makers: True Stories of Nature's Undead*, 2013. There are monsters that can take over innocent creatures, turning them into senseless slaves! They include a fly-enslaving fungus, a suicide worm, and a cockroach-taming wasp. Fun!

King, Mac, and Mark Levy. *Tricks with Your Head*, 2002.

Macauley, David, and Neil Ardley. *The New Way Things Work*, 1998.

McManners, Hugh. *The Outdoor Adventure Handbook*, 1996.

Recommended Reading!

Miles, John C., senior editor. *The Ultimate Book of Cross Sections*, 1996.

Ogden, Tom. *The Complete Idiot's Guide to Magic*, 1999.

Ripley's Believe It or Not! Special Edition (read the most recent version!).

Robinson, Nick. *Super Simple Paper Airplanes*, 2000.

Schyffert, Bea Uusma. *The Man Who Went to the Far Side of the Moon: The Story of Apollo 11 Astronaut Michael Collins*, 2003.

Scieszka, Jon, editor. *Guys Write for Guys Read: Boys' Favorite Authors Write About Being Boys*, 2005. This collection of stories, advice, poems, and comics comes from the Guys Read website (www.guysread.com), which has even *more* recommended books!

——. *Knucklehead: Tall Tales & Mostly True Stories About Growing Up Scieszka*, 2008.

Sheinkin, Steve. *Bomb: The Race to Build—and Steal—the World's Most Dangerous Weapon*, 2012.

Solheim, James. *It's Disgusting—and We Ate It! True Food Facts from Around the World—and Throughout History!* 1998.

Spignesi, Stephen J. *The 100 Greatest Disasters of All Time*, 2002.

Taylor, Barbara. *How to Save the Planet*, 2001.

Tunis, Edwin. *Weapons: A Pictorial History*, 1954. Reprinted, 1999.

The Visual Dictionary of Flight, 1992.

The Visual Dictionary of Special Military Forces, 1993.

The Visual Dictionary of Ships and Sailing, 1999.

Watkins, Richard. *Gladiator*, 1997.

> "The best remedy for being bored or sad is to *learn something*. That is the only thing that never fails. You may be frightened or old, you may miss your only love, you may see the world about you being ruined by nitwits, or know that small-minded people are against you.
>
> "There is only one thing for it then—*to learn*. There is a reason for everything. Learn why the world wags and what wags it. That is the only thing which the mind can never get tired of, never be tortured by, never fear or distrust, and never dream of regretting."
>
> —*Merlyn* (paraphrased) in T. H. White's *The Once and Future King*

FICTION!

Adams, Douglas. *The Hitchhiker's Guide to the Galaxy*, 1997.

Adams, Richard. *Watership Down*, 1989.

Alexander, Lloyd. *The Illyrian Adventure* and *The Book of Three*, 1999. A lot of boys like his books, particularly *The Illyrian Adventure*, etc.

Amato, Mary. *Snarf Attack, Underfoodle, and the Secret of Life: The Riot Brothers Tell All*, 2007.

Angleberger, Tom. *The Strange Case of Origami Yoda*, 2010. I can't describe how weird and wonderful this book's idea is. Just read it!

Avi. This writer has a lot of books out, and he's got fans. Try *Crispin: The Cross of Lead* or *"Who Was That Masked Man, Anyway?"*

Barry, Dave, and Ridley Pearson. *Peter and the Starcatchers*, 2004. Wacky humor and adventure. As my friend Jen said, "How can you not love a book that depicts a giant bra as a sail for one of the ships?"

Basye, Dale E. *Heck: Where the Bad Kids Go*, 2008. This first book in the Heck series starts with a marshmallow-bear explosion—and *then* it gets crazy. Dale Basye is so funny, some readers swear by him. ("*By Dale Basye, this is a good book!*")

Bauer, Marion Dane. *On My Honor*, 1987.

Bellairs, John. *The Eyes of the Killer Robot*, 1998.

Boule, Pierre. An interesting writer! Try *Bridge Over the River Kwai* or *Planet of the Apes*.

Brooks, Bruce. *The Moves Make the Man*, 1984.

Brown, Fredric. Somehow, this very funny and creative author has been forgotten, and if you can get your hands on *Martians, Go Home!* or *The Best of Fredric Brown*, you'll wonder why.

Card, Orson Scott. *Ender's Game*, 1994.

Cashore, Kristin. The Graceling Realm series has a protagonist who's an expert at killing, so that's nice.

Colfer, Eoin. *Artemis Fowl*. This is the first book in the Artemis Fowl series. It's funny, high-tech, and magical. (Other titles include *The Arctic Incident* and *The Eternity Code*.)

Cooper, Susan. She is the author of the much-praised The Dark Is Rising series of books. The first book in the series (but maybe the weakest) is *Over Sea, Under Stone.*

Cormier, Robert. This author is great, but can also be a little bit "adult" for some readers. Try any of his titles, especially *Fade, I Am the Cheese*, or *The Chocolate War, We All Fall Down,* and *After the First Death.*

Coville, Bruce. *Jeremy Thatcher, Dragon Hatcher,* 1991.

Cresswell, Helen. *Ordinary Jack,* 1987.

Crutcher, Chris. Try *Chinese Handcuffs* or *Ironman.*

Cussler, Clive. I don't know if he's a great writer, but many boys like him, plus the word "cuss" is in his name. Try *Cyclops* or *Floodtide.*

Dahl, Roald. In addition to the classic *Charlie and the Chocolate Factory,* try some of his other titles, like *The BFG, The Witches,* or *Danny the Champion of the World.*

d'Aulaire, Ingri, and Edgar Parin d'Aulaire. Both of these books are great: *d'Aulaires' Book of Greek Myths* and *d'Aulaires' Norse Gods and Giants.*

Deuker, Carl. *On the Devil's Court,* 1991.

Doyle, Roddy. *The Giggler Treatment,* 2001.

Dumas, Alexandre. This French writer wrote GREAT stories, including *The Count of Monte Cristo, The Man in the Iron Mask,* and *The Three Musketeers.*

Flanagan, John. Ranger's Apprentice is an excellent fantasy adventure series (which began with *The Ruins of Gorlan,* 2006) that gets better as you go.

Fleischman, Sid. *The Whipping Boy,* 2003.

Funke, Cornelia. *The Thief Lord* and *Inkheart* are sort of modern classics.

Gantos, Jack. *Dead End in Norvelt* (2011) is one funny book. This author is also known for writing about a hyperactive kid in *Joey Pigza Swallowed the Key.*

Gidwitz, Adam. *A Tale Dark and Grimm,* 2010.

Gould, Steven. *Wildside,* 1996.

Haddix, Margaret Peterson. *Among the Hidden,* 2000.

Herbert, Frank. If you think you can handle it, *Dune* can be a great book to read and reread. Be sure to look in the back of the book before you begin to get crucial information that helps the story make sense!

Hinton, S. E. *The Outsiders,* 1967.

Hobbs, Will. *Jason's Gold,* 1999, and *Downriver,* 1991.

Howard, Robert E. *The Coming of Conan the Cimmerian.* Robert E. Howard died at an early age, and many Conan books have been written by other authors, but you can't top the original. Excellent adventure.

Jacques, Brian. Any and all of the Redwall books, including the one called *Redwall.*

King, Stephen. He has written an incredible amount of books, and the odds are you will like some of them. **WARNING:** He's good at being too scary for younger readers. Try *Salem's Lot* or *Pet Sematary.*

Klass, David. Try *Danger Zone, Wrestling with Honor, California Blue,* or *You Don't Know Me.*

Konigsburg, E. L. *Silent to the Bone,* 2000.

Korman, Gordon. *No More Dead Dogs,* 2002.

Lawrence, Louise. *Children of the Dust,* 1985.

Lewis, C. S. If you haven't read *The Lion, the Witch, and the Wardrobe* yet, hop to it. Then read the rest of the Narnia series too.

Lipsyte, Robert. One of his best titles is *The Contender,* and you should also try *One Fat Summer.*

Mazer, Harry. Give *Snowbound, The Last Mission,* or *A Boy at War* a shot.

Myers, Walter Dean. *Scorpions,* 1988.

Palacio, R. J. *Wonder* (2012) is about a kid with extreme facial abnormalities. He's home-schooled till fifth grade, then goes to a private middle school . . . and it's not a smooth move.

Patterson, James, and Chris Grabenstein. *I Funny: A Middle School Story,* 2012. Jamie Grimm is going to be the best stand-up comedian in the world, even if he *is* in a wheelchair.

Philbrick, Rodman. *Freak the Mighty,* 2001.

Pinkwater, Daniel. This guy is very funny. His many books include *Alan Mendelsohn, the Boy from Mars* and *Lizard Music.*

Pratchett, Terry. The writer of many imaginative and funny fantasy/science fiction books, Pratchett's best-known works may be the books in the Discworld series, which begins with *The Colour of Magic.*

Pullman, Philip. He's a great writer. You really have to read *The Golden Compass* and its sequel, *The Subtle Knife.* There is also another great series he wrote about a girl (!) that starts with the book *The Ruby in the Smoke.*

Rockwell, Thomas. *How to Eat Fried Worms,* 1973.

Sachar, Louis. In addition to *Holes,* he also wrote *Sideways Stories from Wayside School* and *There's a Boy in the Girl's Bathroom,* which has a title I'm sure you can relate to.

Salisbury, Graham. *Under the Blood Red Sun* and *Shark Bait* are good titles.

Schwartz, Alvin. *Scary Stories to Tell in the Dark,* 1981.

Scieszka, Jon. *Knights of the Kitchen Table,* 1991.

Shan, Darren. He has a vampire series that begins with *Cirque du Freak.* I really liked these books.

Shiga, Jason. *Meanwhile,* 2010. In this graphic novel, a mad scientist makes a boy choose between testing a mind-reading device, a time machine, or a doomsday machine.

Sleator, William. *Interstellar Pig,* 1995.

Smith, Jeff. *Bone, Volume 1: Out from Boneville,* 2005. What can I say about this funny graphic novel? How about "I LOVE IT."

Smith, Roland. *Sasquatch,* 1998.

Snicket, Lemony. These books are funny and a little annoying, but they're good for a rainy day. Start with the *The Bad Beginning* and take it from there.

Spiegelman, Art. *Maus* and *Maus II.* The most powerful "comics" you'll ever read.

Spinelli, Jerry. The author of *Crash* and *Maniac Magee.*

Springer, Nancy. *Toughing It,* 1994.

Stine, R. L. He writes so many books, it's useless to try and keep track of them all. Try *Welcome to Dead House* (the first book in the Goosebumps series) and see what you think.

Taylor, Theodore. *The Bomb,* 1997.

Tolan, Stephanie S. *Surviving the Applewhites,* 2002.

Vanderpool, Clare. *Navigating Early* (2013) is a cool adventure tale of two boys on the Appalachian Trail. They deal with the usual things: bears, pirates, buried secrets, and extraordinary encounters.

Westall, Robert. *The Machine Gunners,* 1999.

Westerfeld, Scott. *Leviathan* (2009) retells World War I with fantasy elements. See, the *Leviathan* is a flying ship that is actually a whale, and uh, just read it.

White, Robb. *Deathwatch,* 1972.

Yang, Gene Luen. *American Born Chinese,* 2006. This graphic novel tells three stories of young Chinese Americans trying to figure things out.

Zelazny, Roger. A great writer. Try *Roadmarks* or *Unicorn Variations* for starters.

BIBLIOGRAPHY

AirDisasters.com: Solutions for Safer Skies, www.airdisaster.com (accessed March 5, 2014).

Albregts, Lisa, and Elizabeth Cape. *Best Friends*. Chicago: Chicago Review Press, 1998.

Armstrong, Nancy, and Melissa Wagner. *Field Guide to Gestures: How to Identify and Interpret Virtually Every Gesture Known to Man*. Philadelphia: Quirk Books, 2003.

Attanasio, Paul. "Harrison Ford: Currents of a Collaborator." *Washington Post,* December 24, 1986.

Baden-Powell, Sir Robert. *Scoutmastership*. New York: G. P. Putnam's Sons, 1920.

Beard, Daniel Carter. *The American Boy's Handy Book*. 1882. Reprint, Boston: Nonpareil Books, 1988.

Berkenkamp, Lauri. *Kid Disasters and How to Fix Them*. Norwich, Vermont: Nomad Press, 2002.

Blaine, David. *Mysterious Stranger: A Book of Magic*. New York: Villard, 2002.

Blakey, Nancy. Go *Outside!* Berkeley, California: Tricycle Press, 2002.

Branzei, Sylvia. Grossology, www.grossology.org (accessed March 5, 2014).

Brown, Patricia Leigh. "Enthusiasts Gather to Salute G.I. Joe, a Man of Action." *New York Times,* June 30, 2003.

Burroughs, Edgar Rice. *Tarzan of the Apes*. New York: A. L. Burt, 1914.

Cassidy, John, and B. C. Rimbeaux. *Juggling for the Complete Klutz*. Palo Alto, California: Klutz, 1988.

Cirillo, Joan. *The Complete Idiot's Guide to Cooking with Kids*. New York: Alpha Books, 2000.

Cobb, Vicki. *Magic . . . Naturally! Science Entertainments & Amusements*. New York: T. B. Lippincott, 1976.

——, and Kathy Darling. *Wanna Bet? Science Challenges to Fool You*. New York: Lothrop, Lee & Shepard Books, 1993.

——. *You Gotta Try This! Absolutely Irresistible Science*. New York: Morrow Junior Books, 1999.

Cordingly, David, and John Falconer. *Pirates: Fact & Fiction*. New York: Artabras, 1992.

Coren, Stanley. *The Pawprints of History*. New York: Free Press, 2003.

Crayola, www.crayola.com (accessed March 5, 2014). Company website, includes information on crayons and Silly Putty.

De Govia, Mario, with Joe Arnold and Thaddaeus Winzenz. *Yo-Yo Tricks: From Beginner to Spinner.* New York: Prima Games, 1999.

Dickson, Paul. *The Mature Person's Guide to Kites, Yo-Yos, Frisbees, and Other Childlike Diversions*. New York: New American Library, 1977.

Dispatch Magazine On-Line, www.911dispatch.com (accessed March 5, 2014). News and information about public safety communications since 1982.

The DK Nature Encyclopedia. New York: Dorling Kindersley, 1998.

The DK Science Encyclopedia. New York: Dorling Kindersley, 1998.

Dotz, Warren, Jack Mingo, and George Moyer. *Firecrackers: The Art and History*. Berkeley, California: Ten Speed, 2000.

Dumb Warnings, www.dumbwarnings.com (accessed March 5, 2014).

Elsaeed, Rasha, and Chris Oxlade, editors. *150 Great Science Experiments*. New York: Lorenz Books, 2001.

Ficarra, John, and Nick Megline, editors. *The Mad Gross Book*. New York: DC Comics, 2000.

"Fireworks!," PBS: Nova Online, www.pbs.org/wgbh/nova/fireworks (accessed March 5, 2014).

Fletcher, Colin, and Chip Rawlins. *The Complete Walker IV.* New York: Alfred A. Knopf, 2002.

Frey, William H., III. *Crying: The Mystery of Tears*. New York: Harper & Row, 1985.

Godfrey, Neal S. *Neale S. Godfrey's Ultimate Kids' Money Book*. New York: Simon & Schuster, 2002.

The Great Idea Finder: Invention Facts and Myths, www.ideafinder.com/history/of_inventions.htm (accessed March 5, 2014).

Green, Joey. *Paint Your House with Powdered Milk*. New York: Hyperion, 1996.

——. *The Mad Scientist Handbook*. New York: Perigree Books, 2000.

——. *Amazing Kitchen Cures*. Emmaus, Pennsylvania: Rodale, 2002.

Gregory, Leland. *What's the Number for 911? America's Wackiest 911 Calls*. Kansas City, Missouri: Andrews McMeel, 2000.

Griffin, Margot. *The Sleepover Book*. Tonawanda, New York: Kids Can Press, 2001.

Gurstelle, William. *Backyard Ballistics: Build Potato Cannons, Paper Match Rockets, Cincinnati Fire Kites, Tennis Ball Mortars, and More Dynamite Devices*. Chicago: Chicago Review Press, 2001.

Hawkes, Nigel. *Planes and Other Aircraft*. New York: Copper Beech Books, 1999.

Harding, David, editor. *Weapons: An International Encyclopedia from 5000 B.C. to 2000 A.D.* New York: St. Martin's, 1990.

Herbert, Janis. *The American Revolution for Kids*. Chicago: Chicago Review Press, 2002.

Hibbert, Christopher. *The Virgin Queen: Elizabeth I, Genius of the Golden Age*. New York: Addison-Wesley, 1991.

Hillcourt, William. *Official Boy Scout Handbook*. Irving, Texas: Boy Scouts of America, 1979.

History House, www.historyhouse.com (accessed March 5, 2014). An irreverent history magazine.

Hodgson, Michael. *Camping for Dummies*. Foster City, California: IDG Books Worldwide, 2000.

Hoffman, David. *Kid Stuff: Great Toys from Our Childhood*. San Francisco: Chronicle Books, 1996.

Hoge, Warren. "Haggis, the Food of the Poets (Well, One Scottish Poet)." *New York Times*, November 19, 2002.

Holtzman, Debra Smiley. *The Panic-Proof Parent*. Lincolnwood, Illinois: Contemporary Books, 2000.

HowStuffWorks, www.howstuffworks.com (accessed March 5, 2014).

Jay, Ricky. *Learned Pigs and Fireproof Women*. New York: Farrar Straus Giroux, 1986.

——. *Jay's Journal of Anomalies*. New York: Farrar Straus Giroux, 2001.

Jell-O Gallery, www.jellogallery.org (accessed March 5, 2014).

Jillette, Penn, and Teller. *How to Play with Your Food*. New York: Villard Books, 1992.

——. *How to Play in Traffic*. New York: Boulevard Books, 1997.

Johnstone, Leslie, and Shar Levine. *Silly Science: Strange and Startling Projects to Amaze Your Family and Friends*. New York: John Wiley & Sons, 1995.

——. *Everyday Science: Fun and Easy Projects to Make Practical Things*. New York: John Wiley & Sons, 1995.

——. *The Optics Book*. New York: Sterling, 1998.

Jones, Charlotte Foltz. *Accidents May Happen*. New York: Delacorte Press, 1996.

Kawamoto, Wayne. About.com: Magic & Illusion, http://magic.about.com/mbody.htm (accessed March 5, 2014).

King, Mac, and Mark Levy. *Tricks with Your Head*. New York: Three Rivers Press, 2002.

Kohl, MaryAnn F. *Making Make-Believe: Fun Props, Costumes and Creative Play Ideas*. Beltsville, Maryland: Gryphon House, 1999.

Leeming, Joseph. *Things Any Boy Can Make*. New York: Century, 1929.

——. *More Things Any Boy Can Make*. New York: Appleton-Century, 1936.

Limburg, Peter R. *What's in the Names of Wild Animals*. New York: Coward, McCann & Geoghegan, 1977.

Maguire, Jack. *Hopscotch, Hangman, Hot Potato, & Ha Ha Ha*. New York: Simon & Schuster, 1990.

Marin, Doug. "Ed Headrick, 78, Designer of the Commercial Frisbee." *New York Times*, August 12, 2002.

Martin, Eric B., editor. *The Campfire Collection*. San Francisco: Chronicle Books, 2000.

Masoff, Joy. *Oh, Yuck! The Encyclopedia of Everything Nasty*. New York: Workman, 2000.

McManus, Patrick F. *Kid Camping from Aaaaiii! to Zip*. New York: Lothrop, Lee & Shepard, 1979.

McPhee, Nancy. *The Book of Insults: Ancient to Modern*. New York: St. Martin's, 1978.

Monroe, Bill. "Chance Encounter Leaves Pooch with Painful Reminder." *Oregonian*, November 1, 2001.

The National Council on Fireworks Safety, www.fireworksafety.com (accessed March 5, 2014).

Newman, Frederick R. *Mouth Sounds: How to Whistle, Pop, Click, and Honk Your Way to Social Success*. New York: Workman, 1980.

Novobatzky, Peter, and Ammon Shea. *Depraved English*. New York: St. Martin's, 1999.

——. *Insulting English*. New York: St. Martin's, 2001.

O'Connor, Anahad. "Snakebite Advice Is Close to Snake Oil." *New York Times*, August 1, 2002.

Ogden, Tom. *The Complete Idiot's Guide to Magic*. New York: Alpha Books, 1999.

O'Neil, John. "For Warts, the Duct Tape Cure." *New York Times*, October 15, 2002.

Panati, Charles. *Panati's Extraordinary Origins of Everyday Things*. New York: Perennial Library, 1987.

Perry, Charles. "Forklore: Homely Cooking." *Los Angeles Times*, February 3, 1999.

Phillips, Kenneth M. Dog Bite Law, www.dogbitelaw.com (accessed March 5, 2014).

Piven, Joshua. *The Worst-Case Scenario Survival Handbook*. San Francisco: Chronicle Books, 1999.

Pogue, William R. *How Do You Go to the Bathroom in Space?* New York: Tor, 1999.

Powell, John, editor. *Weapons & Warfare, Volume 1*. Salem, Massachusetts: Salem Press, 2001.

Presto, Fay. *Magic for Kids*. New York: Larousse Kingfisher Chambers, 1999.

Raab, Evelyn. *Clueless in the Kitchen: A Cookbook for Teens*. Willowdale, Ontario, Canada: Firefly Books, 1998.

Reynolds, Doris. "Let's Talk Food." *Naples Daily News*, September 23, 1998.

Robinson, Nick. *Super Simple Paper Airplanes*. New York: Sterling, 2000.

Rogers, Nicholas. *Halloween: From Pagan Ritual to Party Night*. New York: Oxford University Press, 2002.

Roy, Thomas, and Ruth Roy. Wellcat Holidays, www.wellcat.com/holiday.html (accessed March 5, 2014).

Schiffman, Nathaniel. *Abracadabra: Secret Methods Magicians & Others Use to Deceive Their Audience*. Amherst, New York: Prometheus Books, 1997.

Schilling, Kim. *Ferrets for Dummies*. Foster City, California: IDG Books Worldwide, 2000.

Schmidt, Norman. *Great Paper Jets*. New York: Sterling, 1999.

Sefton, Dru. "Hand-to-Hand Combat." *Oregonian*, October 20, 2003.

Shimizu, Takeo. *Fireworks: The Art, Science, and Technique*. Austin, Texas: Pyrotechnica, 1988.

Solheim, James. *It's Disgusting—and We Ate It! True Food Facts from Around the World—and Throughout History!* New York: Simon & Schuster, 1998.

Spignesi, Stephen J. *The 100 Greatest Disasters of All Time*. Sacramento, California: Citadel Press, 2002.

Stine, G. Harry. *Handbook of Model Rocketry*. 6th edition. New York: John Wiley & Sons, 1994.

Sullivan, Robert. "Man and Beast Dept.: Critter Flicks." *The New Yorker*, September 30, 2002.

Swanson, Diane. *Burp! The Most Interesting Book You'll Ever Read About Eating*. New York: Kids Can Press, 2001.

Templeton, Brad. Rec.Humor.Funny, www.netfunny.com (accessed March 5, 2014). Humor magazine.

Truzzi, Marcello, and Massimiliano Truzzi. "Notes Toward a History of Juggling." *Bandwagon* 18 no. 2, March–April 1974. Also available online at www.juggling.org/papers/history-2/ (accessed March 5, 2014).

Tunis, Edwin. *Weapons: A Pictorial History*. 1954. Reprint, Baltimore, Maryland: Johns Hopkins University Press, 1999.

Uncle John's Bathroom Reader Plunges into History. San Diego, California: The Bathroom Readers' Hysterical Institute, 2002.

van Straalen, Alice. *The Book of Holidays Around the World*. New York: E. P. Dutton, 1986.

The Visual Dictionary of Special Military Forces. New York: Dorling Kindersley, 1993.

Walkowicz, Chris. *Choosing a Dog for Dummies*. New York: Hungry Minds, 2001.

Wallechinsky, David. *The Complete Book of the Olympics*. New York: Viking Penguin, 1984.

Weber, Bruce. *You Can Yo-Yo!* New York: Scholastic, 1998.

Weeks, Linton. "Worst Foot Forward: A Guide to Foreign Insults." *Washington Post*, April 11, 2003.

Bibliography

Wiese, Jim. *Magic Science*. New York: John Wiley & Sons, 1998.

Wiseman, Richard. LaughLab, www.laughlab.co.uk/home.html (accessed March 5, 2014). A project aimed at finding the world's funniest joke.

World Eskimo-Indian Olympics, www.weio.org (accessed March 5, 2014).

Yates, Raymond F. *Model Jets and Rockets for Boys*. New York: Harper Books, 1952.

Zinsser, Hans. *Rats, Lice, and History*. New York: Little Brown, 1984.